IGNITE JOY

WRITE WITH US

Have you ever had a powerful moment in your life that transformed you, and now you want to write about it? At Ignite, we publish Ignite Moments™, those pivotal moments in a person's life that created positive change that resulted in them becoming a better version of themself.

We've all had life-changing moments like these, and it is when you share those moments you transform your life and Ignite the lives of others. Whether you consider yourself an author or not, we want to invite you to write about your Ignite Moment in one of Ignite's upcoming books. We're always looking for new people with important messages to share, and we help our authors through every step of the publishing journey in a powerful four-month process.

If you feel ready to share your story and support someone who may be going through what you went through, let us be your guide in igniting others around the globe.

SEE OUR UPCOMING BOOKS AND APPLY NOW.

GET TO KNOW IGNITE.

Hundreds of authors have come to us, and we have made them international best-sellers in both our compilation books and their own solo projects. People who were terrified to write have succeeded. Authors who have struggled with writer's block have become victorious. Individuals who longed to be published but didn't know how to begin have reached best-seller status in a matter of months—delighted, triumphant, and empowered. From homemakers to teenagers, from nomads to successful CEOs, we have joyfully assisted authors in fulfilling their writing goals and reaching their publishing dreams.

Learn more about our White Glove Program for one-on-one support at www.igniteyou.life

Or join our monthly **Solo Book Club**, where you learn everything you need to know to write a life-changing book in an online group environment.
Use the QR code to find out more.

Visit: igniteyou.life

YOUR PURCHASE SUPPORTS LITERACY

Our mission to Ignite lives includes igniting the minds of children and igniting literacy. Our commitment to bettering others drives us to use all of our online profits made from Ignite books to build schools in places of need.

Through the Ignite Humanity Foundation Fund, every online book sale goes toward building schools in rural and impoverished areas. Ignite is proud to be supporting education and literacy around the world. If you would like to add yours, donate to our initiative, and find out more, use the QR code. Every book purchased makes a difference.

GET IGNITE'S *100 WRITING PROMPTS*...FREE!

At Ignite, we encourage and foster writing as a healing and introspective tool. To support you in enhancing your writing we are happy to offer you a complimentary eBook, where you will find powerful writing prompts for you to use daily to gain confidence in yourself and your writing. Use these inspiring writing prompts designed to Ignite and unleash the powerful writer in you.

Each prompt will get you started on your amazing writing journey. Access this incredible and FREE resource using the QR code.

IGNITE Joy

STORIES THAT SHOW ENRICHING WAYS TO
ENLIGHTEN AND BRIGHTEN YOUR DAY

INTRODUCTION BY

Lady JB Owen

23-time International Bestselling Author, Global Publisher,
Award-winning Humanitarian, World-Class Speaker, and Legacy Mentor

FOREWORD BY

Jennifer J. Hammond

YAY! Inspirational Speaker, Author, and Real Estate Expert

PROJECT LEADERS

Nicole Shantel Freeman

Christian Life Coach, Faith Activator, Financial Consultant, and Encouragement Speaker

Cheryl A. Rafter

Entrepreneur, Connector, Inspirer of Life, and Courageous Comeback Coach

OTHER FEATURED AUTHORS

Ashley Fry • Allison Prince • Christine von Pander •
Ciara Caston Finley • Corinne Erickson • Elaine Valerie Thompson •
Hollis Baley • Jennifer M. Moore • Joanne Gauthier • Karen Whelan •
Kari Berridge • Katarina Amadora • Katie Allen • Leona Wallace •
Liliana Avila Roque • Lydia Burchell • Melissa A. Corrion •
Melody J. Carberry • Nicole Shewaga • Shirley Jones •
Stacey Tompkins • Stacie Callan • Tanya Dow • Tina Ritchie •
Vanessa Rivers • Dr. Willo Boniface

PUBLISHED BY IGNITE PUBLISHING™

Other international best-selling compilation books
by IGNITE for you to enjoy:

Ignite Your Life for Women

Ignite Your Female Leadership

Ignite Your Parenting

Ignite Your Life for Men

Ignite Your Life for Conscious Leaders

Ignite Your Health and Wellness

Ignite Your Adventurous Spirit

Ignite Female Change Makers

Ignite the Modern Goddess

Ignite Happiness

Ignite Love

Ignite Your Inner Spirit

Ignite the Entrepreneur

Ignite Possibilities

Ignite the Hunger in You

Ignite Your Wisdom

Ignite Forgiveness

Ignite Your Faith

Ignite Your Courage

Ignite Your Purpose

Ashley Fry

Cheryl A. Rafter

Christine von Pander

Ciara Caston Finley

Corinne Erickson

Elaine Valerie Thompson

Hollis Baley

Jennifer M. Moore

Joanne Gauthier

Karen Whelan

Kari Berridge

Katarina Amadora

Katie Allen & Allison Prince

Lady JB Owen

Leona Wallace

Liliana Avila Roque

Lydia Burchell

Melissa A. Corrion

Melody J. Carberry

Nicole S. Freeman

Nicole Shewaga

Shirley Jones

Stacey Tompkins

Stacie Callan

Tanya Dow

Tina Ritchie

Vanessa Rivers

Dr. Willo Boniface

Published and printed by Ignite Publishing™ a division of JBO Global INC.
5569-47th Street Red Deer, AB
Canada, T4N1S1 1-877-677-6115

Book designer and Editor-in-Chief Lady JB Owen
Cover design by Brent Casteling
Typesetting by Kristine Joy Magno
Edited by JB Owen, Mimi Safiyah, Michiko Couchman, Sarah Cross, Steph Elliott, and Zoe Wong.
Designed in Canada, Printed in China
ISBN 979-89-8721-218-9

Ordering Information: Quantity sales. Special discounts are available on quantity purchases by corporations, associations, and others. For details, contact the publisher at the above address. Programs, products, or services provided by the authors are found by contacting them directly.

I loved every part of this experience, including knowing that I had help along the way, meeting new people, and learning how to write.

—Ashley Fry

This is my second time working with Lady JB and the Ignite Team. The training, development, and support that I have experienced have been at an even higher standard than I expected. They have grown in so many ways professionally, giving me the tools to learn and grow in my life and business. I highly recommend that if you want to write your story, contact their team. You will not be disappointed.

—Cheryl A. Rafter

Working with the Ignite Publishing Team made me feel so supported throughout the journey of writing my story. I know that if/when I write again, I will certainly use their team, systems, and processes to bring it to its full power and help change lives for the better.

—Christine von Pander

I can't even speak of how amazing this journey was without tears. I am overwhelmed with gratitude.

—Ciara Caston Finley

I'm profoundly grateful to Ignite for the incredible opportunity to share my story. It was truly amazing to meet so many new faces in such a close and supportive community. Special thanks to Lady JB and her exceptional team of writers and editors, whose dedication and talent made everything possible. The warmth, encouragement, and professionalism I encountered have left a lasting impact on me. This has been an unforgettable journey of connection and empowerment. Thank you for making it so meaningful.

—Corinne Erickson

Thank you to the Ignite Joy family for this opportunity and to Lady JB and Peter for all your incredible work for humanity. You lift us up and encourage us, igniting us all with joy and possibilities. Thanks to your wonderful team, whose huge hearts and talented gifts have blessed me. The Ignite experience will be one I will never forget and always want to belong to. I am grateful for the transformative journey!

—Elaine Valerie Thompson

My experience with the Ignite Team was far beyond my expectations. Each person I met drew out a new depth to my story, shaped me as a more talented writer, and gave me confidence in the creation process. I went from feeling as though I loved writing, yet was too afraid and ashamed of sharing my writing with anyone other than in short posts on social media; to having the full confidence to call myself an author and more importantly have the motivation to write consistently. As more and more strength is coming in my writing; I want to share more and more with the world!

—Hollis Baley

This has been an amazing and therapeutic experience. I am very grateful for the opportunity. Thank you!

—Jennifer M. Moore

I cannot thank the team enough for this wonderful experience. I have learned so very much through the process. How lucky was I to be connected with Lady JB. I have grown; I am now a writer. Thank you, Team Ignite!

—Joanne Gauthier

Ignite has been an extraordinary community. I have been gifted with so much being in this space. Lady JB Owen, your services to humanity are so sincere and inspiring; thank you for loving all of us. The team is incredible and engaging. Thank you all.

—Karen Whelan

I am immensely grateful for stumbling upon Ignite. It's more than just a community; it's a sanctuary where I feel embraced, heard, and valued. Lady JB's dedication is unparalleled; she generously shares her wisdom without reservation. In just two months, I've experienced profound growth in my writing skills and personal development. Look no further if you've ever felt the urge to share your story with the world. Ignite Humanity is the nurturing haven you've been searching for.

—Kari Berridge

I have been with Ignite since the first book, and I have seen it evolve. Writing and editing my stories has been a tremendous part of my personal journey of growth and transformation. Learning to tell your story in an empowered way can help you heal your past and challenge you to take full responsibility for your own part in creating your story. I have loved sharing my story and am grateful for those who have been inspired by my words. Lady JB really cares about helping each author find his or her voice and creating books that inspire humanity. I have met many amazing people and love being part of the Ignite community.

—Katarina Amadora

We so greatly enjoyed this process. The editing team was fantastic, extremely professional, and they helped us bring our story to life! Thank you!

—Katie Allen & Allison Prince

This process has been enlightening and beautiful, as I was supported every step of the way by an amazing team of experts. The systems and resources put in place created an environment that lifted me so I could connect with words that would inspire and impact lives. Thank you. I am eternally grateful and feel I have come into my own author space now. I would do this again and would highly recommend that if anyone feels they need to share their story, this is the place to say yes.

—Leona Wallace

I had no idea how to share my story with others, but I had a huge desire to do so. Thanks to the Ignite Family, writing about my experience and sharing it with the world was easy, joyful, and magical. Thank you!

—Liliana Avila Roque

While writing this chapter, my inner writer emerged. It gave me a new level of confidence in myself and what is possible through writing. Although I have been writing for many years, I was afraid to let anyone see it. Writing with Ignite was a transformational experience. They show you, guide you, and even hold your hand so you have the greatest writing experience possible.

Thank you to Lady JB and the amazing staff at Ignite Publishing. You have ignited me as a writer and author.

—Lydia Burchell

This has truly been a life-changing experience with so much growth and healing from within. Collaborating with so many knowledgeable and kind souls whose warmth and understanding created a safe space for vulnerability and creativity to flourish has made this process deeply meaningful and rewarding.

—Melissa A. Corrion

This is my first experience with Ignite Publishing, and I believe it is the beginning of something great. From introduction with Lady JB to support and through to publishing—a masterpiece of like-minded souls that have taken me through a process with such care, making sure not to miss a thing. I look forward to working with these amazing souls again and perhaps contributing to their Humanitarian efforts. Thank you for all that has been done to help me reach a new level of perspective. I am honored to have been part of this book.

—Melody J. Carberry

Working with Ignite Publishing has been an absolute blessing from start to finish. From the moment I embarked on this journey, I was met with unwavering support, guidance, and encouragement every step of the way. The team's dedication to excellence and their passion for helping authors bring their stories to life is truly inspiring. They provided invaluable insights, resources, and expertise that empowered me to elevate my writing to new heights.
What truly sets Ignite Publishing apart is their genuine care and commitment to their authors' success. I am grateful for the opportunity to collaborate with Ignite Publishing, and I recommend them to any aspiring author seeking to share their story with the world. Thank you, Ignite Publishing, for making my writing dreams a reality!

—Nicole S. Freeman

The opportunity to work with Ignite was something other than what I sought. It fell into my lap unexpectedly, and with cautious skepticism but a willingness to explore, I said yes. The experience far exceeded my expectations. Writing my story brought me healing, clarity, and purpose. The Ignite team gave me the structure, tools, and support I needed to reflect on and share my truth. It has been an absolute gift to be pushed out of my comfort zone, to feel validated and supported in my creative explorations, and to connect with a community of people who genuinely want to do good in the world. Working with Ignite has been a meaningful and life-changing experience. 10/10, I would recommend them!

—Nicole Shewaga

I have received a lot of attention and care, and it is most rewarding that I have already attracted clients, which is very rewarding.

—Shirley Jones

Through Ignite, I have connected with so many amazing people, entrepreneurs, and writers. The journey has helped me transform my writing skills and impacted my healing through human connection and telling my story.

—Stacey Tompkins

My experience with Ignite has been so supportive and helpful. I have felt nothing but encouragement and that I truly have a story that will help people along their healing journey. It is so nice to feel part of a community of like-minded people.

—Tanya Dow

Working on Ignite Joy was an incredible experience. I found the support I received, especially the editing sessions, invaluable.

—Vanessa Rivers

My experience with the team at Ignite has been life-changing. I felt completely supported as I crafted my story and experienced professional editors for the first time. I felt seen, and my story was honored every step of the way. Lady JB, in particular, was generous with her time and expertise and encouraged me to step confidently into my brand to see out my vision. The connections with co-authors enriched the experience, and I'm certain that life-long friendships are being forged. I'm grateful I said yes to this. Thank you.

—Dr. Willo Boniface

Dedication

Ignite Joy is dedicated to everyone, from the joyous newborn baby to the joy-filled grandparent. From those who love their job, enjoy their talent, joyfully give their gifts, and rejoice in their unique styles of enjoyment, this book is for everyone who loves to feel joy. We all deserve to live in the center of our joy and we each have the ability to offer joy to everyone we meet. We dedicate this book to those who radiate joy in every area of their lives.

Ignite Joy is also dedicated to those seeking more joy and those wanting to attain the inner peace and contentment that joy brings. It is for the ones in search of a new experience via joy and those open to embracing a different way of living that is more joy-infused, enjoyably abundant, and filled with the fun that comes while on the joyride of new ideas and experiences.

Joy is free, and costs nothing — available to all who desire it. Joy is an emotion that touches us deeply and rises us up to our greatest potential. If we can all give one thing to another, let it be unencumbered joy.

ASHLEY FRY

I dedicate this chapter to my Auntie and Uncle, whom I call my mom and dad. They took me and my sister under their care. Showed us love and helped us grow into the people we are today. They mean the world to me.

CHERYL A. RAFTER

My family and friends are the joy in my life. To all who are shining a light and bringing joy to their world, thank you for everything you do. Know you make a difference.

CHRISTINE VON PANDER

This writing is dedicated to every woman who still has that little girl inside who needs healing.

CIARA CASTON FINLEY

Dedicated to my late mother and brother, Relda Kaye Anderson and Troy Magee. Thank you for believing in me. Thank you to every reader who gives my words a chance. Blessings to those of you who find a piece of yourself in my story.

Corinne Erickson

To Rachel and Nathen, whose love and patience supported my recovery, and to my husband, David, whose unwavering support became my strength—this book is a testament to the power of family. A special acknowledgment to Alexis Stanhope of Stride Vestibular, whose expertise and care guided me in the healing process. Thank you all for your support, which inspired every word on these pages. Thank you all for being my lighthouse.

Elaine Valerie Thompson

I dedicate my chapter to all those reading it and needing Hope. To those who may feel life is dark right now, may you be filled with a shining light of joy. I also thank my wonderful Mum, my steadfast soulmate and partner, and my friends and family. To my partner, you are my rock. To my Dad, I know you are also looking down upon me and cheering me on. I pray you will be proud of me.

Hollis Baley

To my Creator, God,
For the gift of life and the blessings bestowed upon me. To my parents,
For nurturing and guiding me with love and wisdom. To my daughter, Sofia,
Who chose me to be her Mama,
Your presence brings immeasurable joy to my life. To my ex-husband,
For the lessons learned and the growth experienced, and for being the father of our beloved daughter. This story is dedicated to all those who have played a role in shaping my journey, with gratitude and love.

Jennifer M. Moore

Thank You, Jesus. Without You, I wouldn't have had the strength or the courage to write this. Thank you to my children, who are my three biggest cheerleaders, heroes, and inspiration; my siblings, for always making sure I laugh every day; my mom, for always loving me; and my dad, whose love and memory I will always cherish. He didn't live to see the free me, but one day, we will experience the joy of being free forever—together.

JOANNE GAUTHIER

This story is dedicated to my hero, Monique, and all the many other cancer warriors out there who never give up shining their light so that others can see. Through their courage, we find ours.

KAREN WHELAN

I dedicate this chapter to all the beautiful souls in my life who see the best of my light, particularly my husband Jeff. Your love is magical. My son and daughter, Aaron and Fia, you both fill my heart. I love being your mother and thank you for that gift.

KARI BERRIDGE

I would like to dedicate my story to all of those that have wrestled with crippling self-doubt and teetered on the brink. Your struggles are recognized, and your anguish is acknowledged. May you find comfort in shedding blame, shame, and guilt, embracing your true essence. In the depths of despair, remember you are not alone. Let this dedication serve as a guiding light, illuminating the path to a future where your value is unwavering and your presence celebrated.

KATARINA AMADORA

I would like to dedicate this chapter to my partner Tim, my life's love, and Lewys, whose wise words inspired me to embark on this journey. May we each have the courage to find what ignites joy within us and find a way to bring that joy to the world.

KATIE ALLEN & ALLISON PRINCE

We are so incredibly grateful to our parents for empowering us to pursue our dreams and passions. For our husbands (Jason and David), family, and friends who support us; as well as our BTC staff and community who cheer us on and make this all possible. We'd like to thank all of our teachers for preserving and sharing life-changing wisdom. And of course to our little boys Summit and Aiden who inspire us to be the best versions of ourselves.

LADY JB OWEN

I dedicate this to my amazing husband who shows up each and every day to help make my dreams come true. I thank all my kids, Jackson, Adonie, Jorja, and Lydia who teach me endlessly how to be a better person and show me the power of compassion, acceptance, and understanding. They bring me so much joy so that I can spread joy around the world. Thank you.

LEONA WALLACE

My story is dedicated to my Twin Flame, my two amazing sons, and my Saint of a sister, who all inspired and supported me to step into my joy and say yes to my deepest heart's desires.

LILIANA AVILA ROQUE

To my dad, my friend and Wise Old Man, whose advice continues to guide me today. Thank you, Mom, for the greatest gift of all ... LIFE! To Andrea, Roberto, and Santiago, thank you for your love, advice, and support. You are my greatest inspiration. Thank you for making us a great team. Thank you, my dear friend David Jamieson, for motivating me to write and share this story with the world.

LYDIA BURCHELL

I dedicate this chapter to my Dad, Ross Burchell, for always being my quiet hero and to all women on their path to finding inner confidence.

MELISSA A. CORRION

I dedicate this book to my husband, whose love, support, and encouragement fuel my dreams, my two cats, whose healing love brings joy to our home, and my children, who are my pride and joy. A heartfelt thank you to all the beautiful souls writing in this book for your love, support, and compassionate listening. Lastly, to all who have suffered from the 'mother wound,' your resilience and strength are undeniable. Healing starts by learning to re-parent yourself, found by looking deep within.

MELODY J. CARBERRY

I am dedicating this story to my family. I am grateful to my children for teaching me nothing short of love, kindness, courage, and self-reflection. I have learned from you more than I could have ever taught you. You are the center of my heartfelt joy and gratitude.

NICOLE S. FREEMAN

To my beloved daughters, Alli and Ainsli. You are the brightest stars in my sky, the greatest blessings in my life, and the purest embodiment of joy. From the moment you came into this world, you have filled my heart with indescribable love and brought endless light into my days. Your laughter, your smiles, and your unwavering spirit have been my constant inspiration and the driving force behind everything I do. Watching you grow, learn, and flourish fills me with pride beyond measure, and I am endlessly grateful for the privilege of being your mother. As I dedicate this chapter to you, my sweet angels, my Warrior Princesses, know that you are the truest joys of my life. May the words within the pages of my chapter serve as a testament to the boundless love and happiness you bring into my world each and every day. With all my love, Your Mommy

NICOLE SHEWAGA

To my honey-bunny boo-boo-boo, my strong-willed, perseverant, sweet little mini-me. For being my beacon of light and a wellspring of strength for me to continue the forge on the path to freedom and authenticity. And to anyone who has ever experienced the all-consuming, existential dread of a life without passion.

SHIRLEY JONES

I dedicate this chapter to my three sons, two daughters, and my grandchildren, hoping they follow their inner GPS.

STACEY TOMPKINS

I dedicate this story to my wonderful husband, who has supported me, encouraged me, and been my rock through tough times. I also thank my family and friends for always listening and the many patients I have met over the years who have inspired me with their mindset, perseverance, and resilience.

STACIE CALLAN

This chapter is dedicated to all of those who have traveled down those bumpy roads, only to come back and find their purpose. For everyone who has reached the bottom but has found their way to the top again, here's to you!

TANYA DOW

To the beautiful souls who may have given their power away and lost their light, may my chapter inspire you to rise again, reclaim what has always been yours, and stand boldly in your truth.

TINA RITCHIE

Dedicated to my children and grandchildren, each a unique star in their own right. They have challenged me to stretch and grow, while embracing our differences with love. Grateful for my children's understanding as they navigate change alongside my free spirit. Gratitude to my kindred spirits, great friends who lift and support me, you know who you are. To Brian Ashton a father figure who imparted wisdom in navigating markets and the great saying, "We become who we hang out with." Lastly to my Angels looking over me, including my loving mother and graceful Grandma; they taught me the importance of interdependence and gifted me their timeless wisdom.

VANESSA RIVERS

For my daughter, Sadie, my greatest wish is that you live a life filled with joy, love, and adventure. I am so proud to be your mother!

DR. WILLO BONIFACE

I dedicate this book to any young mother facing her mortality. May you find inner strength to cherish the moments and experience blissful joy, even as you face the unimaginable. And when you are ready, share your glow and your story, you never know who needs your light.

Contents

Preface

In the quiet moments of reflection and amidst life's tumultuous waves, women often find solace in the pursuit of joy. It's a journey uniquely theirs, woven with threads of resilience, courage, and unwavering hope. Within the pages of *Ignite Joy*, we embark on a voyage into the hearts and minds of women who have dared to embrace life's challenges and emerge victorious — their spirits illuminated with the radiant glow of joy.

These stories, penned by women from diverse walks of life, resonate with the raw authenticity of lived experiences. They speak of triumph over adversity, of navigation through a labyrinth of emotions, and of the discovery of hidden treasures of joy nestled within the folds of everyday existence. Each narrative is a testament to the indomitable spirit of womanhood, a celebration of the strength that defines them, and a reminder that joy is not merely a temporary emotion but an intrinsic part of our being.

In a world that often seeks to dim our light, this book serves as a beacon of hope, shedding light on the path to inner peace and contentment. It reminds us that joy is not found in the absence of challenges but in our ability to rise above them, to find beauty amid challenges, and to cherish the moments of joy that bless our lives.

As you embark on this journey, may you be inspired by the courage and fortitude of the women whose stories grace these pages. May you find comfort in the shared humanity of our experiences and discover that, amongst life's trials and tribulations, joy remains a dependable companion — ever-present and ever-true.

For in the journey of life, it is the moments of joy that lend texture to our existence, infusing even the darkest of days with a promise of a brighter tomorrow. When we embrace these moments, cherishing them, and sharing them with others — we find a joy we are eager to share.

Welcome to *Ignite Joy* – may it ignite a flame of hope, inspiration, and boundless joy in your soul.

WHAT MAKES IGNITE BOOKS SPECIAL?

At Ignite Publishing™, we're not just about publishing books; we're about igniting transformative experiences. With *Ignite Joy* being our twenty-third compilation book, we continue our mission to empower others, Ignite lives, and make a profound difference on the planet for future generations. What makes Ignite books truly unique is our focus on capturing those pivotal moments of insight and growth – what we call Ignite Moments™.

An Ignite Moment isn't just a fleeting realization; it's a profound, life-altering experience that reshapes your perspective and sets you on a new path. These moments are the heart and soul of our books, offering readers the opportunity to witness authentic stories of personal transformation. From overcoming adversity to discovering inner strength, each Ignite Moment is a testament to the resilience and fortitude of the human spirit.

What makes Ignite Moments so powerful is they are universal. Regardless of background or circumstance, we all experience moments of clarity and revelation that propel us forward on our journey. By sharing these stories, we hope to inspire readers to recognize and embrace their own Ignite Moments, leading to greater self-awareness, growth, and fulfillment.

At the heart of every Ignite Moment is a lesson waiting to be learned – a nugget of wisdom that has the power to change lives. It is through these moments of insight that we discover our true potential and unlock new possibilities. Whether it's a small epiphany or a monumental breakthrough, each

Ignite Moment is a reminder of the resilience and capacity for growth that lies within us all.

As you delve into the pages of an Ignite book, we invite you to open your heart and mind to the transformative power of these moments. May they inspire you, challenge you, and ultimately Ignite a spark of change within you. It is in these moments of insight and growth that we truly discover what it means to be human – to strive, to overcome, and to Ignite the flame of possibility within ourselves and others.

As a publishing house dedicated to Ignite lives, we stand as a beacon in Empowerment Publishing, championing powerful, authentic, and heartfelt stories aimed at transforming lives. The word "Ignite" encapsulates the essence of our books, symbolizing our goal behind every story we share. We view our books as gifts to the world, igniting ideas, sparking thoughts, kindling feelings, and awakening desires. Each publication is meticulously crafted to inspire and uplift readers toward greater personal fulfillment. Our books and the stories they contain foster connections, cultivate love, bridge divides, and deepen understanding. Every story within these pages is carefully designed to resonate with you profoundly, stimulating your mind and touching your heart while instilling a sense of hope and possibility.

As you embark on your journey through an Ignite story, each one commences with an inspiring *Power Quote*. These empowering statements are intended to propel you forward, encouraging you to break free from your comfort zone. Power Quotes offer insights and hope, serving as catalysts for ideas, actions, and change. Crafted with the intent to Ignite new possibilities within you, these quotes aim to infuse your life with joy, regardless of the challenges you face. Joy, after all, is often found in the simplest of moments and manifests in myriad ways unique to each individual. While joy may be personal, its transformative power is universal, binding us all together in shared experiences.

Following the Power Quote, you will encounter the author's *Personal Intention*, offering their heartfelt insights and aspirations for you, the reader. Each author enters this book with a singular mission: to *Ignite joy within you*, a sentiment they lovingly express in their opening intention. Their stories, derived from personal experiences, reveal moments of transformation, enlightenment, and newfound understanding. These Ignite Moments illustrate how life's challenges can lead to profound growth, offering valuable lessons and insights. They transcend barriers of race, religion, and gender, highlighting our shared humanity and interconnectedness.

Ignite books extend beyond mere storytelling; they provide actionable steps for personal growth and transformation. At the conclusion of every chapter, you will discover *Ignite Action Steps* – practical exercises designed to empower you on your journey. Our authors share these actionable insights drawn from their own experiences, hoping to spark positive change and foster a more joyful existence. Each step is as unique as you are, offering the potential for transformative results when implemented with dedication and consistency.

The Ignite experience is tailored to accommodate your unique reading style. Whether you choose to read cover-to-cover, randomly select a page, or follow a recommendation from a friend, we trust that you will find the perfect approach for you. Our aim is simple: to Ignite joy in your life and inspire you to share that joy with others. We invite you to share your experiences with our authors and community, as your feedback has the power to uplift and inspire. Together, we can continue to ignite lives and spread joy throughout the world.

May your journey through these pages be filled with profound insights, heartfelt connections, and abundant joy. As you immerse yourself in the stories that lie ahead, may you discover new perspectives, find solace in shared experiences, and embark on a journey of personal transformation. May each Ignite Moment you encounter bring you closer to a life filled with joy, purpose, and fulfillment. May this book and all its stories spark joy, create joyful and joyous new thoughts, and bring you a sense of joy-filled enjoyment.

***May all your Ignite Moments be filled with both joyful lessons
and heart-filled blessings.***

IGNITE
Joy

Lady JB Owen

INTRODUCTION

By Lady JB Owen

THE SPARK JOY CREATES

Welcome to the vibrant world of *Ignite Joy: Stories That Show Enriching Ways to Enlighten and Brighten Your Day*. In the following pages, you'll embark on an exhilarating journey filled with laughter, tears, and heartwarming moments that will leave you with a smile on your face and a bit of joy in your step. This book has been written so that you feel swept away by a whirlwind of inspiration and lifted by a bevy of delight. Each story in the book has been penned by a unique individual who has bravely faced life's challenges and emerged on the other side with a heart ablaze with joy.

In a world often overshadowed by chaos and uncertainty, the pursuit of joy becomes not merely a luxury but a necessity for the soul. Joy is a vital emotion that nourishes the body, uplifts the spirit, and binds humanity together in a tapestry of shared understanding. At its core, joy serves as a beacon of light amidst life's darkest moments, offering solace, hope, and a renewed sense of purpose. It has the power to transcend individual suffering and connect us on a deeper level, fostering empathy, compassion, and understanding of one another's journey and experiences.

When we allow joy to permeate our lives, we cultivate a mindset of gratitude and appreciation for the beauty surrounding us. Joy opens our hearts to the wonders of the world and invites us to savor the many pleasures of life; from a sun-kissed, dewy morning to the deep belly laughter of loved ones, joy can be found everywhere. The best part is that joy serves as a catalyst for connection, inspiring acts of kindness, generosity, and love that will ripple outward, touching the lives of those around us and countless others we may never meet.

On a collective level, the presence of joy in our communities fosters harmony, camaraderie, and a sense of belonging. It strengthens the bonds that unite us as human beings, transcending barriers of race, religion, and culture. In a world often divided by strife and discord, joy is a unifying force, reminding us of our shared unity and interconnectedness with all living beings on our planet.

Ultimately, joy holds the power to transform not only individual lives but also the world at large. It is the fuel that propels us forward on our collective journey toward a brighter, more hopeful future. By embracing joy in all its forms, *joyful, joyous, enjoyable, rejoicing,* and *enjoyably*, we become agents of *joy-filled* change, spreading light and love wherever we go and leaving a lasting impact on our world.

Even in the midst of life's challenges and difficulties, joy has a remarkable way of finding its way to us. It often emerges unexpectedly, shining through the darkness of hardship, adversity, and unexpected challenges. It's in these moments that we realize the true power of joy — its ability to elevate our spirits, give us hope, and remind us of the beauty and strength present in every human being.

WHY JOY MATTERS

Joy isn't just something we experience individually; it connects us to each other and to the world around us. When we share moments of joy with others, whether through laughter, acts of kindness, or simply being present with one another, we strengthen our bonds and create a sense of belonging and connection.

Joy plays a crucial role in fostering unity, understanding, and empathy in our communities and societies. It transcends differences and brings people together, reminding us of our shared humanity and our capacity to value each other and honor our diversity. Joy is a powerful force for healing and reconciliation in a world that can often feel divided and fragmented.

Most importantly, when we embrace joy and Ignite it in our lives, we become examples of light and hope, spreading happiness and giving more support wherever we go. It is through the collective experience of joy that we can create a more *joyful*, compassionate, and harmonious world for ourselves and our future generations.

In our individual lives, joy holds immense significance in serving as a vessel of promise that enlightens our journey through beneficial and challenging times. Emotionally, joy is a powerful antidote to feelings of sadness, despair, and loneliness. When we experience joy through moments of silliness, connection with colleagues, or achievements that bring us fulfillment, feeling joy uplifts our self-worth. It infuses us with a sense of belonging and personal contentment. This emotional resonance enables us to navigate life's difficulties with greater ease and grace, fostering a positive outlook and a deeper sense of well-being.

Physically, the experience of joy has tangible effects on our bodies and overall health. Studies have shown that joyful experiences can lead to the release of endorphins and neurotransmitters that act as natural painkillers and mood enhancers. Additionally, joy has been linked to lower levels of stress hormones such as cortisol, which can positively impact our immune system, cardiovascular health, and overall resilience to illness. By *enjoying* activities and experiences that bring us joy, we can cultivate a healthier, more vibrant physical state and enhance our overall quality of life.

Similarly, joy plays a vital role in shaping our thoughts, beliefs, and perceptions of the world around us. When we cultivate a mindset of joy and gratitude, we train our brains to focus on the positive aspects of life, even in the face of adversity. This shift in perspective fosters greater resilience and mental fortitude and enables us to approach challenges with a sense of optimism and creativity. By embracing joy as a fundamental aspect of our lives, we empower ourselves to live more fully, love more deeply, and find meaning and purpose in every moment.

Ignite Joy in One Another

As you turn the pages of this book, prepare to be inspired, uplifted, and transformed by the power of their *joy-filled* stories. From tales of overcoming loss and grief to narratives of self-discovery and acceptance, each author offers a glimpse into their unique journey toward uncovering the blessing amidst finding joy. Through their stories, we are reminded that joy is not merely a momentary emotion but a desired state of being — a choice we make to overcome the opposite of joy and embrace life with thankfulness, appreciation, and serendipity.

Ignite Joy is not just a collection of stories; it is a celebration of the human spirit and the enriching lessons of the human heart. Each author shares their joyful "Ignite Moment" to awaken the idea that joy is possible. They show that joy is not an elusive treasure reserved for a select few; rather, it is a universal experience available to every one of us. Regardless of our circumstances, background, or life events, joy is within reach, waiting to be discovered and realized. Joy is not dependent on external factors or material possessions; rather, it arises from within, rooted in our capacity to learn from another who has walked the path to joy before us. Each one of the stories you read here is an authentic representation of that.

We like to say that *joy* is a choice — a conscious decision to focus on the positive aspects of life and cultivate a mindset that will serve you going forward. To choose joy requires us to shift our perspective away from what we lack or what is going wrong toward what we have and what is going right. By practicing mindfulness, self-awareness, and intentional appreciation, we can train our minds to recognize and savor the moments of joy that exist all around us, even during challenges or difficulties; like a lotus flower emerging from the mud, joy finds its indelible way.

Best of all, *joy* is contagious — when we experience joy, we naturally spread it to those around us, creating a ripple effect of positivity and connection. By sharing our joy with others through generosity and understanding, we not only enhance our own sense of well-being but also contribute to the collective happiness of our communities, society, and humanity as a whole. Joy inspires us to embrace diversity and celebrate every individual's unique gifts and talents. When we approach life with a mindset of joy, we recognize all people's inherent worth and dignity. *Joyful* inclusivity and enjoyable acceptance pave the way for greater unity and togetherness as we celebrate our shared commonalities and work toward a brighter, more harmonious world.

Ultimately, joy is a birthright — a fundamental aspect of the human experience that is inherent to our nature. It is not something to be pursued or achieved but rather something to be embraced and celebrated. By recognizing the infinite potential for joy within ourselves and the world around us, we can cultivate a life filled with meaning, purpose, and endless *enjoyment*.

That means, dear reader, we invite you to embark on this joy-inspired journey with us — to open your heart joyfully and expand your mind joyously. Allow the stories within these pages to Ignite the flame of joy within your own soul. May you find inspiration, comfort, and solace in knowing *joy* awaits you. May you discover, as we have, that joy is not merely a destination but a sacred journey to be discovered, felt, and *rejoiced*.

With gratitude and joy,

Lady JB Owen

IGNITE
Joy

Jennifer J. Hammond

FOREWORD

JENNIFER J. HAMMOND

"Lift your voice with positive energy and say YAY as you pave the way to creating a better world. With YAY in your heart, every moment is a work of art."

YOU HAVE THE POWER TO CREATE JOY EVERY DAY, WILL YOU?

Welcome to a journey of joy, positivity, and transformation! As you embark on the pages of this book, *Ignite Joy*, allow me to extend my heartfelt gratitude for choosing to explore the boundless potential of ways to create joy in your life. Each chapter will be an opportunity for you to look at your life journey and find new ways to create joy.

In a world often filled with challenges, uncertainties, and obstacles, it's easy to lose sight of the simple yet profound essence of joy. Yet, amidst the chaos and noise, there exists a powerful force waiting to be unleashed. For me, the way I express joy is by saying the simple yet impactful word — YAY!

YAY! is just one of many ways to create a joyful life. It is more than just a word; it's a beacon of your inner light, a source of inspiration, a high frequency, and a catalyst for change. It embodies the essence of celebration, gratitude, and positivity. It's a reminder that regardless of our circumstances, we have the power to choose joy, embrace life with enthusiasm, and find beauty in the ordinary.

For me, YAY isn't just my brand; it's a way of life — a philosophy that has guided me through the ups and downs of my journey. From the bustling streets of Washington, DC, to the serene shores of Key West, YAY has been my constant companion, guiding star, and source of strength. Yet, my life hasn't always been filled with YAY moments. Like all of us, life has also had its challenges.

As a high school student in Key West, Florida, I remember sitting in my guidance counselor's office, noticing the rust around the metal framed windows and the black mold growing on the air conditioner vent. The smells of Cuban coffee filled the air in this quaint coastal town. Many people consider the beautiful islands of the Florida Keys as a 'paradise' filled with endless joy. However, as I sat listening to my mother explain why I was not intelligent enough to be in college prep classes and that I didn't have what it took to succeed in anything, joy drained from my spirit. She recommended that I take auto mechanics instead. I watched the reaction on the face of the high school guidance counselor as she agreed with my mother, and I was filled with sadness as I thought: *I guess I am stupid and worthless.* I sat in silence and wondered: *Why was it that no one believed I was smart or had the potential to be successful?*

The family secret that we, as children, were never allowed to speak was hidden deep inside. I felt like an invisible robot that no one even noticed as I walked the halls of high school. My sister was brave, and she spoke about the family secrets; thus, my mother sent her to live in foster care in New York. My brother was brave and revealed some of the family secrets; he soon ran away from the violence and the drug/alcohol abuse from my mother. I was left alone to face the abuse and find a way to survive.

When the day came, I walked across the stage to receive my diploma. My mother's voice was still haunting me from her grave: "You will never be successful at anything, and you most likely won't even graduate." As I looked at the huge crowd in the stadium, I realized I could create any success I wanted. I can create joy even when life doesn't make it easy. I am a success. My mother had thought that I would never graduate from high school, yet as I was walking across the stage to receive my Master's Degree from The University. I thought, "YAY! I did it!" and I was filled with joy. I had overcome obstacles, the doubts of others, and a very challenging childhood. I discovered my joy that day and from then onward, I celebrated every day with my unique YAY!

From that moment on, I have incorporated that important YAY ingredient in my career in real estate as a SiriusXM™ radio talk show host, currently a podcast host, a best-selling author, a worldwide educator, and someone who is honored to have been inducted into the Happiness Hall Of Fame with trailblazers such as Deepak Chopra, Tony Robbins, and Reggie Jackson, Olympic gold medalist Kristi Yamaguchi, Dolly Parton, and Dr. Wayne Dyer. *What an honor.* YAY! I've witnessed firsthand the transformative power of igniting your YAY. I've seen how a simple shift in perspective, a moment of gratitude, or a burst of enthusiasm can change the course of someone's day, their week, or even their entire life.

As you begin reading the stories in *Ignite Joy,* let it be a burst of inspiration to shift your viewpoint and explore new ways to create more joy in your life. In this book, you'll discover practical strategies, powerful stories, and heartfelt reflections to help you cultivate a deeper sense of joy, purpose, and fulfillment. Each author has a unique viewpoint on joy, and each story is designed to bring you insights that will help you discover and manifest the deep feeling of joy you desire.

From the importance of gratitude practices to the impact of positive thinking, from the art of celebration to the science of happiness, *Ignite Joy* offers a roadmap for embracing the full potential of YAY in every aspect of your life. Whether you're seeking to overcome challenges, pursue your passions, or simply infuse your days with more joy, this book is here to support and inspire you every step of the way.

As you journey through the chapters ahead, I encourage you to approach each page with an open heart and a playful spirit. Allow yourself to fully immerse in the wisdom, insights, and joy that await you. And remember, no matter where you are on your journey, you have the power to Ignite joy in your life and the lives of those around you.

So, dear reader, *are you ready to embark on this joyful adventure? Are you ready to embrace the power of YAY and Ignite the spark of joy within you?* If so, then let's dive in together and let the journey begin!

With love, light, and a resounding YAY, let's Ignite Joy!

Jennifer J. Hammond — United States of America
YAY! Inspirational Speaker, Author, and Real Estate Expert
www.JenniferjHammond.com
Jennifer Hammond
jenniferjhammond

Nicole S. Freeman

NICOLE SHANTEL FREEMAN

"Let joy be your flaming sword, lighting your way and giving you strength."

As you immerse yourself in this chapter, may its words envelop you like a shield of resilience, fortifying you with comfort and strength during life's toughest trials. Sometimes, life delivers powerful blows capable of staggering even the strongest among us. Yet, in the midst of adversity, I want to impart this essential truth: *joy remains within reach. Through life's chaotic twists and turns, joy can still be discovered, guiding us through the complexities of our journey with an unwavering sense of peace and grit.*

WHEN LIFE PUTS YOU ON NOTICE, PERSEVERE WITH JOY

The autumn breeze turned to a winter chill, and the excitement of Thanksgiving break filled my children's hearts. The delightful aromas of apple crisp and pumpkin spice kept every one of us in a pleasant mood, spreading joy all around. Amidst the changing seasons, I found fulfillment in tending to the needs of my two precious daughters, who were my greatest pride and joy. I cherished every moment of motherhood as a single parent, and ensuring their well-being with love and compassion was not just a responsibility but a joyful commitment I held dear in my heart. Our evenings were filled with laughter as we sang at the top of our lungs and danced around the house, creating beautiful memories together. There's a special kind of contentment in the simple pleasures of eating my favorite foods and baking desserts, surrounded by the love of my playful children.

While dedicating myself to my daughters, I also nurtured my entrepreneurial endeavors, continuously investing in my personal growth and development. Juggling the responsibilities of parenthood and entrepreneurship, I dedicated myself to a nine-to-five career, striving to excel in every aspect of my multi-faceted life. Embracing these roles with unwavering commitment, I navigated the challenges with a heart full of love and optimism.

However, that optimism would be tested when I grappled with an unexpected challenge that shook me to my core. It was a typical morning, returning home after dropping my daughters off at school and daycare, in the routine of our daily lives. However, as I approached my front door, something caught my eye — a piece of paper, seemingly unimportant at first glance. To my disbelief, it was an eviction notice demanding that we vacate our home. The weight of the situation hit me like a ton of bricks, flooding me with a sense of dread and uncertainty. This was the third such notice in a week, following the disconnection warning for our electricity and the threat of repossession of our transportation. Over just a few days, I wondered if baking cookies, dancing in our living room, and even getting my angels to school would be possible again. As I stood there, reading the eviction letter, a wave of fear washed over me, leaving me questioning, *What am I going to do?*

Receiving those notices felt like a crushing blow, triggering a whirlwind of emotions. The weight of the situation descended upon me like a boulder, leaving me gasping for air amid overwhelming feelings of inadequacy, despair, and unworthiness. A thought echoed relentlessly in my mind: *I failed my children.*

As those three notices loomed in my mind, I consciously focused on my tasks — finishing my project, engaging in meetings, and tackling the day's to-do list. Yet, in the thick of the hustle and bustle, a whirlwind of questions and doubts crept in as I pondered where I had gone wrong and where I was headed next. Despite these swirling thoughts, I persevered through my workday, meeting deadlines, connecting with clients, and leading discussions. As the day wound down, I found myself sinking into the comfort of my sofa, which felt unusually enormous. At that moment, I couldn't shake the feeling of shrinking, shame, fear, and embarrassment, as if the sofa was swallowing me up, leaving me feeling minute and alone on a deserted island.

Drowning in fear, I found myself yearning for solace, seeking refuge in a familiar comfort I've always turned to when life throws unexpected challenges my way… junk food! Slowly, I went from the living room to the adjacent kitchen. Each step felt like an eternity as I was drawn to the pantry where my toddler's snacks awaited. For quite some time now, I've struggled with this habit. I turn to my daughters' gummy bears, cheese puffs, and chocolate wafers for comfort when life throws its curveballs. It's not about hunger or a genuine need for sustenance but rather a craving for something to soothe me and momentarily uplift my spirits. Devouring those gooey treats is not just a fleeting desire, it is almost like an urgent need. I can't control myself, as if indulging in those snacks to ease my turmoil is the only option.

As I approached the pantry, I felt a gentle tug in another direction. It was as though something beyond myself was calling out to me, urging me to step outside and bask in the warmth of the sun. I yearned to feel the presence of something greater, something more nourishing that would serve me. My body craved the sunlight to warm my skin and lift the weight from my shoulders. Instantly, I realized it wasn't just the sun I needed, but *The Son* — God's presence wrapping me in His love and grace. I stood at a crossroads, faced with a decision that would determine my path forward. Would I retreat to the familiar by using the unfulfilling comforts of food, or would I dare to embrace something new and transformative, something I deeply desired — *Jesus*, God's son? Making this choice felt monumental, especially for a creature of habit like me, accustomed to routine security. Breaking free from the chains of addiction required an epic shift.

With determination in my heart, I took a bold step in the opposite direction. Instead of succumbing to the allure of sweet treats, I consciously chose to try something new, to embrace the light and love that surrounded me. I ventured outside. I paused in my tracks, soaking in the beauty around me. The sunlight embraced me; its warmth reminded me of God's divine presence. As I gazed towards Heaven, I whispered, *How are you going to help me this one, Lord? For I am in need of a miracle.*

As I embarked on my walk, contemplating the harsh reality of impending electricity cutoff, vehicle repossession, and losing our cherished home, it felt like a downpour of emotion flooded my eyes, like raindrops cascading down a windowpane on a stormy day. Though I sought solace in God's love to carry me forward, the weight of the situation brought forth an inevitable stream of tears. Yet, in that moment of vulnerability, a voice within me thundered:

Remember who you are, Nicole.

You are victorious!

In the chaos and uncertainty, you remain unshakeable and steadfast.

The words were profound and life-changing. I knew the Holy Spirit gently reminded me of my identity and reassured me of God's unwavering care. With newfound resolve, I stood tall, shoulders squared, with a smile gracing my lips. With reignited conviction, I declared:

I am unshakeable! I am unstoppable! I am unbreakable!

The joy that surged within me felt like a glorious symphony, resonating from the core of my being and igniting every corner of my soul. Despite the chill in the late afternoon air, I basked solely in the warmth of the radiant sun, echoing the words, *The joy of the Lord is truly my strength* (Nehemiah 8:10). With renewed grace and gratitude, not only did I experience joy, but an all-consuming peace that settled within me, assuring me I could find rest in God's embrace, even with the looming threat of disconnection, eviction, and repossession notices overhead.

As I twirled back into my home, blowing kisses toward heaven in gratitude, I retreated to the comfort of my favorite spot on the sofa, wrapping myself in my cherished blanket. This time, it fit me perfectly.

I felt hesitant as I reached for the remote to turn on the television. A gentle nudge from God stirred within me, urging me to confront the three companies behind those daunting notices. Tilting my head towards the sky, I whispered, "Lord God, they've already demanded their dues. What else can I do?" Yet, sensing His persistent guidance, I reluctantly dialed the numbers, believing *something* could be done.

First, it was the property management company behind the looming eviction notice. With a tremor in my voice, I pleaded for a payment plan, fully expecting rejection. I grew increasingly frustrated as I attempted to communicate with the company again, a sense of hopelessness creeping in. *Why bother*, I wondered, *when it hadn't worked in the past?* These companies seemed unwilling to negotiate, leaving me questioning the value of my efforts. But to my astonishment, they agreed. In a wave of divine intervention, an empowering sensation washed over me like a beacon of hope, illuminating the darkness of uncertainty. Tears of gratitude flowed, for God had intervened when my eviction seemed imminent.

With renewed faith, I moved on to the electric company, bracing myself for another round of negotiations. Despite my already extended deadline, they, too, granted me an extension, asking *me* to choose a new date. It seemed surreal — first, the property company, now the electric company offering me mercy and favor. Truly, God was at work! With newfound confidence, I made the final call to the vehicle finance company, the bearer of the repossession notice. And just like the others, they too offered me the chance to choose a new date for partial payment. Immediately, I felt the presence of God's grace and provision, a triple blessing bestowed upon me in a single day. Joy radiated from within me, transforming the atmosphere around me. *I could breathe again.*

As all three companies agreed to grant me an extension, a wave of relief washed over me and I felt a weight lift from my shoulders. It was as if a door of opportunity had opened before me, offering a glimmer of hope amidst the darkness. With gratitude overflowing in my heart, I whispered a silent prayer of thanks, knowing that this victory was a testament to the power of faith and perseverance. Truly, when God moves, miracles happen.

Graced with the opportunity to regain my footing, I turned to God, seeking His wisdom and direction for the path ahead. As I reflected on my circumstances, I resolved to maintain an unwavering sense of peace and joy, recognizing that even through adversity, God is good and faithful. With my eyes fixed on Him, I adopted a posture of thankfulness, choosing to appreciate the blessings in my life rather than dwelling on what I lacked. Focusing on the solution magnified the situation. Embracing this mindset shift, I implemented practical money management practices with diligence and discipline. I regained a sense of control over my financial situation and secured a stable future for myself and my girls. After doubting my abilities as a mother and provider, engulfed in shame and guilt, I was empowered by the joy that was now lighting my path.

Today, I find myself enveloped in peace and joy, once again relishing moments spent dancing with my daughters, sharing laughter, driving them to school, and baking together in harmonious bliss. I carry that same empowered joy into my new professional endeavors. With God-given confidence and strength, I am proud to facilitate the "Create Your Financial Freedom" summit and also spearhead in-person workshops, supporting individuals to seize control of their finances and powerfully move forward into renewed financial freedom. I proudly launched my Wealthy Worthy Woman leadership program, designed to encourage women to embrace their financial independence and cultivate a mindset of abundance. Through these transformative programs, participants are equipped with the tools and strategies to build wealth, step into their leadership potential, and create a lasting financial legacy. I am devoted to helping as many women as possible to avoid the pitfalls of what I went through.

As I look back, I value the experiences I endured to be able to teach these skills. God allowed me to see how one can take a difficult time and use it to realign, reconnect, and reinvigorate oneself. In being closer to Him, I could take hold of my life and persevere. I used His belief in me to find belief in myself.

As I reflect on these blessings, I'm reminded of the words from Romans 15:13, a prayer I extend to you: "May your trust in God fill your heart with boundless joy and peace. In the midst of life's highs and lows, I encourage you to find joy in the chaos. Allow yourself to acknowledge the pain, but also pivot towards gratitude, for in doing so, you'll rediscover *your* joy and peace."

As I faced the daunting prospect of eviction, repossession, and disconnection, the notices reminded me of life's uncertainties. I now choose to take notice of God's presence and cling to joy. Even amid life's storms, you too can take heart, for joy is not elusive but ever-present, waiting to be embraced. In the tumultuous sea of uncertainty, let the unwavering goodness of God anchor your soul, providing a steadfast foundation in the midst of that turmoil. Notice how His faithfulness knows no bounds, a beacon of hope guiding you through the darkest of nights. Choose joy, for in the noticing, you'll find the power to rise above life's storms and discover the boundless grace that awaits.

The mantras I impart to my daughters are, "We do hard things" and "Everything is possible," all while encouraging them to take deep breaths. Life indeed presents us with joyful moments, challenging obstacles, and heart-wrenching sorrows. Yet, I want to instill in you the belief that you can overcome these challenges. You possess the strength and resilience to tackle life's difficulties head-on. Remember, you are more than capable of doing hard things. When life puts you on notice, let joy light the way and be the sword you carry into the realms of possibilities.

Ignite Action Steps

To cultivate a deeper connection of joy in any situation, incorporate these action steps into your daily routine. As you take intentional strides to prioritize these action steps in your life, allow them to guide you toward greater spiritual, emotional, and mental well-being. Let's GEAUX! (In Louisiana, this is how we say "Let's go.")

- **God first.** Start each day by dedicating time to connecting with God through prayer, meditation, or scripture reading. Prioritize your relationship with God above all else, allowing His guidance and presence to illuminate your path.

- **Gratitude.** Cultivate a habit of gratitude by regularly reflecting on the blessings in your life, big and small. Keep a gratitude journal or simply take a moment each day to express thanks for the people, experiences, and opportunities that enrich your life.

- **Get outside; get some sun.** Make it a point to spend time outdoors, soaking in the sun's healing rays. Whether it's a leisurely walk in the park, gardening, or simply sitting outside and enjoying nature, prioritize getting fresh air and sunlight to rejuvenate your mind, body, and spirit.

- **Get out of your head; Remain positive.** Challenge negative thoughts by practicing mindfulness and focusing on the present moment. Engage in activities that bring you joy and uplift your spirits, whether it is pursuing a hobby, spending time with loved ones, or practicing acts of kindness. Choose positivity and optimism, even in the face of challenges.

- **Give grace.** Extend grace and compassion to yourself and others. Recognize that we all have our struggles and imperfections, and choose to approach yourself and others with kindness, empathy, and understanding. Embrace forgiveness toward yourself and those around you, allowing room for growth, healing, and transformation.

Nicole Shantel Freeman — United States of America
Christian Life Coach, Faith Activator,
Financial Consultant, Encouragement Speaker
Nicole Freeman
nicoleshantelfreeman
nicole-freeman-33aba096

Cheryl A. Rafter

Cheryl A. Rafter

"When you take responsibility for your life, you will find joy."

May this story encourage you to discover your inner child, to love, forgive, and find the hidden joy that we all have inside of us. I encourage you to play like a child every day and embrace the moments. Live life like there is no tomorrow. I hope that by reading my journey, you find inner peace and love within you. Embrace the freedom to be yourself and do things by yourself with joy and happiness.

Free to Discover Who We Are

I heard high-pitched yelling from the tiny upstairs bedroom next to mine. My two younger sisters were in the middle of another loud argument over who knew what. I ran in to try to calm the situation, wanting to protect my sisters from getting into trouble for fighting.

"What's going on up there?" my dad angrily shouted from downstairs, following a daily pattern of my sisters misbehaving and him getting overly upset. I didn't want them to set him off. I would respond by saying, "Nothing, Dad," as I tried to calm down my middle sister, who was quick to get upset and mean. "Shh!" I would direct both of them before he shouted, "Get down here!" I knew if he called us downstairs, we would get a spanking, and my dad's verbal rage would be thrown at us. I was scared. I lived in the suspense of never knowing when the next time would be that he would get enraged at my mom or us over any little thing. I tried hard to be the peacemaker as I didn't want anything to happen to my sisters or me.

Growing up as the oldest child, I learned early on that I had to be responsible because my mom worked full-time and needed my help. I was always doing things around the house, like taking care of my sisters, making dinner, and doing daily chores. Sometimes I felt resentful for having so many duties, unable to go anywhere after school or spend time with friends at their homes. I could play outside in our front yard, but only once my chores were done and I had ensured my sisters had finished their homework. My little sisters always wanted to go everywhere with me, which I thought was a burden as a teenager, wanting my own space. I now know all they wanted was to spend time with me because they loved me very much — even though I loved them deeply, my obligation to my family often felt too much to carry, overwhelming and disconnected.

Despite these feelings, my family also provided a sense of joy. I remember the happiest times as a child were when we all went to see my grandparents each summer. We would climb into the back seat of my dad's big truck and drive for a day and a half to get to Vancouver Island, which was over 1500 kilometers away in a different province. I remember being in awe at the beautiful snow-covered mountains and their size as I would gaze at the amazing lakes and different kinds of trees along the way. I loved being on the ferry and feeling the freedom of the wind tossing my hair as the water splashed and the boat rocked me rhythmically.

The drive was always a bit of a challenge as all three of us were stuck in close quarters for such a long period of time, taking up too much room and sleeping on each other as the journey continued. We definitely got on each other's nerves, but we were also singing, laughing, and playing games — creating great memories as a family. I would not have changed anything as we were bonding and learning how to be with each other. I cherished these moments as they were filled with relaxation, connection, and ease.

It was fun to be able to be at my grandma's house with no yelling or getting into trouble. Grandma, a strong-willed and strict lady, would not tolerate shouting — I had the freedom to be a kid with no worries. I had a glimpse of peace there as I didn't have to be the peacemaker. The joy we would have as a family was an unbelievable feeling that I didn't get to feel very often. It was a happy, blissful time, even for my mom and dad, as they, too, could forget about their life struggles for a while.

I still had responsibilities, but it felt different when we were at Grandma's house. My sisters and I would always get to go to the small town corner store by ourselves. It was exciting to pick out our favorite penny candies, and I felt grown up as I skipped down the street to the end of the block, laughing and playing with my siblings. Opening up the door to the store, and hearing the doorbell ring, we felt so important being greeted by the owner. I remember a few times when he would give us one of our favorite candies, jawbreakers with different layers of colors, to eat right away. It was a special time that gave me the belief that life had good things to come.

I created a special bond and connection with other family members, something I never had at home. I loved seeing my cousins as they were older, and I could relate to them; we laughed and played cool games together, enjoyed dinner, and just hung out having fun. In those moments, I felt special and seen. It was always exciting when we would extend our trip and go see my Great Aunt Jean, who lived on the other side of the island. The beautiful drive along the coastline was always magical; sometimes, we even got to stop at the little towns in between to look in the souvenir shops, hoping to get a little memory gift. We would spend the whole day with Aunt Jean and Uncle Reg, having a delicious homemade lunch and devouring her yummy baked goodies. I remember her always knitting us sweaters to take home, and to this day I still have the last sweater she made for me.

The highlight of the day was going to the park, where there was a petting zoo. I loved being able to pet the goats and little ducks and smell the beautiful flowers. It was magical when I found a magnificent peacock feather to take home as a memory of the day; I was free to be a child running around, playing tag, and having fun with no worries. It was such a different life than being at home.

I never wanted those easy-going summer days to end. It was always hard to say goodbye, and tears of sadness flowed, knowing it would be another year before I got to see them again. We made the best of our few days together at Grandma's, spending time outside, seeing cousins, and having a final day at the beach. It was joyous and sad all at once. When the time came for us to say goodbye, I hugged my grandma and cried, not wanting to leave her. I was left with the heartbroken feeling of knowing all that I would have once we left was a weekly phone call with her.

Then, we were back in the car on the long, cramped trip, returning to the real world we called home. Once home, it was always nice to sleep in my own bed again. Being home, I enjoyed the final weeks of the summer holidays being with my friends, riding my bike, and making the best of things before school began.

I dreaded the first days back at school, a little scared to meet new people. It was difficult to get back into the routine, and I never r got a lot of new clothes, like the other kids, which made me feel different than everyone else. I would do extra jobs like babysitting to make money to pay for the nicer things I never got from my parents — it was a great feeling of accomplishment and I was proud of myself when I was able to buy a brown leather jacket that I saved for months to get. As a teenager, it was important to me how I dressed as I always felt I was the 'different one.'

I struggled to know who I was, defining myself by my responsibility to my sisters and parents and my role in their lives. I wasn't good at school, and I didn't have a lot of friends; I ever wanted was to fit in like the other kids. I was the only one in my class who wore glasses and had super curly hair making me stand out from everyone else. The other other girls had long, straight hair, which I wished for. I knew I was different, which made me often shrink back and not say too much. There were many times when I was made fun of; I was the last one picked for any sports team, and often left out of group conversations, which did not help my self-esteem or my inner self-worth. It was a sad and lonely time and made me want to find what I had to do to create joy in life.

Going to a new school in grade ten was overwhelming, as I was shy and never spoke to too many people. I would find a quiet place in the hallway, outside the classroom, to eat my lunch so I wouldn't have to sit at a table alone. Eating my homemade lunches, I felt even more isolated from the main crowd who had the funds to buy things from the cafeteria.

One day, my mom gave me fifty cents, which I knew was a lot as we didn't always have money. I was able to buy my own lunch, which was a nice treat: a burger, fries, and a pop; the food was delicious. A few girls from one of my classes asked me to join them that day. It was amazing to feel like I belonged: a cafeteria lunch and a group to sit with. It was one of the best days I had in high school.

After that lunch, those girls and I became friends and started to hang out every day (to this day, I still keep in touch with them). It was not easy being a teenager trying to discover who I was, but those friends gave me the confidence to explore my inherent value and focus on who I was becoming. Without the weight of so much self-criticism, I was able to grow and accept myself and my circumstances. They influenced me in positive ways, and I was joyful to know I was finally being appreciated.

I was truly excited when, in grade twelve, I was able to go on my first big trip to London, England. The strong work ethic I had learned by caring for my sisters and buying my own clothes gave me the discipline to save enough money to pay for the trip all by myself. It was a huge confidence builder! I felt so proud and ecstatic that I made this happen by myself. Exploring all the amazing sites in London was memorable: the hustle and bustle of the people, the cars driving on the wrong side of the road, and me trying to cross the street was a challenge, but it was filled with the beginnings of knowing that my experiences were the results of my efforts. It was comforting to experience such a life-changing moment with my other classmates, as the trip was very eye-opening and revealing at the same time. I could never have imagined traveling alone despite earning the money for it by myself. Nor could I have predicted that the same girl who sometimes felt so unworthy had found her inner worth.

I know now that without the encouragement of my teacher, I never would have taken that leap and gone on that trip of a lifetime. I believe people are put in our lives to teach us at the right time when we need it: teachers, employers, friends, and even strangers we meet in passing. They all have a message of learning to take you into the next stage of life.

I remember a friend I worked with during my high school years. She was a few years older than me; a big sister I never had. She was someone who taught me that everything would be okay even when home life wasn't that great; a true confidant who believed in me when I didn't believe in myself. We would hang out, laugh, go out partying, and have fun as we were finding our way in life. There was a sisterly bond with her; I felt like she was a lifeline when my confidence was at its lowest. I depended on her for guidance, and she was one of those people I respected and cherished.

That made it difficult when she found the man of her dreams and moved away to get married. It felt like my heart was torn out. I was devastated and didn't think I would find another friend like her; this was not true. I went on to meet new girlfriends who I have created long-lasting memories with to this day. They are dear friends, and they became that because I knew I kept moving forward, making an effort, and knew that it was up to me if I wanted to feel joy.

As I got older I had an opportunity to move out of my parent's house with a girlfriend, so I did. I saw it as a way to break free from a home that was not always supportive. I was eighteen, yearned for my independence, and decided to embrace freedom. I was too young to think about the impact of leaving home on my sisters and mom. It wasn't until years later, when my sister and I had a heart-to-heart conversation that I learned that she had to endure the abuse of my dad in my absence. I felt a sense of guilt having left them with him, but I was young and wanted my independence.

Soon after moving out of the family home, I met the man of my dreams, or so I thought. We had ups and downs like any relationship, but we worked things out and managed to remain married for twenty years until things ended permanently. Over those two decades, I did what many people do: I felt joy, lost joy, searched for joy, and went on the elusive hunt to make joy a permanent fixture in my life

Years later, after the breakup of my relationship, I had an opportunity to go on a trip of a lifetime to Las Vegas. I hadn't left Canada since my high school trip. Seeing the sparkle and lights of Vegas was a huge dream. Even though I was meeting up with others there I was terrified to get on the plane alone. I had always had friends close by, for better or worse, and people I relied on or who were responsible. Despite all the times I had worked for the freedom to be independent and self-reliant, being *alone* was something I struggled with. If I went, it would be the first time I would travel alone. The feeling in my chest was heavy as my heart was beating fast. Yet, there was another feeling speaking to me from within, a longing for adventure. If I could do this, I knew that I could do anything. If I could overcome the anxiety in my mind, I could overcome almost anything, so I pushed past the fears and decided I *had* to do it.

After days of arguing and talking to a few friends about it, I finally found some clarity. I realized that if I didn't go, I would miss out on a great opportunity. Not going and experiencing what it was like would have been a big regret. I pushed through my fear, got excited, and away I went.

Venturing through the airport with the crowds of people from around the world, all traveling to different destinations, was thrilling. Flying over Vegas with all the bright colored lights was magical, like nothing I have ever seen in my life; the tall buildings, the energy, and the noise of the strip were liberating. I was in awe and had not experienced anything like it: the energy of the casino, the sound of the slot machine going off, happy people everywhere; it was certainly a city that never sleeps. As I stood in the center of the busiest place on earth, I realized that I had overcome so much in life: adversity, challenges, fears, and limiting beliefs from my childhood. I saw how I had made fear less important and myself the winning prize. All that was 'out there' in my life suddenly became less amazing than what I had 'inside' of me. In a jewel-encrusted mirror, I caught a glimpse of myself and saw the *real* me. *I did it, I'm here, and I made it!* I am where I wanted to be… living with joy radiating *from* me.

That experience taught me that it's okay to do things by yourself and have fun doing it. To this day, I go out to concerts, movies, and festivals, and I am fine to travel by myself. If you don't get comfortable being with yourself, you will never go and experience the joy life has to offer.

I was planning to go to New York by myself for my 60th birthday and got a big surprise from my younger sister. She decided at the last minute to join me. We had so much fun together; this was the first time in our adult life that we spent such precious time alone. We walked the streets, visited tourist attractions, and ate new delicacies. The time we had was joyous. We now have a more sisterly bond than ever before, and that trip brought us closer, talking more and connecting on a deeper level. On the last day of our trip, after spending all that time together, and as we were leaving the big city in the cab, I came to realize how lucky I was to have a sister like her. I am so blessed to be getting to know her in a different way than as her older, protective sister. The fear I was carrying before our trip of being alone with my sister melted away, bringing our relationship closer together. The barrier that was there after many years of different lifestyles disappeared. I got my sisterly relationship back like when we were kids.

Enjoy being by yourself; make it magical. There's *freedom* in being capable and confident enough to have a good time with yourself. Life is too short not to enjoy what you love, even alone. Joy comes in many packages, and each one is a treasured gift. Whenever you look back on all the good or bad times, know that your destiny brought you to where you are today. I am grateful for all the good times and memories that were created along this journey we call life.

They say the best three people you can spend time with are ME, MYSELF, and I.

I would like to leave you with this: embrace the present moment, enjoy life along the way, and be happy being *you*. There's freedom in being alone and that doesn't mean you are lonely. By taking responsibility for your life you gain your freedom, and when you are brave enough to show yourself that being alone *is* the gateway to a deeper connection, you forge your inner strength. Time with yourself is how you discover the freedom to simply… be you.

IGNITE ACTION STEPS

- **Keep that child-like feeling inside** of you by doing the things you love and playing every day, such as going to the beach, dancing, singing, coloring, or drawing.

- **Embrace the freedom** by doing things by yourself, with just you as your only companion.

- **Take yourself out on a date** to the movies or out to dinner.

- **Go on that holiday** you've always wanted to go on.

- **Go dancing** or to a new coffee shop to meet exciting people.

- **Let go of what doesn't work** and surrender the control of what we think it should look like or how it should be. There is no right or wrong way; it just is!

- **Decide to get lost in a market** or go a different way to work — let go of control, and be free. Freedom is a conscious choice.

Cheryl A. Rafter — Canada
Courageous Comeback Coach
www.courageouscomebackcoach.com
cherylrafter.ignite@gmail.com
cherylrafter
cherylrafter60

Ashley Fry

ASHLEY FRY

"The storm you survive can be the source of your strength."

I hope that within your Ignite Moment, you find the joy you've been searching for. Within each of our spirits lives a bright halo that is full of passion, love, and beauty. May you leave your humble mark on this captivating place we call our eternal home.

GREENER ON THE OTHER SIDE

I was five years old, dishing up my plate for supper before sitting at the dinner table with my sister while my birth parents, whom I'll name as R and T, sat watching TV in their bedroom. We rarely ate as a family, only for special occasions like Christmas. I soon realized my eyes were bigger than my stomach. I had taken too much food, nervously I threw. What I couldn't eat into the garbage. Unexpectedly, R saw what I had done, and without hesitation he aggressively rushed over, grabbed me by the back of my neck, and threw me across the dining room floor.

That was my earliest childhood memory.

Using his massive hands, R picked me up and took me to his room filled with cigarette smoke. He threw me on his bed and pressed my face into the comforter as he pulled my pants and underwear down. All of it happened within seconds. R took his belt off and started hitting me across my butt. I was petrified, shaking, and confused about why this was happening. With every slash of the leather belt hitting me came unbearable pain; I felt like a piece of meat, tossed around worthlessly. I tried to hold my breath to help with the torment, but it felt like my skin was being torn from my body. I was yelling and crying while in a state of shock. I was overheating, and I could feel the adrenaline rushing toward the wounded area; I thought I was dying. While all of this was happening T just watched TV within arms reach; she was close enough to stop it but didn't. My sister cried while listening from the dining room, trying to finish her supper. Even with family around me, I felt so very much alone.

Finally, R decided he was done, proud of what he had accomplished. He looked me in the eye without regret or sympathy for what he put me through. He yelled, though I was already scared for my life, to get downstairs and stay down there till morning — tears were running down my burning red face. With my bruised body, I gathered what dignity I had left and grabbed my pants, still half-naked. I ran downstairs to my room like my life depended on it. I jumped into bed and threw all the blankets over my head; sobbing in pain and fear, I lay there alone, confused, and lost.

If you look at me today, you would have never guessed that I hold so many scars within me from being brought up in a physically and mentally abusive household. Seventeen years of having my body always in fight-or-flight mode caused intense stress and anxiety, making it hard to enjoy life. Many day-to-day activities were a great challenge, especially fitting in at school. Not only were my sister and I getting abused at home, but R controlled everything, all the way down to what clothes we wore. My baggy, tomboy clothes drowned me out and did not win me any popularity votes. I had no confidence in the way I looked or felt; I was bullied by my classmates for my appearance and demeanor. I was the quiet, awkward, scared little girl with my head down, keeping eye contact with my feet. I tried to go unnoticed, sitting in the back to stay under the teachers' radar.

Keeping everything a secret is how dysfunctional my family lived. Anytime my sister or I fell below the expected grade percentage we would get that many slashes with the belt; one slash for each percentage point we missed. Being a kid for me was learning how to survive in an abusive household day to day. It was like learning how to swim for the first time, paddling desperately, taking in water, and trying to stay afloat without drowning.

Both R and T smoked profusely and were closet alcoholics but didn't want anyone to know. R especially didn't want my Grandpa to know that his son smoked, drank, or hit us kids. Whenever we went over to my grandparents' house, R enforced that whatever happens in our household does not leave. So we stayed quiet, or we would get into trouble with a belt, a punch, or a slap across the face. We obeyed; I pretended like everything was fine and that we lived in a happy, healthy family. I thought everyone was punished and disciplined in this same way.

We only got to see R's side of the family even though T had lots of brothers and sisters. I hardly knew the names of many of the immediate family on her side since I only saw them at big family functions. I could never have guessed the role that T's family would play in my life later on.

I repeatedly remember R telling us he never wanted children. He threatened to kill us more than once, a threat that felt very real. I felt like he went out of his way to find something wrong so he could beat us. As I got older, it seemed his attacks escalated and became more intentional and cruel. I once warned T that I was going to run away; I was positive it would be better somewhere else. She said, "Go ahead and see if it's greener on the other side."

I asked myself why things happened the way they did as I continued to grow toward womanhood. As my body developed, I wanted to fit in with the rest of the girls. But R wouldn't allow that. So, I did what any teen would do and rebelled. I would hide my clothes and make-up in my bag and change on the bus on the way to school as I was the first one on and last on off. That made it easy to slip on my favorite clothes and do my make-up before anyone saw me, and then change back before I got home.

Until one day in May, my junior year of high school, I put on some mascara on the bus before school and forgot to take it off. The bus driver wasn't dropping us off at our place; she was dropping us off at my grandparents' lumber yard, where both R and T worked. It was just up the road from our place. I got off the bus and went straight to work helping R in the shop with building the roof of a horse shelter. He was on one side of the roof, and I was on the other. As I stood on a scaffolding, he looked up at me and asked, "Are you wearing makeup?"

I looked over and lied, saying "No" sarcastically, fearing what he would do. My deception sparked a huge tantrum, as he started swearing at me, calling me horrific names and horrible insults. Tears instantly start running down my cheeks; I knew that I had crossed his unachievable line and something really bad was about to happen.

"Get the hell out of here; I don't wanna see your disgusting face until I get home! Go find your sister. I will deal with you when I get home!"

Anxiety started to fill my chest, noises around me blended into one, and my eyesight became a blur. I could feel my body heating up, I began sweating, my adrenaline surged, and all my senses were shutting down. Terror set in. I was in panic mode. I ran out of the shop trying to find my sister, who was cleaning up lumber by the piles in the front of the yard. As I got closer, I could see the look of worry and confusion on her face; she asked me what was wrong.

"I messed up!! I wore mascara when I shouldn't have, then I lied about it."

I had to wait two hours until we were headed home, and all I could think of was what awful things were going to happen to me once we got there, and I tried to keep it together. My sister and I hid in T's car, where I started bawling my eyes out. Once T arrived, she looked over at me and smirked, "You deserve whatever is going to happen to you." Those words cut through me like glass. I wanted her to protect me, and she wouldn't. I felt more upset than ever. "When you get home, start doing your outdoor chores and then get in the house," were her only instructions, removing herself from any parental responsibilities.

Not even five minutes had passed when R showed up, revving his truck and spitting rocks everywhere as he pulled into the garage. He slammed his truck door and yelled, "Ashley, get get in the house RIGHT NOW!"

I was shaking and had enough tears to soak my T-shirt. I ran into the house and waited nervously, pacing back and forth. He came into the house with a 2" × 4" block of wood. I screamed in terror as he threw my face down against the wooden shoe bench. He ripped my pants and underwear, then hit me across my bare cheeks with the massive chunk of wood. *This is it. I am about to die.* My body was now working in overdrive from the extreme pain and trauma. There was so much happening: yelling and screaming and wood hitting my bare skin so many times I lost count. I went in and out of consciousness until the pain made me completely black out. I wasn't sure where I went, but I wanted to go somewhere peaceful.

My body went so hot, boiling; I could feel my blood surfacing to my skin, the adrenaline kicked into my body. He then threw me outside on the ground with my underwear and pants still at the bottom of my knees. I was face down in the dirt; I was sobbing in so much pain with the cold air hitting me from outside. I lost consciousness again. When I came to, I looked up to see my sister being grabbed by her neck and then thrown on the ground because she was trying to help me. He snarled, "If you touch her, you'll be next." I tried to gather myself together and pull the rest of my pants and underwear up. I was on my knees, sobbing with agony. Both my sister and I weren't allowed to eat supper that night — all because I was wearing makeup.

That was the day I started praying. I prayed to God over and over again. *Please, God, get my sister and me out of here.* Over and over, I asked him. *Please, God, please, this is not fair. Why? Please, I'll do anything. Just please get me out of this place.*

I was praying for a miracle, a God-inspired lifeline that would deliver me to a better place where I could be free.

The next morning, R acted like nothing happened, like everything was normal as he left for work and we went to school. My sister and I waited at the end of our lane for the bus; the pain of the bumpy ride to school on gravel roads was like a bad burn, just throbbing. It was the longest bus ride of my life.

The first class I had was gym class. I went into the girls changing room. We switched out of our street clothes into our gym clothes—it must have been how I was sitting or facing because one of my friends looked at me and asked if I had my period.

"No, why?" I responded.

She pulled me aside and started crying. She normally never showed any emotion. I knew something was wrong for her to be this upset; she asked, "Did your dad do this to you?" I cautiously replied, "Yes." Apparently, because of what happened, I bled through my underwear. I had no idea. I started crying as my friends encouraged me to tell someone about what had happened. I was embarrassed and scared that any confirmation of the abuse I endured would just make things worse at home. I asked my friends not to tell anyone, got hold of myself, cleaned up, and went into the gym.

Instead of joining me there, my two friends snuck out and told the principal, who immediately called social services. I got pulled from my class, and I went to the office. I was introduced to a social worker and a police officer. They asked what had happened, and I told them that if I explained, I would probably die when I got home. "Honey, you're not going home," the social worker said with a soft, safe-sounding voice. It was the first time in my life I felt sympathy and caring from someone willing to help.

I told her everything.

The police officer took a picture of my bare bottom for evidence. Despite all the times I had been bare-bottomed in front of R, it was completely embarrassing to pull my pants down and bend over in front of a total stranger. Yet, it was the price I had to pay to finally have my freedom.

I wasn't allowed to go home and had to choose which family member I would live with. I decided to go to my Auntie Sandra and Uncle Tommy's. I had to ride a different school bus, which took me to my new home, their home.

I was scared and yet relieved. That was the day I got proof that miracles *do* happen — that God carries each one of us through our hardest times.

To this day, I still do not understand how no one knew that this was happening to us kids. When social services removed both my sister and me from the house, my auntie Sandra and uncle Tommy gained full custody of us both. Despite having children of their own, they took us in and raised us, becoming our real Mom and Dad. This was probably the hardest and most overwhelming experience of my life. Realizing that for seventeen years, I endured something that didn't need to happen helped prompt me to want to assist others in similar situations. I realized that we weren't living a normal life and that people don't abuse their children mentally, physically, and emotionally. Yet, I was able to use what I went through to blossom into being an advocate for myself. As soon as I was able to leave that house, I found the strength to stand on my own.

Being in the care of my auntie and uncle was hard, but not how people may think; the hardest part was trying to realize that I was no longer living in a stressful situation and was now in a healthy, loving family. Anytime there were fast movements of any sort, my sister and I would flinch and duck, thinking we would get hit. We were automatically put in therapy; we talked about our feelings, how we felt, how it made us feel in the situation. Once in a while, I went by myself just to talk. I remember I wanted to have a therapy session with just me and T to let her know how I was feeling and doing in a different household. I wanted her to get out of the situation that she was in. I was so excited, but unfortunately, our therapy session only lasted about five minutes. She sat down, looked at me, and said, "If you think I'm going to leave him, you're wrong. He came first." Those words hurt, but at the same moment, they gave me the ultimate permission to heal. I was released from holding on to toxic connections and free to live a life filled with joy. I no longer carried the weight of staying bonded to those who had hurt me. Finally, I could breathe!

Without the worry of not reaching unrealistic standards, I could take my time and take everything in. I loved being free to express what I wanted to wear and who I wanted to be; it felt like I earned back my stolen time. A new feeling rushed into my body and filled my spirit with laughter. That was followed by the affection I allowed myself to feel and be unconditionally loved. I had never known what it was like to have someone genuinely care for my well-being. Something as little as a hug brought instant tears to my eyes, the warmth of arms being secured around my body, the feeling of being safe in another human's presence, speaks louder than words. Feeling okay and that no one will hurt me ever again grew within me. As I continue to reclaim the years of innocence and love that I lost, I recognize the strength I gained from the storm I survived. That storm gave me a perspective not everyone has and the eyes to see that it truly can be *greener on the other side.*

Find your miracle. Gain your strength. Embrace the person you are. Realize how beautiful life can be. There are always two perspectives when it comes to life — choose to see the path you can control. Map out your vision and cultivate the place that brings you happiness, freedom, and endless joy

Ignite Action Steps

- **Fill your life with lots of love**, including self-love. Go outdoors, camping, and take long walks. Work out, move your body, and express yourself. Taking care of you will create positive feelings and allow you to see things with a better perspective.

- **Surround yourself with positive**, outgoing people who will have your back. Go to classes, take training, educate yourself, read lots of books, find a hobby, and get therapists. When you do these things your life becomes more involved, in tune, and interconnected to those with the same vibration. When you do positive things, you connect to those with a positive outlook and well-being.

Ashley Fry — Canada
Humble and Outgoing Individual
Ashleyfry04@gmail.com

Christine von Pander

Christine von Pander

"Joy comes in moments; recognize and appreciate them."

My hope is when you're reading my story, you will recognize that joy comes in moments, like the feelings you get on Christmas Eve being a carefree child, knowing magic is in the air. Sometimes, these moments are shadowed by trauma and unwanted experiences. Other times, they allow you to open the imaginative boxes in your mind, filled with joyful memories, and own the power of making your own choices.

Unpacking Boxes

As I opened the front door, I saw two policemen standing there. I felt frozen with fear from what was happening inside our home, yet the fear was lessened by relief once I knew they were there to help me. They were tall and in uniform, wearing their police hats and looking very crisp and official. Dad was standing behind me. I could feel his eyes burning through the back of my head, staring blankly, drunk and void of emotions. As I took a breath, I found myself saying in an incredibly calm voice to the two policemen, "He has a knife behind his back."

One of the officers slowly reached over and pulled me by the shoulder out onto the front porch of our house.

The second officer asked me, "Where is your mother?"

"She's in the living room near the fireplace," I responded.

Then they said, "Stay out here."

They entered the house and found my dad holding a large carving knife behind his back. They were able to quickly disarm and handcuff him. As I watched one officer walk him out to the police car, my heart fell into my stomach. I was part of the reason he was taking that walk. My ten-year-old self had learned how to call the police to come pick up my daddy, and on that night, I had made the difficult but powerful choice to make things right. I felt as though I had been holding my breath my whole life, and now I was finally breathing. Seeing my father in handcuffs walking by me, not looking at me, gave me the chills, the feeling as if I had betrayed him. Yet, in that same moment, I knew in my heart I did the right thing to protect us all.

The other officer got to my mother as soon as they had my dad out in the car. Thankfully, he hadn't used the knife. But he had used his fists. Her face and shoulders were already changing color and bruising. I felt guilty that I hadn't woken up earlier to stop him before he could hurt her again. She looked so broken and ashamed. They asked if she wanted to go to the hospital, but she refused. She begged the officers to keep him in jail so she could sleep (in those days, they only kept a drunk in holding until they woke up and were sober enough to go home). The officers agreed.

She took me back to bed. I was exhausted and could not keep my eyes open any longer. I was relieved that we were safe. That night, I slept deeply, without dreams or nightmares.

Before that night, these events had only happened on paydays. Then, they progressed to at least once a week. When I was much younger, I would be awakened by yelling. I would toddle out to the living room, rubbing my eyes and saying something like, "What's happening?" Dad would stop, scoop me up in his arms, and put me back to bed. I was completely unaware of what would happen once my eyes were closed again.

Eventually, there came a time that I didn't go back to sleep — the time I learned what was happening after I went back to my room. Soon enough, I found out that he resumed beating her.

The way I learned that he was beating her, I got out of bed as Dad was carrying Mom toward their bedroom. I looked at her face. She had a black eye. I asked, "What happened?" And before mom could say anything, dad said, "Oh, I gave her a love bite." Then he kept walking with her into their room, telling me to go back to bed. I wandered into my room and lay on the bed, trying to understand what a 'love bite' was. *How could it be love if it hurt?* I was so confused. I had nightmares about his reference for a couple of weeks, as my confused young mind could not rationalize love and pain existing at the same time.

At that moment, I learned that the only two people in the world who had one job—to love and protect their family, to protect ME—weren't even capable of looking after themselves. From that point on, I felt there was no safety, no security for any of us. The result was I wouldn't go to sleep at night until I heard my dad come home. I listened to ensure he was calm when he came into the house. And, even when he was calm, I still wouldn't fully rest.

Sometimes, coming out of my room would stop him from beating my mother, so I would call grandma (mom's mom) and ask her to drive to our house. Grandma would verbally go at him and get him to smarten up. Then he'd sleep it off on the couch. But when grandma said she wouldn't come anymore because mom wouldn't leave dad, this created a new level of desperation for me. She became another adult in my life who was supposed to love and protect us yet abandoned us.

Soon enough, I felt I was the only one who could protect us. I don't even remember how it came about that I knew how to call the police. This was long before the days of 911 and caller ID. So, I had to be able to tell the dispatcher my name and address. The memory of that first night is still incredibly vivid in my now adult mind: the heaviness of the responsibility on my shoulders. It was the beginning of shoving my feelings into a box to cope. Over time, I discovered that I had created many of these mental boxes, each holding a different memory. For most of my childhood, only some of the boxes held good, joyful memories.

It took me years to learn how to sleep through the night without "Sleeping with one eye open." It was a saying my dad used when I was little and afraid of monsters. He would announce, "It's okay; I'll sleep with one eye open and ensure nothing bad happens while you sleep." People should be more careful what they say to small children. To this day, when I am under exceptional stress, I sometimes wake up with my eyeball stuck to my pillow.

Not every box was filled with sadness, though. Despite this terrible trauma, I experienced as a ten-year-old, my life was also peppered with incredible moments of youthful joy. I was very fortunate that my mom's mom came from a big Italian family. Every year, as is a tradition in Italian culture, we'd gather on Christmas Eve for a celebration of *family*. There's always so much fun, food and sweets, and, of course, gifts and games for the kids.

That year, I called the police. It was the first time mom got us dressed up and drove us *without* dad to my grandmother's sister's house. I had conflicting emotions. I wanted to celebrate with dad, but I didn't want him to destroy the memory by being with us at home after the celebration. Mom had asked him to move out a couple of months earlier, and we would see him every second weekend if he wasn't drinking.

That year, the party was at my Great Aunt Irene and Uncle Bill's, a lovely two-level house with enough room for all of us. As soon as we arrived, my brother and I went into full kid mode, taking off our shoes and dropping our coats on the floor, running through the house looking for our cousins so we could play. I felt so free and light and happy in their home. It was like the whole world had changed, and I was able to be a kid. We ate pretzels and chips, garlic sausage, cheese, and crackers all night, and we got to drink soda pop! We played so hard and had so much fun; my sides and face hurt from laughing. During that family time, none of the bad things were anywhere in my thoughts.

That night, it was like all the grown-ups there were our parents; what parents are supposed to be. When I'd run too close to a table or the counter, someone would put their hand on my head, without breaking stride in their conversation, to ensure I didn't hit my head on the table as I flew by. When I ran out of steam for a few minutes, the nearest grown-up would pick me up and put me on their lap to ask me what I asked Santa Claus for that Christmas. I was so excited I gave a huge list! I could feel the love being given freely and without any pain. I was safe, secure, and protected.

At ten o'clock, Christmas dinner was served, and all thirty of us sat down for supper: kids at the kids' tables and the grown-ups at their tables. We were three generations deep. I could feel the love, joy, peace, and gratitude in the room filled with delicious food. I thought my tummy would burst, eating the marshmallow yams, so sweet, and the moist turkey and gravy. With our bellies full, we waited for Santa Claus to come at midnight!

Santa would start yelling "Ho, ho, ho" before he even got in the house! The first grown-up that heard him would shush us and say, "Listen, I think Santa is here!" We would stop in our tracks and listen hard. As soon as we saw him, we all ran to him and wrapped our arms around his legs before he had a chance to get into the house. He almost fell over; there were so many of us! Santa laughed and told us to go to the living room so he could come in and bring us our presents. We didn't waste any time! We all gathered on the floor, sitting and waiting for what felt like so long. Santa asked, "Who's been a good girl or boy this year?" and all of us kids would scream, "MEEEE!" Then Santa got quiet and said, "Who's ready for presents?" "USSS!" We all squealed. He reached into his big red velvet bag and brought out the presents one at a time, calling us each by name. We ran up and hugged him and said, "Thank you," definitely trying to get 'goody' points for next year. I can still hear the sounds of wrapping paper being ripped off the boxes of gifts; I still see the moms trying to collect the paper so the gifts wouldn't get lost in the pile and accidentally be thrown out. The exclamations of, "Wow, thank you, Santa. That's what I asked for!" went on for a couple of hours as we embraced the magic wholeheartedly. Opening my gift, I felt like I was a good girl, and someone else knew it. I had no idea until I was in my 40s that "Santa" was my Aunt and Uncle's next-door neighbor!

I don't remember what my gift was. I remember mom in a long dress trying to wake us up in the car when we arrived home. I woke up, still holding my present, awake enough to walk into the house. She ended up carrying my brother in, taking his coat off, and putting him to bed in his clothes. It had been a perfect night.

Perfect doesn't last. Once my brother was settled, mom went to the basement because it had been raining all day and night. I followed her and saw there was so much water it went all the way up to the fifth stair from the bottom. She hiked up her dress to her waist, and I watched as she carefully walked through the water toward the sump pump and felt around for why it wasn't working. It turns out that a pile of newspapers on the floor had floated over and blocked the pump's float. She pulled out all the paper, and the pump started working again.

We went upstairs, and she got me into bed, kissing my forehead and telling me she loved me. I didn't know that hours later, she would call my dad to help with the basement cleanup.

Christmas morning was wonderful. I don't know how she did it. She was able to get us to stay in our rooms for an extra hour, but after that, we couldn't hold back anymore. Then dad came over, and we opened presents and had breakfast. Mom and dad left us to play with our toys while they worked together to clean up the basement. Of course, that didn't mean they would make up. I am not sure I wanted them to. I had come to a place in my childhood knowing that I didn't want dad to be living with us anymore. I needed safety and security, and even though I was a child, I loved the feeling of being joyous, joyful, and around people who brought joy into my life.

When I was twelve, mom and dad finally got divorced. It was so strange to know and understand what that meant. Dad would not be moving back in with us. I had such mixed emotions. I was sad about my child's wish to have a happy, complete family, even though I was glad that those nights of being woken up by the sounds of abuse were finally over.

My brother and I had very different experiences around these events. He was fortunate to be able to sleep through *everything*. I was a little jealous that he wasn't tarnished by the abuse the way that I was. Since dad was gone, I watched over my brother more closely. Though he was only a year younger than me, I felt responsible for keeping him safe and everything as 'normal' as possible.

Suddenly, the boxes in which I had stored my memories burst open, flooding my consciousness like the water that had filled our basement all those years ago. When I was nineteen, my brother killed himself. I felt it the moment it happened. In my body, physically, I felt like I had been punched in the stomach. I was overcome with emotion and didn't understand what was happening to me. I was at work on the ferry in the middle of a morning shift. My coworkers immediately took me to the lunch room and sat me down. Then, the Chief Steward came to find me and asked me to follow her to her office. She told me that when we got into port, I would get off the ship and go home. I was confused. "Which home?" I asked. I lived alone in an apartment, so why would I need to go there? She said, "Your stepfather called and told you to go home as soon as possible." I knew at that moment that someone in my family had died. But I had no idea who. My mind was racing. To get through the next hour, I again put fear into a box until I could arrive at my mother's home to learn who had passed away.

For a month, the blame, guilt, and shame were flying in the air all around my family. My parents were flinging it back and forth through me at each other. I was finally able to get them to meet at my apartment so they could process their grief. I laid out the ground rules. They were to "figure it out" between the two of them, as I would no longer be the go-between. It was causing me so much pain on top of the devastation I felt from losing my brother.

After calming down from the initial shock, I began to look within myself. I realized that I had put my memories in different boxes in my mind throughout my life, stacking them higher and higher.

The other thing I noticed was that the boxes would open on their own when my psyche was ready to learn, understand, and deal with what was inside each one. Realizing that my life journey wasn't all bad—it had moments of joy—seemed to help me get past my painful addition to my box collection. I stopped talking to both of my parents for a while to open each box and process what was inside. I looked at it from an adult perspective, factoring in a more mature understanding to help distinguish between what I saw, what I heard, what I experienced, and what lies I was told.

Then, I made the most significant realization of all! I was a grown-up. I could *choose* how I wanted my life to be. I could *choose* who I wanted in it and what kind of person I wanted to be. I *decided* to be happy and conflict-free wherever possible. I could *choose* to feel comfortable putting those memories away — the good ones and the bad ones. Because I *chose* every time, I thought I didn't have a *choice*.

Now, I am who I've always been: a loving and caring person. I *choose* that when I am in a relationship with someone, I am "all in" because if the relationship does break down, I never want to feel regret or wonder if it was because I held back or played it safe to protect my heart. I know what love and joy are. I learned that from my extended family during those joyful Christmas holidays. And. I know what love is not. I also know that there is more than enough happiness in life that you can control. You simply need to go looking for it; you can choose to create it, stay in it, and share it with others.

Always remember, you can *choose* to open one or more of the memory boxes in your life when times get rough. Choose the good ones. Choose the ones that empower you. Then, sit with them for as long as you need to realize that you can improve anything because as long as you positively use those memory boxes, you have the full choice and the power to make your life radiate joy.

Ignite Action Steps

- **Remember to allow the positive moments** to be stronger than the negative ones.

- **Take a pause, and ask yourself,** *Will this choice only make me temporarily feel better, only to make the future me feel worse?*

- **Have a person in your life that truly has your back**. If you don't feel like you have a person like this in your life right now, call a Helpline. They were created for this exact reason. It is a sign of strength to make that call, and it could be your first step in making choices by *YOU* for *YOU*.

- **Listen to yourself**. Your mind and body will let you know if *and* when you're ready to open your boxes. If some of them don't get opened, that's ok. Trust yourself.

Christine von Pander — Canada
Entrepreneur & Speaker
www.ihavepeopleforthat.com/cookies-from-the-universe
www.ihavepeopleforthat.com
christinevonpander
i-have-people-for-that
christine.von.pander
ihavepeople4that
christinevonpander

Ciara Caston Finley

Ciara Caston Finley

"Focus on what is right, pure, and lovely, and joy will become your strength."

It is my hope that you will find peace in knowing that all things work together for your good. You don't always have to know the answers. Sometimes, the solution is all in how you handle your adversity and, ultimately, who you become. Drowning in distractions keeps you from feeling the full experiences; it robs you of the good and prevents you from seeing yourself as you truly are. I want you to realize the importance of self-love, self-care, and self-value. I want you to know that it is okay to stop and allow yourself to feel every emotion you desire. The answer, simply put, may just be your presence. You are enough. You are worthy of joy.

The Woman I Left Behind

Fear gripped me as I moved from the sofa to the corner of the hospital room. I was watching myself through a lens, an out-of-body experience. The space seemed darker, as if a cloud had started to hover over it. "Pump epi," the doctor proclaimed. I didn't see the doctor. I could only hear him. My eyes were fixed on my brother in the hospital bed. "Troy!" I screamed, but nothing came out of my mouth.

"Clear!" the doctor yelled. My blood ran cold, causing freezing jolts to shoot through every inch of my body as insurmountable fear took over. The air in the room was so, so cold. I wanted to run, but I was still frozen in the corner of the room. It was extremely chaotic, with nurses scrambling and moving around, constantly grabbing items, checking monitors, and crowding around the bed. "Troy!" I yelled again. And then there it was… the long, drawn-out BEEEEEEEEEEEP.

How could this be?

We prayed earlier that day, and I had confidence that everything was going to be okay.

I don't understand.

Deadly bacteria had entered my brother's lungs from an unknown source. Within hours, he suddenly went from a healthy 39-year-old to an intubated patient being airlifted to an advanced hospital. He was placed in intensive care, and in two days, he passed from acute respiratory distress syndrome.

Standing there, frozen in fear in his hospital room, was a nightmare that replayed every night after his death for two weeks. Each time, the dream became more intense and more devastating. I entered a prison of my own thoughts, tumbling uncontrollably in the wake of my loss. *Why was I unable to do anything? Was my faith not strong enough to save him? I should've prayed harder. I should've been a better sister. Could I have done more? God, Why did this happen? Why him? Where does this leave me now?*

Then, silence.

Two weeks later, the nightmares suddenly stopped.

As I shifted the blame away from everyone and everything else, trying to own it all myself, the time for dreams faded. I increased my workload, my responsibilities, and the tasks that took my time—anything to avoid the agony. But that avoidance just attracted more chaos.

Oh, how my mom loved her baby boy! He was the apple of her eye, the kind and generous 'help whisperer.' People would always say he just appeared out of nowhere with the bandaid, the tire, the food, the money, the hug, and the laughter. Whatever the need was, he showed up for anyone without being asked and never expecting recognition. He was a Fire Captain, a hero in our eyes. He loved God and was a true man of service. He was healthy. He was on the brink of finding joy in his life.

Why, plagued me again.

My anxiety over his death triggered a quest for answers. I reviewed his medical records, consulted specialists, and sifted the internet to no avail. The anxious thoughts got more invasive as I wondered if something so sudden would happen to me, also. I had full-on panic attacks as I imagined daily the ways I might die or lose other loved ones.

Cue my next nightmare.

Three months after my brother passed away, I began to notice a change in the way my mom communicated. She had so much personality; she was the loudest and friendliest person in the crowd with an infectious laugh. She suddenly became more and more withdrawn. This woman who had always loved a classy outfit, flawlessly healthy skin, and a clean house now wanted to lie in bed most of the day. She became a shell of the person she was. She would look right through me, hardly communicating and repeating the same childhood stories whenever she spoke.

I learned to go with the flow and adjust to each change, as it allowed our time spent together to run seamlessly. Still reeling from my brother's death, I realized I was also losing my mom. Several months later, she was diagnosed with dementia. I was scared, sad, and overwhelmed. But I didn't give myself time to process that information. I took it on as a new problem to figure out. *This should keep me busy for a while*, I thought, constantly staying in a fight-or-flight state of mind.

One moment, my mom thought I was her aid, so that's who I became. At least she was talking. The next moment, she thought I was one of her sisters, so that's who I became. At least she was laughing. The next day, I was one of my sisters because it made her feel special to know we were visiting. But I was scarcely Ciara. If I gave her the truth contrary to what she thought at the moment, it would have created a bigger problem for us both. Saying, "Mom, I am Ciara," meant she would either call me a liar or get upset that she didn't know it was me. She would shut down, often several times in one visit. Each day, I did what was necessary to get through our time together, then sat in my car and sobbed before going home drained. Walking through my front door meant it was time to be what I needed to be for my daughter, son, and husband. Sometimes with all the joy I could muster and other times with a half smile. I didn't give myself the time to grieve or take care of my needs. Getting help just wasn't in the cards. Too much needed to be resolved, and I felt I was the fixer. Through empathy, I garnered strength, allowing me to have my heart broken over and over again and to keep myself afloat in the small moments of joy when my mom had clarity.

The entire time I was coping with loss, I had also been trying to nurture my 2-year-old daughter, who had developed allergies to eggs, dairy, wheat, nuts, fish, and soy (along with environmental allergies), all of which would manifest in severe eczema and inflammation. We stopped eating out. I cooked and baked all of her specialized food from scratch, dedicating hours upon hours to learning about alternative ingredients. I also made her dish soap, laundry detergent, and body products. I removed the window blinds and carpet and purchased hypoallergenic bedding, clothing, and cloth diapers. Her condition was so severe that I would have to give her bleach, oil, and oatmeal baths and wrap her limbs with gauze to keep staph infections away. It tore me apart seeing her fragile skin rip and tear with each movement. Over sleepless nights, I'd cry and pray while gently cleaning and wiping away the tacky blood and plasma. My poor baby spent at least six years of her life in constant pain. I wanted so badly to absorb all the pain and discomfort she felt.

I journaled and logged my daughter's reactions to food and environments, tracking what not to eat, where not to go, and what not to do. All this constant work brought out a gift lying dormant inside me: the gift of service, creativity, love, and inclusion. From this, a small-scale catering business was born. I was a great home cook and baker, but when I could attach my love for my daughter to food and my passion for others, it became my ministry, eventually leading me to culinary school.

I was wearing every nametag: Caretaker, Chef, Businesswoman, Mother, Wife, Tutor, and Volunteer. I believe I said yes to it all because it gave me the false sense that I was doing something to overcompensate for my problems. I didn't want to be the person who complained about my circumstances without putting full effort into the solution. I *was* the solution; I *had* to be.

I tried to pick up everyone and carry them… and left myself behind in the process.

I never said yes to the crisis that was happening inside of Ciara, whoever she was. I gave myself nothing. I would skip doctor's appointments and ignore aches. My mom couldn't be left alone. The parent-teacher conference was more important. I needed to advocate for my daughter. I didn't need 'me time.' My marriage and husband mattered more. My son had baseball games and school plays, and I *had* to show up because I was always "busy and unavailable." It was easier to ignore my needs, whatever those were. I was utterly depleted and had absolutely nothing left to give to me. I hated myself and resented others.

I had *forced* myself to become an expert and an advocate for everything my family needed: dementia, allergies, ADHD, you name it. But really, I had become an expert on how to *not* truly exist and how to avoid feeling trauma through unceasing work and projects.

I still hadn't faced my brother's death. Though, sometimes, I felt I was channeling his inner champion. I tried to replace him through my actions. I was a friend to whoever needed one. I laughed, prayed, and brought hope to so many, yet I was plagued with fear, depression, and anxiety and hid the fact that I was having panic attacks all the time. My brother's absence was still affecting me mentally and physically, but I buried my feelings. I read a few self-help books, borrowing a little hope from this person and stealing a little joy from another to get me through each day. Some days, I felt like I was suffocating, but holding onto the tiniest morsel of joy somehow preserved me just enough to keep depression from swallowing me.

Six years passed, and things began to level out a little. I had developed systems to help navigate my overloaded life. My mom was in a nursing home, which helped tremendously as her condition rapidly progressed. My daughter had outgrown her soy and egg allergy and was less sensitive to environmental changes. It was still tough to navigate, but I was getting through it. My catering business was now large-scale and thriving. I was reading more books, had more intentionally positive thoughts, and was attempting to do more for myself.

Then, BAM, my mom takes a turn for the worse.

She was found unresponsive and eventually placed in hospice care, passing away in April 2021. There was no system, book, or way I could have prepared. I had been losing her mentally, but having a piece of her was still so much better than not having her at all. I would toggle between feelings of relief and guilt, and it was too much to take.

I did what I knew best: I drowned myself in more work, taking on every event that came my way. I was working myself into the ground, causing internal damage, and spending the only time I had off very sick. I knew something had to change, but I had no idea how. I thought I was doing the work, and maybe, just maybe, I would get through it.

Then, one cool, wintery evening, I was finally forced to embrace all the challenges that had occurred in my life. I was at a special church service, where a guest prophet from South Africa was visiting. He carried with him a presence that could be felt as soon as he entered the room. There was an altar call in which the prophet asked people who felt they wanted a touch from God to come to the front. I knew that I needed God's hand in my current situation and to be freed from my past circumstances. I had been up for altar calls several times before and typically would feel joy descend upon me as if a weight had been miraculously lifted. But somehow, I always felt I was still holding on to my 'human strength' or that something was holding me back. Yet, that evening was different. I lay on the floor weeping loudly. As the tears rolled, I felt a gentle hand on my shoulder and an assertive whisper in my ear. The soft female voice was like a direct message from the Almighty:

"You've been holding on for too long. Let it go; release it. It's time for you to get your joy back."

Those words weren't new to me, but I sensed something different happening deep inside this time: a sudden shift. I began to *feel*. I felt every muscle in my body loosen. I felt my heartbeat. I inhaled and knew that I was breathing life in. I exhaled and knew that I was letting go. Heat consumed my body; I felt blood rushing through my veins. This was the complete opposite of what I felt in my brother's hospital room. I was completely present and more aware of my body, thoughts, and emotions than ever before. I left church that evening feeling whole and continued to rejoice in all the good God had given to me.

I surrendered it *all* and life was returned to me.

Any one of my circumstances could have been God seeking my attention, but I didn't see it because I was running. I was busy focusing on the complete overwhelm of my life. I was trying to carry the weight that I never intended to carry alone. *He* made every effort to tell me, "Be still." *He* would locate me right where I was. *He* wants to tell us that His grace is sufficient for us so that we can allow peace and joy to rest upon us. *His* grace forced my heart to smile even when the world around me seemed to be falling apart. *His* love showed me that I had the strength and the ability to make it through. That's the power of joy!

It's been said that time heals all wounds. I believe what we do with our time truly heals us. We just need to slow down, turn off everything, and be present with a renewed way of thinking. In silence, we learn that life can come at us or life can come *from* us. You have a choice. When you decide to listen to the voice inside you, you'll hear the truth: self-care, self-worth, and self-value matter. It is pure, it is beautiful, it is lovely. When you listen, you'll hear yourself say, "I am enough. I am worthy of joy. JOY resides in me."

IGNITE ACTION STEPS

Practice focusing on what's right, pure, and lovely
- Love and trust in God; he will teach you to recognize the beauty in you and the world.
- Develop simple habits for self-love and see yourself as worthy of these things.
- Create a gratitude journal and write one thing you are grateful for daily.

Allow yourself to grieve
- Be gentle and kind to yourself. Your grief won't, nor does it need to look like anyone else's.
- Examine the deepest parts of your soul to expose your trauma. You need to be willing to *feel* in order to spring forward.
- Know that brokenness doesn't make you less than or inadequate, but embracing your brokenness in truth leads to healing.
- Seek help from a grief counselor if necessary.

Change the lens through which you view your life
- Don't know? Be still and ask! Prioritize your peace: Find time for prayer, positive affirmations, meditation, and those things that nurture you.
- Monitor your inner dialogue and speak life into your circumstances.
- Lean into beautiful, positive people who may be divine connectors and destiny helpers.

Find joy in the POSSIBLE
- Create exciting possibilities in your mind; be childlike and enthusiastic.
- Use your imaginative power to *Provide, Be,* and *Ignite Joy.*

Ciara Caston Finley — United States of America
CEO, Executive Chef, CC, CPC
www.desideratakitchen.com
CiaraFinley
Ciara Caston Finley
Desiderata Kitchen by Chef Ciara
ceeceefinley

Corinne Erickson

Corinne Erickson

"When you twirl on your mountaintop, with arms open wide, give into your surroundings, and miracles will come your way."

Sometimes, when we least expect it, our lives can change in an instant! I wish to remind the reader that if we open our minds to new possibilities of what may be, we open ourselves to opportunities, adventures, and a whole new story filled with joy.

Joy on Top of the Mountain

That night, the snow was blizzarding hard, and it was difficult to see where I was driving as the fresh snow blew wildly, pounding across my windshield. There were cars in all three lanes, everyone on a mission to get wherever they were going as quickly as possible. It was not a good night to be out driving, as it was the first snowfall of the winter season. Drivers were learning how to maneuver icy roads once again.

It happened so quickly, and yet when I look back, it seems like a slow-playing movie inside my head. On this crowded highway, I remember seeing cars swerving all over the place to miss one another. From the corner of my eye, I noticed a dark vehicle sliding sideways out of control and heading in my direction. I had NOWHERE to go! To my left was a solid concrete median;

to my right, cars were scrambling to get out of the way. Vehicles around me swerved in panic so as not to hit the oncoming car, but I was not as fortunate. I could see the driver inside as the dark car slid uncontrollably toward me. As our eyes met, my first thought was, *If I hit the driver's door, I might kill her on impact.* I turned my wheel slightly to the left, missed the driver, and sent the car sailing back into the traffic. There was grinding metal, a deafening crash, and a blood-curdling scream from me. The sound of metal on metal was deafening and haunts me to this day.

I opened my eyes, so grateful to be alive, as I sat for a moment in shock. I don't remember what happened after our two vehicles collided, but I woke up on the left side of the road, not knowing how I stopped or avoided the concrete median. I had angels watching over me that night and truly experienced a miracle.

There was a searing pain in my head and chest. My airbag had gone off, crushing the front part of my body. It felt like my ribs were broken, my glasses were missing, and there was a slash on my forehead. I did not realize that my car was a total write-off. Oncoming traffic swerved around pieces of broken metal scattered everywhere.

At that moment, my life changed.

Backtrack twenty-four hours before the accident; you would have seen me in my prime. The definition of joy in the dictionary is "*a feeling of great pleasure and happiness that comes from good fortune, or a sense of well-being.*" This is how I felt. I was on top of the world with my career, family, friends, and life in general. I was a wife of thirty-eight years, mother of two children, and grandmother to three wonderful grandkids. Being active and staying in good physical health were essential components of my life. Every weekend, we did fun things such as hiking, cycling, dancing, golfing, and other spontaneous activities. I truly felt joy in my heart with all the wonderful opportunities that blessed my life.

Not only was my personal life in a good place, but my professional life and new business were starting to show profits. I owned and operated two companies for income while working for almost twenty years at my full-time job. I had worked hard for many years to be in that position. Safely heading into retirement, I felt security, purpose, a sense of accomplishment, and great happiness in my heart. Volunteering was a big part of my life, filling my soul with extra purpose and a sense of well-being. I have followed my passions throughout my life and felt complete and successful. If I could describe a picture of myself before the accident, I was on the mountaintop, spinning with my arms open wide, not a care in the world, enjoying the family and friends I had been gifted with.

Sometimes, however, the Universe has different plans for us; in my case, the story changed drastically. I am a believer that things happen for a reason. When I look back before the accident, I thought things were wonderful, and I was busy from early morning until late in the evening. My family always came first, but sometimes, I would work on my days off or later into the evening and even holidays to fit the family in. After speaking with my family and co-workers, I realized that they believed I was heading to a dangerous place of exhaustion. I was trying to juggle three jobs and fulfill my role as wife, mother, grandmother, and volunteer. It was taking its toll.

This may sound strange, but prior to that terrifying night, I had the same vision, three different times, in detail, about a car accident. It happened around a corner on a highway. I could see the reactions of all the moving cars and knew there was an imminent crash. But, the vision always ended before I could see the final outcome. Little did I realize that these dreams were foreshadowing what was to come. I believe the vision gave me the clarity to maneuver through the accident. That divine intervention was my own little miracle that helped save my life.

My journey over the next three years became a very difficult one. I had received injuries to my lower back and right rotator cuff. These required so many appointments and so much time to heal. The worst injury for me, however, was a visual concussion. Not having my brain functioning like it was before the accident was frustrating and debilitating in so many ways.

Being the positive person I am, I thought my injuries would be short-term, and I would return to work in a few months. Running my two companies was the hardest since I was the only employee; no one could take over my tasks. I had some support at my full-time job, but even then, my husband was doing all the data crunching for me at home. I pushed through for a year as the pain increased in my head until I had continual dizziness and discomfort. I was having problems driving and analyzing data, and I was messing up my words and numbers. I would read my work repeatedly, not fully understanding and absorbing what the documents were saying. I became dizzy and nauseous when I scrolled up and down in my emails. Watching TV with the flashing commercials also made me sick. It was like my brain was not fully connected anymore.

By the end of the first year, I ended up closing one of my businesses. Mentally, this was one of the toughest decisions I had to make, but my health was more important since the pain would not subside in my head. The frustrating part is that people asked me why I didn't sell. If you can't analyze and handle data and thought patterns, it is hard to put together proposals and do number-crunching to sell a business.

The dominos had begun to fall. The next thing to go was my second business, then my full-time job. I was asked to go on disability since I was making huge errors with the data I was supposed to be analyzing. My heart was broken as I left the office and my co-workers, not knowing how long this situation would continue. I was sure I would have been healed by now and back to work after a year. The opposite was true. My symptoms in my head and back had not become better; they were worse.

I started to sink into a state of frustration and anger. I had done everything that my doctors, concussion specialist, and physio had told me to do. Why wasn't I getting better? I was terrified of what might happen to me. I had always had control over my life and my situation, never dependent on anyone. Now, I relied on my husband to drive me. I had problems with elevation hikes in the mountains. I would lean to the left when I was tired. There were limitations on things that I could do with my kids, grandchildren, and friends. I felt like a burden to everyone. People saw me differently. I saw myself differently, also.

I spent two more years in constant turmoil, waiting to return to my job. I did not want to accept the changes that had occurred in my life. Desperately trying to heal myself, I didn't take the time to slow down and continued pushing myself. I consistently felt pressure to work full time and pull my weight financially in the family. I was declining physically and mentally. I lived in a place of frustration and anger, my negativity attracting negative energy. Before the accident, I felt like a superstar. After the accident, I was dealing with doctors, lawyers, and insurance appointments. There was loads of paperwork and more paperwork, which was difficult to go through with a post-visual concussion. I felt like I was trapped in the insurance bubble. I was making thirty percent of what I used to make, and that was stressful. Each time I went to the chiropractor or physio, I had to prove it was needed. Each month was spent anticipating whether I would be covered by insurance for the next month. Unlike physical injuries, head injuries are hard to see. I looked normal, but my head was still not working right.

Then, in November, I became very sick. I was on medications for some type of respiratory illness, and I felt like I would not pull out of this massive hole of darkness and sickness. I was having problems with breathing and suffering from additional head pains. I believe the Universe was trying to tell me something about taking time to heal. I felt ashamed in front of my friends and family that I was not strong enough to push through everything. I felt obligated to my employer to get back to work and the people around me to keep up a good face and continue to push through life as usual. I was not allowing myself to heal; I kept trying to fight what was in front of me.

The unrelenting respiratory sickness was forcing me not to move or think, and I was very angry. It was getting harder to be that joyous self I once knew. At Christmas, my favorite time of the year, I normally would spend hours decorating and entertaining family and friends. This year, I felt like I would not make it through Christmas. My body was shutting down from being sick, and I didn't even want to get up. I had gone to the doctors who had me on antibiotics and medication. It felt like I was just getting worse and fading. I was tired of fighting the situation; I just wanted to go to sleep through life. I didn't want to be that person.

After three years of fighting for control from such a helpless place, I knew I needed to regain my mojo, magic, spark, and love of life. I was tired of surviving, not living. I told my husband I wanted to go to the mountains to my favorite waterfall and hike. He was surprised that this was what I wanted to do and mentioned that it was cold out and I was quite sick. It didn't matter to me; I just needed to get out and find a place where I used to feel joy and happiness in my body and soul. It was important to find a piece of me that had control over what I did and not be around doctors, lawyers, physiotherapists, and concussion specialists. I just wanted to be free of it all, if only for a short while.

We headed into the mountains, where fresh snow and white peaks surrounded us with their beauty and majesty. As a young adult, I would go to the mountains to ground myself and breathe in the fresh air. It was my place of peace. It is where I studied and thought of big and new ideas.

As we started our hike, I could feel the tingle of cold air on my cheeks. I could barely breathe because I was so sick, but I didn't care as I continued up the path. The clear blue icicles' natural beauty hung from the canyon's sides and shimmered like aquamarine crystals. I felt my body and soul soaking up the incredible energy of my surroundings. At the bottom of the canyon, I could see small openings in the frozen ice, where the stream continued to push powerfully down to the bottom of the trail. Even in the cold, I could smell the fresh spruce trees that towered on the sides of the path. This was Mother Nature at her best.

As we approached the waterfall, I could see the cascading water behind the frozen sculpture of ice. The sound was soothing as if speaking only to me, very slowly and concisely, nothing like the summer sounds of water roaring into the pool below. I felt tears coming down my cheeks. I snuggled up against the rocky side of the canyon as it supported me, and held me up, and I stared in amazement at the beauty, peace, and serenity before me.

With the snow glittering at my feet and the water babbling in the distance, I shifted into a different reality. *Wow, can life be that simple? How did everything become so complicated? Why did I carry so much anxiety and anger inside me?* At that moment, I realized all the events in the past three years had made me forget what it was like to have myself grounded and my soul full of joy. How could I have lost my drive and flair for life? I closed my eyes, and the tears continued to mirror the waterfall cascading down my face. I decided at that moment to stop fighting everything around me. My shoulders dropped, and I stood in silence, with the movement of the waterfall following in the path of least resistance, simply going where it was meant to be. It was the first time in a long time I felt tranquility.

With the deepest sigh of peaceful acceptance, I saw where I was in life. I wasn't going back to my old work, and I wasn't going to keep fighting the insurance company. I was going to recreate myself and accept my current limitations. This was me — here and now.

Surrounded by the beauty of all creation and the power of nature, I had one of the most transformational and life-changing experiences of my life. It reminded me how simple it can be to bring joy, peace, and love into your soul. Before the accident, I used to run all the time, but now it was time to slow down and enjoy new possibilities. I had to open my eyes and love myself in the present.

I could have stayed all night listening to the water caressing the ice with its soothing and loving splashes. My husband finally pulled me away from the falls as the late afternoon settled in. I was excited to go back home and face myself in the mirror. I would release things that were not feeding my soul and re-evaluate my situation. I was just as smart as I was before, but not as fast. I could figure out problems, but not for long periods. I could spend time with my kids and grandchildren, but the activities would have to change. I had to acknowledge things were different but could still be as fulfilling and rewarding. I was blessed with my family and friends, and I had an abundance of love that hadn't changed.

My life had transformed within three weeks of my hike to the falls. I decided to start another company at sixty-four years old called *Freelance Writers* so that I could work with my limitations. I was terrified and scared, yet excited that I was starting a new journey with my new company. I could feel the joy of accomplishment as I learned and rediscovered new computer applications and skills. I rekindled my love for writing and started putting a plan together for timelines to accomplish my new vision. During this new journey, I paid attention to my body and limitations, listening when it told me to rest and honor self-care.

Life used to be a big race every day, every week, and every month. For the first time in a long time, I felt like I was in control of my body, thoughts, and feelings; my new perspective on work is about balance, happiness, and love of writing. It was a long three years where I had to overcome physical and mental challenges. I am so thankful I went through this journey of change and rediscovery to the place where I am now. I have accepted certain limitations and have made them part of my life. Over time, things may become better, but I feel joy in my heart RIGHT NOW and the true love of life around me. I feel like I am twirling on the top of the mountain even higher now, with my hands spread out, catching better opportunities and miracles that are sent my way.

I encourage you to find the top of your mountain and the joy that fills your heart. Look for the strength inside you to move forward and Ignite your life.

IGNITE ACTION STEPS

- **Take a hard look at what brings you joy and fulfillment in your life and make a list**. What makes you feel powerful? It is easy to slip into frustration and anger when you feel like you have lost control over things.

- **Call someone who will support and encourage you**. Have them just listen and support you mentally so you can express how you are feeling.

- **Write down your happy place and strengths**: one that reminds you that you are strong, beautiful, and worth fighting for. If you can, go to that place physically or visualize yourself being there.

- **Meditate daily**, and be thankful for the simple things that bring joy to your life.

Corinne Erickson — Canada
BKn, DipCIS, DipICL
www.freelancewriters.ca
freelancewriters.ca
corinne-erickson-01082a5b
erickson.corinne

Elaine Valerie Thompson

ELAINE VALERIE THOMPSON

"Hope is the magnet that attracts Joy."

I pray this story Ignites your belief that even in the darkest of times, there still exists a glimmer of hope. Its sole purpose is to shine a deep sense of reassurance that you can navigate the shadows of adversity and emerge into the light of renewed possibilities through the transformative process of rewriting your mental scripts. My *soul purpose* is to encourage women to recognize their strength and see that through our energetic belief system and accessing the right holistic tools, it is possible to transcend even the darkest moments in our lives and attract infinite joy.

WHEN THE BOTTOM FELL OUT

I found myself curled up, rocking in a fetal position, sobbing. All hope seemed lost. Yet in that dark moment, my innate sense knew that one day, I would find the hope I needed that would be the catalyst for change.

An active, positive, and sporty child, I traversed tumultuous waters that came with successful grades and top student awards. My journey through School and Beauty Therapy College was met with female rivalry, leaving me a loner. I felt unworthy and introverted. I would get caught in the trap of comparing myself to other girls, taking me deeper into my downward spiral. The real pain, though, that could have crippled me was the raging furnace boiling in my torso, an undiagnosed severe medical condition that was apparently "all in my head."

I felt unseen and unheard in the health system throughout my teens and early twenties. My innate gifts of perception and intuition led me to believe deep down in my heart that the health system had it wrong. Tattooed with acne, my self-esteem rapidly crumbled; just a glance at my skin forced me to dig deep, swallow back the tears, and put up my floodgates.

Suppressing the pain, I focused on striving to be my best. At twenty, I graduated in the top three beauty therapists. My vision was unfolding. Through my hard work and dedication, I was awarded a position in my dream vocation. Working at an elite spa in the North of England. My shifts began with a uniform parade; I felt proud and accomplished. Gradually, pride soon turned to anxiety as I began to feel like a soldier going into battle. Adorned in a pristine white dress with my shoes glistened white, I felt a bit angelic and as if a dream had come true. Yet, it was a competitive, female-dense environment. I wore multiple badges of success only to feel quite isolated and often lonely. No token of merit could heal my pain. Every day, my emotional struggles were layered with gritting my teeth through painful ten-hour shifts, giving and giving. I sobbed behind the scenes with physical pain that felt like burning flames and daggers in the center of my belly. I wiped away the tears and grabbed my inner strength. Resetting my makeup, I painted on my smile as I attended to the next client and the next.

I had big plans to conquer the world and fill it with joy. My healing hands and huge heart were my gifts. I knew that my soul purpose was to sprinkle pink glittery sparkles over my clients, turning sadness into joy and pain into ease. That was my mission, and with unicorn zest, I seemed oblivious to defeat and innately bulletproof. I stuffed down the pain I was feeling to make sure I finished the work. I had signed a contract, and with every achievement badge I had reached, my work contract was extended. Encouraged to shine and succeed, I felt I was walking a path to entrapment. Every new course I took meant I had to stay longer to fulfill my obligations. Months and months were added; how *would I cope*?

My mum wanted to pay my way out of my contract; she always stood by my side. She was also trying to help me uncover the source of my mystery pain and had already spent a fortune on private healthcare. Trading funds for freedom was not an option. I had reached the breaking point that had ended in a breakdown. Thankfully, I was saved from my financial obligations at the eleventh hour. The news was released that the elite spa I worked at had entered receivership. My contract was no longer binding. Through grace, I was bailed out and set free. All of my years of study to attain my dream job, and my self-esteem and dignity were washed away. Blindsided, I returned home to live with Mum, feeling like I was half the young woman I once was.

Back in the solace of my pink childhood bedroom, I felt defeated, disappointed, devastated, and destroyed. The once golden light that was my aura, the twirling happy child with a smile that lit up a room, had morphed into a weeping silhouette I no longer knew. Self-loathing was rife. I could barely find the will to dress myself. I was plagued with the scent of the burning cinders of my life; the furnace inside me wouldn't cease. *Why was no one hearing me?* Like an artist with a brush, I described the pain of my insides to multiple specialists. The sensation of the soccer ball lodged in the left side of my torso. The swelling and inflammation that grossed me out. I detested my body. The food that would not digest festered like a daily cesspit in my gut. I was agonizing for answers, yet the health system said again and again it was all in my head. I was stuck in a quagmire going ten feet under. *I am a high achiever,* I told myself; *I must get back up.* The medical solution was for me to begin antidepressants.

I struggled to understand what my life had become. *Aren't our twenties supposed to be fun?* I questioned. I wanted to make a difference in the world. Yet, I couldn't even make a difference in myself. Clutching my pills, hoping for the best, I tried a local job with less stress. My mum longed for me to slow down and rest, but I was born to be ambitious. My intuition led me. When it spoke, I acted. Stuffing down my emotions and opposing the pain, I leaped back onto the high achiever ladder. Next stop, 'the big smoke of London.' *Perhaps now this was my true destiny, the right path*, I thought. I went with courage, shining my light. I longed to believe that I'd numb my pain by sprinkling joy and helping others find their dream jobs. I secured a role in the feisty world of recruitment. Trouser suits my new armor, my briefcase my ammunition. Squeezing my raging, inflamed torso into my clothes, I battled each day not to grimace in interviews or vomit in meetings. My antidepressants sedated my mind for a moment, but the cocktail of drugs did not quell the inner red raging flames of pain. I had thought I had found my future, but it was more like hell.

I lived a facade, thirteen years of painted-on smiles. But nothing stopped my tears each night. *Please, Lord,* I would cry out. *Stop the pain.* Finally, a forced breakthrough came. I collapsed at work. I was whisked to the emergency room. I did not fit the textbook diagnosis, but at that moment, there was hope. It took one specialist to listen. To put aside the textbook and see the picture I had painted. I was one of a few women living the nightmare of the silent disease called endometriosis that is not only contained in the womb. I had it in my bowel, intestines, rectum, kidneys, and bladder. My thirteen years of pouring my heart out to doctors, therapists, and psychiatrists suddenly made sense. The antidepressants had been just one more plaster on a never-ending, gaping wound. Finally, it was not in my head. It was REAL.

So what now? I said to myself. With no family history of endometriosis, my intuition spoke: *had I manifested this disease?* I needed to explore more deeply. What were the underlying emotions of this silent attacker? Most descriptions included a lack of self-love, unresolved sadness, frustration, and insecurity possibly rooted in childhood grief (I had lost my father at age seven), blaming oneself, and even rejecting one's femininity and personal power. I reflected; *I was the dis-ease,* the lead in my own movie. Every harsh emotion, every loathing feeling, had been incessantly flooding my cells with toxic negativity.

Then, a new chapter opened in my life. I met a man. With low self-esteem and still fueled by pain, I was vulnerable, my mind unconsciously tricking me. I was brainwashed that external validation was the magic wand to remedy my crushed self-worth. It wasn't long before his true colors shone. I should have gone with my innate perception, the gut feeling from our very first meeting. Instead, I moved to New Zealand and endured a marriage that would scar my heart and sense of security for years to come — all the while, the torso furnace continued to burn, and the daggers continued to stab. With new levels of grief, loneliness, distrust, and despair, I endured another chapter of pain that deeply branded itself onto my heart, taking me even lower than I emotionally was.

Despite my physical anguish, my hope of a better life never waned. My innate perception told me that even in a future filled with the unknown, my pain would be my purpose one day. *I could help other women*, I would say to myself, *rise up out of the ashes and see that glimmer of hope.* First, I had to feel well. I had endless laparoscopies and endo excisions. I tried pristine diets, naturopathy, meditation, walking, and yoga. Nothing was the golden ticket or relief from the relentless pain.

By the age of forty-nine, my life had been checkered with pain, both physical and emotional. My finances fractured in my divorce. The last thing I needed was a new health mystery. My left leg had lost feeling and gave way without warning. I again dug deep into innate resilience. Umbrella sticks became my new walking aids.

This time, it wasn't "in my head," according to the consultants. It was "hormones and perimenopause." Astounded, my eyes glued to my forehead, I felt a roar deep in my belly. It rose to my chest. For so many years, I had cowered from having a voice. Now, it was erupting. I fired back boldly with courage. "Wow, really?" I said, "That's quite an assumption. If this were true, wouldn't the world be filled with limping perimenopausal women?" Shocked at my own outburst and gingerly shuffling, I left the consultation room, proud of my sarcasm!

Sarcasm alone would not ensure I was heard, but collapsing would. A week later, I was back in the emergency room. Misbelief in my condition was suddenly validated; I needed multiple operations. My trust in my doctors was frayed. I had received so many previous misshapen medical opinions. Patiently enduring more invasive investigations, my new diagnosis was revealed. Endometriosis in my pelvis, hips, and ligaments, two inguinal canal hernias, and a fatty mass pressing on my femoral nerve in my left leg. The demon attacking my torso for so long was now starving my leg from functioning. Every knock, every fracture, every blockage was a sign. A sign I wasn't seeing. I often wish I had laid down sooner and surrendered, but I forged on.

Then, the bottom *really* did fall out of my life.

It was six months after my third operation. My hernias had been darned, and the masses had been rebuked. *Surely, that was it,* I hoped. *Only the Universe had more for me to learn — more than I was ready for.*

On a normal Wednesday morning, I peeled myself from my comfy sheets and my pink fluffy blanket with stars that glowed, my snuggle blanket that brought me hope. I walked to the bathroom in my small city studio without bothering to say hello in the mirror. I knew how terrible I felt; I did not need to check. I sat on the toilet, and in that split second, my life changed. I gasped. My throat seized. My rectum had a dispute with my body and dropped from its internal position. I was sucking in my tummy, contracting my muscles to draw it back in, but it was disconnected, refusing to respond. It just hung motionless externally. My mind was awash with fear and despair; my only answer was to use my hand. I pushed my rectum back up to where it belonged. I felt like I wanted to vomit. I was so afraid of what was happening with my body. I felt like I was falling apart in pieces, my body breaking down, rejecting itself, drowning in a prolapse of helplessness. I didn't think to call an ambulance. I just mustered on. Had I lost my mind? I dismissed the severity of the situation and found a way to simply cope with it.

That was my new normal for the next nine months. I feared coughing, and sneezing caused dread to ripple through me. Each trip to the bathroom caused my body to seize. This was during the pandemic, so doctor appointments were online and weeks away. The following months washed a whole new level of self-loathing and disgust over my soul. Life was a horror movie, I thought. Then the circus really came to town! "I lost my job."

On the Friday before my rectum was to be surgically mended, work called me to a video meeting per COVID-19 protocol. At that meeting, they let me know I was being let go. Jobless and speechless, heaving and breathless, I lay on the floor in a fetal position once again. Facing surgery without an income, I knew I needed to dig deep into my hope and faith. Because of my despair, I had established deeper Christian beliefs. At each eleventh hour, I could see the Lord was saving me. His footsteps were the ones I could see in the sand. He had carried me all my life. I had prayed for financial security, yet the Lord had released me from my job. *How interesting!* I thought. I had to trust His ways were higher than mine. My salvation created a peace that flowed within me. I had felt protected by a Higher Source.

I spent the next ten days in the hospital. The tumultuous operation had ended, and I was back on the ward, my heart joyful as I had been blessed to be in a bed by the window. I sensed the persistent, burning red inferno once raging inside me was slowly subsiding. The pain and discomfort that had been a part of my life for way too long must be nearing an end, I thought. I gazed out of the window, knowing I had a long recovery ahead, but joy was just over the horizon, waiting to be embraced. As the day turned to dusk, I saw the stars beginning to sparkle, and there it was… a vision. A sight so vivid I felt I could touch it. Dense and bleak, the once-black cloud that engulfed my soul was tinged with pink. Its edges were fluffy; it was the hue of hope. I saw an image of the Lord peering in at me through my window. An Angel on each shoulder, supporting Him. I felt it was a sign, a validation that the end of my suffering must be near. A sense of anticipation flooded my body. I believed this sign was one of reprieve, and I could fully begin my healing journey. My vision faded into a distant sketch, and my numb body began to tingle. My faith was so strong that my soul began to sparkle again, and a pink glow surrounded my heart. The news from my surgeon, "All went well; the operation was success-ful." My body felt whole.

Losing my job released me from an old pattern of wanting security over my connection with myself. I see the opportunity I was given, the message He had been sending me all along. Once the bottom fell out of my life and body, I had no choice but to trust His guidance. God was urging me to be released from a pain that had been fueling my flames: the corporate world. When the Lord peered in through my window suspended by Angels, I knew they were carrying Him, and he was carrying me. The fractures in my life were healing, the pink, glittery, sparkly dust of joy once again flickering. I felt the opportunities ahead and a future of untethered bliss.

In the next two years, I magnetically attracted a myriad of opportunities. After much hard work, a grant enabled me to start my own business, *The Wellwishers Haven*. I had chosen the name back in my college days. It is a safe refuge for people in pain, providing them with a toolbox of holistic modalities. *There it was unfolding: my purpose.* I then found physical help using a new cutting-edge science. I was able to relinquish all medications. I embraced a practice called FlowCode™, a Neuroscience with a roadmap to silence my inner critic, once so loud. I was certified as a FlowCode Coach, and I live life without pain to this day. Everything I was learning became my toolkit for freedom. I believed the Lord had designed my entire journey for *my healing.* Changing the pain inside me changed the attraction magnet outside me. It led me to a new chapter, finding Ignite itself. My past pain has now become my intended purpose.

Joy is within us all. Listen to your intuition; it has been there all along. Your life's journey *is* divinely meaningful. Using actionable tools will unleash the joy deep inside you. Stand courageously, and believe in your inner strength; use your hope. Devise your own inner toolkit, and you will discover joy is not illusive; it is just a chapter away.

IGNITE ACTION STEPS

- **Set aside time for yourself** each day to engage in prayer or meditation. Let this practice invite reflection and bring you a sense of higher purpose.

- **Live life in flow,** and view challenges as an opportunity to grow versus obstacles to be avoided.

- **Address your thoughts**; they impact emotions, behaviors, and experiences. Changing your thoughts can influence your outcome to be more positive.

- **Listen to your intuition**; it can be your inner doctor. Be open to alternative paths to wellness beyond traditional methods.

Elaine Valerie Thompson — New Zealand
Holistic Wellness Coach
www.thewellwishershaven.com
thewellwishershaven
the_wellwishers_haven
elainevaleriethompson

Hollis Baley

HOLLIS BALEY

"Joy just happens when you're not looking for it."

I want to convey that joy isn't something we must *strive* for; it can be experienced at any time, especially in the quiet, reflective, sweet moments life delivers! Joy comes when we allow ourselves to receive the life that is coursing through our veins. With each breath, we bring our awareness to the magic and miracles surrounding us. Joy blooms in those who can accept and honor themselves for everything they've been through, especially the losses, failures, and pain. It shows up when we adopt the perspective of being a student of life, accessible in the hearts of those who honor all relationships and life experiences and who live in faith and connection with God.

TAKING THE HELM

Six months pregnant, with the promise of a new life swelling within me, I woke up in bliss as the love of my life, holding my head in his hands, kissed me sweetly and asked, "Will you marry me?" His eyes were sparkling with a mixture of nerves and excitement, and I responded in tears with a kiss that confirmed my "yes." On that beautiful sunny morning, as we made love, I greatly appreciated him. With our daughter growing inside of me, living my dream life in Mexico, and now engaged, it felt like everything was falling perfectly into place. As he prepared to pick up his family from the airport for the weekend, I lay in bed, contemplating our future.

"Do you think we should have the ceremony before or after the baby is born?" I asked. His response took me by surprise: "How about today?" I laughed out loud, thinking he was joking. But he didn't respond with words, and when I saw the smile that stretched across his face, I knew he had something up his sleeve. It turned out everyone knew about our surprise wedding but me. "So, will you marry me today?" he said proudly.

I remember my brain going through the list of questions that one would naturally have upon receiving a proposal like this, but another part of me knew to just be present for what I was about to say. I took a deep breath, smiled, and said, "Okay! Let's get married today!" As we sealed our commitment with a kiss and a long embrace, I couldn't help but marvel at the moment's perfection. Not only were we stepping into a new chapter as parents, but we were also eagerly anticipating the arrival of the charter fishing boat I had purchased for our growing family. It was set to become our second 'baby' together. With our wedding just hours away, life felt surreal and almost too good to be true as we stood on the brink of realizing our shared dreams.

This journey held an extra layer of significance, a triumph over the trials and tribulations of my personal past. Four miscarriages with previous partners had tested my faith and resilience, but with him by my side, every setback had led to this moment of profound joy and fulfillment. In the midst of life's unpredictability, I had found my anchor in him.

With the blessing of the ocean as our witness and the hues of the setting sun as our backdrop, we exchanged vows that evening in an intimate ceremony surrounded by our closest family and friends. The air was filled with magical, loving energy, bubbling with the promise of a future woven together by spontaneity, possibility, and sacred union. As we stood beneath the painted sky, I knew that we were ready to set sail into a future brimming with love, laughter, and endless adventure.

The day our daughter entered the world was also the day our charter boat arrived. Receiving both a baby and a new boat was a mixture of excitement and pressure that quickly took a toll on my new husband. As I rested at home, recovering from the birth and bonding with our beautiful newborn daughter, my husband bonded with his new dream boat and quickly became a ghost in our house. He left at 5 AM, and I waited all day long for him to return. Some days, that meant I didn't see him until after dark! Drinking and fishing immediately took precedence over his new wife and baby. It left me confused and feeling more alone than I'd ever felt in my life.

On one hand, I gave him credit for wanting to build a successful business. Still, as the weeks went on, I saw less and less of my husband, watched our finances dissipate, and felt like he was a thousand miles away; our emotional connection was nowhere to be found. I couldn't find a constructive way to communicate with him. He turned his phone off when he went fishing, and by the time he came home, he was too intoxicated, and I was too tired to talk about anything serious. His few hours at the house were spent drinking with friends after work, and he only held our daughter when I asked him to.

The days turned into weeks, the weeks into months, and the initial clear skies of our union turned dark gray with shadows of doubt and discord. My husband, once my rock and confidant, began to drift away, consumed by the siren call of irresponsibility. The ease and connection we had once shared had been replaced by distance, confusion, and despair. I felt like I was living with a stranger.

Our daughter, the embodiment of our love and dreams, was my beacon of light amid our stormy seas. Yet even this perfect, beautiful gift of life couldn't quell the tempest brewing within our marriage. The joyous chapter of becoming a wife and mother quickly gave way to the harsh reality of a relationship unraveling at the seams. My spirit wavered, and I was adrift from the faith that had used to anchor me. As I navigated these tumultuous waters, I found myself clinging to memories of happier times, moments when our love felt invincible, and our future seemed limitless. But as each day passed, those memories became tainted by the bitter taste of disappointment and betrayal. I succumbed to my own demons of anger and depression, caught in a pattern of blaming him, desperately fighting for his attention, and then shaming myself for getting so upset. Though a part of me knew it wasn't my fault, I would convince myself I had done something wrong. I also expected him to change, making my happiness his responsibility and setting myself up for constant disappointment. I held onto this cycle of anger, blame, and shame like a lifeline.

For a year, I remained trapped in a downward spiral of victimhood and hopelessness, unwilling to confront the reality of my situation. The beautiful visions I had imagined when pregnant — waking up together in bed as a happy family of three — never happened. Instead, I spent my mornings alone with our baby clinging to my breast as I wiped the tears away and tried to calm my racing thoughts. Each day, I worried about where my husband was with no idea what was happening with him or our boat, which had every penny of my savings and inheritance wrapped up in it.

I would struggle to be present with my daughter, my mind a tangled mess of negative thoughts. I struggled to find any thread of hope or happiness; the unanswered calls, hollow promises, and a garage full of beer cans were all painful reminders of what we had lost. I clung to my anger and continued to blame the situation because it was easier than feeling the pain. I knew if I admitted the truth that my relationship had crumbled, I would have to walk away. I felt like a complete failure. As I began to recognize I needed to get out of this marriage for the well-being of all three of us, I was terrified. I resented the woman who was living this story of a failing union. What's more, I judged her for becoming a mother who was completely disconnected from the bliss and gratitude of having created a beautiful little child.

As my daughter approached her second birthday, I found myself standing at a crossroads, faced with two of the most difficult decisions of my life. The first was to leave my husband, to untangle myself from the web of dysfunction and despair that had consumed our once vibrant relationship. The second decision was to sell the boat, the symbol of our shattered dreams, purchased with every bit of money I had to my name.

The thought of leaving my husband filled me with terror. Despite the turmoil and heartache, I couldn't shake the fear of walking away from the life we had built together. But anyone looking in on the situation would have told me the same thing: the hope of things changing was false. During one of my first spiritual awakenings decades earlier, someone had imparted a profound truth to me: "Expectations are premeditated resentments." It was a phrase that lingered in my mind's recesses, waiting to be rediscovered when I needed it most. And, just before my daughter's second birthday, it resurfaced with startling clarity, jolting me awake from my victim mentality slumber.

With tear-stained cheeks and a heavy heart, I made the agonizing decision to let go of the past and chart a new course for myself and my daughter. I might lose the man I love, but I had a daughter to care for, and I refused to lose myself or cause any more damage to her perfect soul in the process. I needed to change before the darkness consumed me. I had hardly any life left in me and couldn't continue to sacrifice my own well-being for the sake of a sinking ship.

I summoned up the courage to walk away from our relationship, but I found myself grappling with the decision to sell the boat. It wasn't just a vessel; it represented my husband's dreams and aspirations. It was the only thing besides our daughter that anchored us together. Selling the boat meant crushing any remaining hope of "us." I didn't know what would become of him if he didn't have the boat to turn to every day and was terrified of taking it away. He was so distant, seemingly lost even when he was physically around, and no matter how hard I tried to communicate with him, he refused to face the situation with a sober presence.

In the midst of my pain and uncertainty, I found solace in the wisdom of my inner voice, the wise woman who knew that healing couldn't happen by expecting others to change. She knew that true love meant walking away, even when it felt impossible. I knew that joy couldn't be found in clinging to material possessions or staying in a toxic environment. It had to come from within, from a place of self-acceptance and resilience. That meant, a few weeks after my husband moved out, I made the difficult choice to cast off the boat, unanchoring myself from the weight of what could have been.

As I navigated divorce and newfound independence, I slowly discovered the power of acceptance and forgiveness, both for myself and for my ex-husband. I learned to embrace *all parts* of myself with love and compassion. And in the quiet moments of reflection amidst the chaos of rebuilding my life, I found glimpses of joy! It was always in the seemingly quiet moments — while I was taking a shower, sitting down to breastfeed, or staring at the stars at the end of a long day. To my surprise, moments of joy began to frequent my days, whether it was hearing my daughter's laughter dance through the air or finding peace in a moment of stillness; I began to understand that joy wasn't something to be chased or attained. It was already within me, waiting to be rediscovered. I realized something so beautiful in that state: *joy is just something that happens when you're not looking for it.*

As I embraced this awareness and resilience, I embarked on a journey of self-care and nourishment, nurturing my soul and my body. In doing so, I discovered that the most challenging things in life are full of nuggets of wisdom, overflowing with miracles, and flourishing with opportunities for growth. Emerging from my despair, I found an unexpected beacon of hope, which is, to this day, the enduring force that illuminates the happiness and joy in my soul: my faith. As I journeyed through the storm of divorce and my transition into single parenthood, I realized my relationship with God was the anchor I had been searching for all along.

The difficult decisions I had made for my own well-being and that of my daughter were buoyed by complete surrender and faith. When I reconnected with God and began nourishing that relationship, I found that I could embrace the uncertainty with a newfound sense of resilience that came from fully trusting in the unknown. Through prayer and introspection, I began to rebuild my life, turning to God and asking for guidance, reading and living by the word of God as the Bible spells it out, and turning my will over and allowing Him to work in my life. I let Him take the helm of my boat, and through the process, I realized a profound truth: real joy cannot be found in external circumstances but rather in the unwavering love of God. The more I surrendered to His will, the more I found peace and purpose amid life's storms. Though my marriage may have ended in abrupt farewells, my faith remains steadfast and is still the guiding light that illuminates the path forward.

Now, on the other side of the storm, I know that the most challenging things that happen in life are the greatest gifts… If we allow them to be. Being human in a dualistic world means that we are bound to experience both ends of the spectrum, and I can't say I would appreciate the joy, happiness, and love in my life today had it not been for the times when I felt pain, fear, and despair. Finding my true north — my purpose and my experience of joy came through the manifestation of the one thing I desired most in life — a family. It was truly a joyful chapter in becoming a wife and mother. I am grateful for the trials and tribulations that have led me to this moment of profound clarity and the realization that joy isn't something I have to strive for. It can be experienced anytime — especially in the quiet, sweet, reflective moments!

In true moments of joy, we can stop to celebrate and tap into a reservoir of strength and power stored in the frequency of the moment. We each have the capacity to recreate ourselves over and over again. We build the boat, and God fills the sails. Faith illuminates the joy that lives inside all of us. It opens our hearts and souls to new perspectives and can restore hope in life, no matter how dark the days have been. Faith is the foundation for living a joy-filled life. In turn, joy catalyzes transformation, propelling us forward with renewed purpose and determination. When we allow joy to flow through our veins in the here and now, we will see that magic and miracles are saturating the lives we live… even when we're not looking for it.

Give yourself the gift of allowing yourself those sweet, quiet, reflective moments, and have the faith that joy will swell in you.

Ignite Action Steps

Restore your faith and open yourself to joy with these daily practices:

- **Prayer & Self-Reflection:** Start your day with a moment of reflection or prayer. Set aside time each morning to connect with your faith through meditation, scripture reading, or expressing gratitude for the blessings in your life. This practice will center your mind and heart, grounding you in your spiritual foundation: Faith.

- **Divine Breathwork:** Your breath is the eternal Spirit of God within you. Practicing conscious breathwork for ten to fifteen minutes or more daily will help you cultivate inner peace, mental clarity, and spiritual alignment. You can find a free seven-day online Divine Breath practice on my website, *www.HigherSanctuary.com,* and discover the power of daily devotional breathwork.

- **Acts of Kindness:** Practice acts of kindness and compassion toward others. Whether it's offering a helping hand to someone in need, listening in the presence of a friend, or performing random acts of kindness, these gestures reflect God's love in action. By spreading love and kindness, you not only uplift others but also deepen your connection to your faith and experience the great joy that lies in being of service to others.

Hollis Baley — Mexico
Transformational Coach, Author, Speaker,
Founder & CEO of The Higher Sanctuary
www.highersanctuary.com
thehighersanctuary
highersanctuary

Jennifer M. Moore

JENNIFER M. MOORE

"Happiness relies on situations and circumstances; joy defies them."

It is my intention that this story helps you to discern the difference between happiness and joy. My hope is that you would not only choose joy, but become more deliberate and intentional in doing so. And, after reading it, you will learn to find joy in everything. I believe what I have written will help you find the real joy that comes from the soul, which is as abiding as it is deep and overflowing. Finally, I want you to learn to "re-joyce" daily, to practice finding joy repeatedly.

CULTIVATING JOY

"Don't marry him!"

The voice seemed to emanate from within me and all around me simultaneously. I was sitting in the bay window of my living room, staring at the Allen Bradley Building on campus across from Raiders Field, where I had my Engineering Dynamics class. I was contemplating whether I would actually go to class that afternoon and process the news I had just received a few hours earlier.

That voice...

I was confused and a little frightened because I was alone in the apartment. As those words echoed in my head, *"Don't marry him!"* I thought I was going crazy because no one had even asked me to marry them. I was in the next-to-last semester of my senior year, and I was looking forward to finally graduating with my BS in Biomedical Engineering from Milwaukee School of Engineering or MSOE (pronounced "mosey"). I was happy to graduate, but it was a real challenge. I worked two (sometimes three) jobs while attending school full-time. I was older than most of my classmates. My struggle with depression was putting a damper on what should have been a joyous occasion: graduation. For the last few weeks, I had been experiencing excruciating stomach cramps, ending up on the floor of my bedroom, silently crying and writhing in pain.

The sudden and very unexpected news that I was now pregnant had thrown my world into chaos. I was so close to graduating and I couldn't afford a child. The day before the voice, I had gone to a neighborhood clinic a few miles from the school, where I was diagnosed with irritable bowel syndrome (IBS). They gave me medication to help with the symptoms and pain, which I took that evening. But just before my morning class, I received an urgent phone call from a nurse at the clinic asking if I had taken the medicine. I was told not to take any more because the urine test they took as a precaution indicated I was pregnant. It seemed surreal. I was twenty-five years old enough to have a child, but I was still so disappointed in myself. I had grown up in the church. Premarital sex, for me, was a sin. And now, I was about to become an unwed mother. I was ashamed.

The father was not who I ever imagined raising a child with. In fact, my plan was not to marry or have children at all. I planned to work in a career that I loved and travel for the rest of my life. He and I met at the water softener company, where I worked part-time as a lab tech. He asked me out one afternoon. He was twelve years older than I was but very charming. No one had ever asked me on a date before, and I was flattered. I had been dealing with deep self-esteem issues after being bullied almost daily because of my deep "frog" voice and thick glasses growing up in Chicago. It felt good to be with someone who I thought really liked me, and I was happy to have the attention. The fact that he was also a recovering addict and alcoholic didn't bother me at the time because there were alcoholics in my own family.

About ten minutes before I heard the mysterious voice, I called the father to inform him that I was pregnant. I was humiliated when he asked, "*Are you sure that it's mine?*" Then, when he suggested that I have an abortion, I became very angry. I didn't believe in abortion, and I told him as much. Then he asked me what I was going to do. Not what we were going to do… what I would do.

"Whatever I need to!" I snapped back before hanging up. For me, it was an easy decision. I wanted to keep the baby, so I had to put my degree on hold. I was scared but had faith I could raise a child. My mom had just retired, and my parents planned to return to Arkansas. It seemed the perfect chance for a new start, so I moved with them to be close to family.

Soon after arriving in Arkansas, my child's father started calling in the middle of the night (the beginning of eighteen years of sleepless nights), wanting to get back together. I wasn't sleeping, and I was both exhausted and annoyed from the nightly arguments followed by drunken, sob-filled apologies. But the stress of fighting him was not good for the baby. So I let the father back into my life, believing the madness would stop. He came to Arkansas, but we couldn't live together or "shack up," so I married him. It was a simple courthouse ceremony — me in a plain white dress covering my eight-month pregnant belly and my parents as witnesses. But it was a fresh start. I ignored the voice and was hopeful that our marriage would be filled with the happiness I felt as we said, "I do."

A month after we were married, I gave birth to my first and oldest daughter. The joy I felt the first time I held her in my arms was unlike anything I had ever experienced before. She was a chunky baby with a full head of hair and beautiful, dark brown eyes. I found a new focus as a mother and a wife. I had someone to care for and love who would unconditionally love me. My daughter had her father in her life, and I believed everything would be fine.

Sadly, the joy I felt in those first few moments following her birth was short-lived. Soon after the nurse came in to take the baby back to the nursery, my mom came into the room and sat in a chair beside my bed. My husband had gone back to the apartment to get ready for work. My mom leaned toward me and whispered, "Is he drinking again?"

The question caught me off-guard.

"I could smell the alcohol on his breath while he was talking to me," she continued. Something in me clicked. I looked away, engulfed with disappointment and shame, remembering how his breath smelled like Listerine mingled with another smell that I couldn't quite identify until she shared her concerns.

After the baby and I were released from the hospital, I returned to work at the telephone company. My husband worked evenings, so he watched the baby during the day. I was apprehensive about leaving the baby with him. But I hadn't seen him take a drink, so I gave him the benefit of the doubt. Right up until the day I came home for lunch and found the baby sound asleep in her crib… all alone. I was frantic and absolutely livid. I caught a glimpse of him through the front window, walking back toward the house, drinking from an upturned brown paper bag. I was frozen in anger, unsure of what to do, yet I knew he wasn't worth going to jail for.

I have been called a "brainiac" all of my life. How could I have been this dumb?

My husband's drinking escalated, and the mental and emotional abuse started. I kept clinging to the hope that he would change. When I was offered a job opportunity at a brand new hospital back in Milwaukee, my parents gladly offered to keep my daughter while we went to get situated. We found a loft apartment, and after I settled into my new job, we were finally able to bring our daughter up to live with us again.

A week after we were back home, he left with the car after dinner. It was our only transportation. I asked him not to drink since he would be driving. My daughter and I were sound asleep when I was roughly awakened around midnight by an obviously intoxicated husband, demanding that I give him the money from the paycheck I had cashed earlier in the day. This 'intoxication' seemed different and was the beginning of the financial abuse. I quietly reminded him that we had yet to pay rent and buy groceries, but he was very insistent and *very* mean. I was afraid for the first time in our marriage, but not the last time. I stood looking down over the railing, begging him not to take the only money we had as the door slammed so violently behind him that it shook the apartment and woke the baby.

I knew I made a huge mistake and needed to leave the marriage. I had already ignored what I now know was the voice of the Holy Spirit when I was sitting in the window that day back in college. However, I felt this new level of aggression was a sign that I needed to reconnect to my faith and pray for guidance. I thought, maybe if I just prayed for my husband and loved him enough, he would change, and everything would be alright. Believing I could help him, I stayed… and it was like watering a poisonous plant.

Our family grew over the next eighteen years as we added another daughter and a son to our dysfunctional family. Then, the sexual abuse started. To outsiders, we were a perfect family. We cultivated the ideal life. After living in several states due to my career, we ended up in Virginia. We were actively involved as leaders in the churches we attended. But no one knew the hell I was going through every day. And… I didn't want anyone to know because I was ashamed. He was so charming. No one would believe he was the jealous, mean, and vindictive man I was living with behind closed doors. As his relapses became more frequent, so did the abuse. I was physically, mentally, and emotionally exhausted. What little self-esteem I had before I met him no longer existed. I no longer knew who I was or even what my purpose was anymore. I was deeply unhappy.

Thankfully, it was joy that allowed me to never look like what I was going through. The joy of seeing my children continue to grow, thrive, and excel in a less-than-conducive environment kept me looking forward to coming home each day with renewed hope that things would get better, even though my stomach was tied in knots. The joy of serving and helping others while dealing with feelings of my own helplessness enabled me to genuinely share a smile as I engaged with others. It was Joy that gave me the strength and the courage to endure. *To persevere. To survive.*

We tried counseling a few times, but he refused to continue when it was not favorable to his side of the story. My depression and anxiety were becoming unmanageable. I hadn't wanted to be married before all of this, and now I had reached a point where I just wanted out, even if it meant suicide. It was then that I knew I needed to finally leave the marriage. Dying was not an option because I couldn't leave my children that way, and I definitely couldn't leave them with him.

With the courage I needed, I took the kids and whatever we could fit into the car and left. I was conflicted about leaving, and even more so about moving forward with a divorce. I felt like I had once again disappointed God. But one morning, while I was taking some time away at a resort during the separation, I woke up early to study and pray about the direction I should take. During my meditation, another voice whispered inside me, *You deserve more.* It was a still, small voice that Ignited the realization that the person who was supposed to cover and protect me was the one who exposed and abused me. Suddenly, the guilt and shame I had felt about divorce began to melt away, replaced with a comforting awareness that my abusive marriage wasn't what God desired for his daughter. Not ever. I decided to proceed, and at that moment, an unspeakable peace filled my heart. I was finally ready to move on.

Of course, ending the marriage did not instantly end the trauma. Over the next few years, my ex managed to find a place close to wherever we lived. He continued to attend the same church, even joining the praise team I co-led. The church was my sanctuary, but it didn't feel like a safe place for me. The stalking was both tormenting and tiring. Despite it all, I was deliberate in continuing to cultivate what joy I had through serving others for the sake of my children.

When my son was accepted into the University of Arizona, and he decided to attend, I felt God was also telling me to go. None of us had ever been to Tucson, Arizona, but over the next month, I sold, gave away, and discarded most of what I could and put everything else in storage. We loaded up my Hyundai Sonata and my daughter's Pontiac with our three dogs and our belongings and headed west. My oldest daughter was also starting grad school in Kansas, and my youngest daughter transferred to an undergrad school in New York in the fall. It was a new start for all of us.

Passing the *Welcome to West Virginia* sign brought such a sense of freedom and release. I felt like I could FINALLY breathe because I was finally FREE. My ex couldn't find us so easily anymore. Seeing the majestic mountains in New Mexico brought a genuine calm that I hadn't felt before or since that moment at the resort. It was then that I felt real joy returning. As we pulled into the parking lot of our new home, I took in the beauty of everything around me and felt grateful for my newfound liberation.

Reflecting back on those years, I was very unhappy but still thankful for the lessons I learned. My children were never without a roof over their heads, even if it wasn't our own. They never missed a meal or class. There is regret and remorse I often feel for staying and raising my children in such an abusive environment for so long, and they have their own mental health struggles as a result. Yet, my heart is full of gratitude, and my soul overflows with joy as I watch them pursue and fulfill their God-given purposes. My oldest daughter is in her final year of medical school as she pursues her dream of being a doctor while garnering scholarships and recognition for her research in the field of hematology. My youngest daughter has obtained her degree in music, her melodic and soulful voice filling music venues around NYC while teaching other young hopefuls to explore their musical talents. My son is pursuing his degree in playwriting, amazing those around him with his brilliant directing skills in the theatrical arena. We all remain close, laughing daily via text messages. Now, the voices I hear most often are the three who feel joy in their lives.

I have become stronger through my relationship with the Lord and my faith. Before, I ignored His voice before, but now I have learned how to lean in and hear His heart and plans for me. I spend less time with my own thoughts and more time with Him because it is in His presence that I find complete and utter joy. In spite of feeling so many times that the Lord didn't hear me, I now understand that He always saw me. Even after making what I felt was the worst decision of my life, He provided a path to my freedom. I am no longer just an abuse survivor. I am a joy thriver.

God always had a plan for my life, and my pain had a purpose. It could have been so much worse. I am still healing and not always happy, but I am choosing to cultivate joy wherever and whenever I can. Apostle Paul said *that we should give thanks for everything and to count everything as joy.* It wasn't easy to do then, and it can sometimes be difficult now. But when we are intentional, it becomes easier to 're-joyce,' even in the worst places, finding joy again… and again… and again.

IGNITE ACTION STEPS

- **Be Grateful** - Gratefulness is more than just being thankful. It's deeper than emotion. It's an attitude of appreciation that flourishes even in the worst circumstances. Knowing this difference, you will find that there is always something to be grateful for.

- **Acknowledge the sovereignty of God** - We may never understand why certain things happen to us and around us. *But He did, and He does.* He knows what He is doing even if we don't. And we can trust that He is working all things, even the absolutely terrible and seemingly unbearable things, together for our ultimate good.

- **Choose Joy** - Be intentional and deliberate about it. Practice it again and again. Exercise it like a muscle. The more you do it, the easier it becomes to find joy and the stronger and deeper the experience will become. *Joy truly is where you find it.*

Jennifer M. Moore — United States of America
Author, CEO of Y.O.U.T.H., Inc.
www.theyouthjoynt.org
jenimoore4
ladij726
jennifer-m-moore

Joanne Gauthier

JOANNE GAUTHIER

*"Every day is a new chance to choose to be happy,
to see the abundance, to choose joy."*

My hope for you is through reading my story, you will find your inner joy. It is there inside of you… waiting for you. Once you learn to believe and accept that everything happens for a reason, you will experience the blessings of joy. I say bring on the obstacles, as it means there is growth about to happen. Adversity will always be in our lives, but it doesn't have to define us. How we deal with the turmoil is on us. I choose to be like bamboo, strong and flexible. In times of immense turmoil, I may sway, and I will bend, but since I am resilient, I won't break.

JOY, I HAD IT IN ME ALL ALONG

Mine was one of those white picket fence childhoods. I grew up on a dairy farm with bail twine swings hanging from the rafters in the hayloft and our very own skating pond in the field. My family was the best. I had amazing, loving parents and five fantastic siblings, and everyone got along. I had over a hundred cousins between my mom's thirteen siblings and my dad's ten. With such a sizable extended family, our front door was more like a revolving one, always someone coming or going. I was so fortunate to grow up embraced by this huge net of support. I was never alone. Amidst that beautiful web, the strongest strand was my sister Monique. She was my constant, my home base. Throughout my childhood, I knew I always had her with me. Through our special bond, she taught me to be strong and, most importantly, to believe in myself and persevere.

Although we were six siblings, Monique was the closest to me in age. We were roommates for the first fourteen years of our lives. In our teen years, whereas Monique exuded calmness, order, and discipline, I oozed an excess of clutter, disorder, and chaos. Her side of the room was always meticulously tidy, books lined neatly on her desk, clothes folded and stored, and her bed was always made. My side was adorned with books lying about carelessly and yesterday's clothing strewn haphazardly on my desk, the floor, the chair, and my unmade bed. As my older sister, she guided me on life skills and advised me on makeup, clothes, hygiene, boyfriends, and anything I would ask her about (and many things I hadn't even thought of). Invariably, she knew the answers to my oh-so-many questions. She was my guidance system, coach, sounding stone, voice of reason, and north star. She always knew what to say, and she always had my back.

By today's standards, I would most likely have been diagnosed with ADHD, but back then, I was just a fidgety, squirmy handful of a child. My strobe light-like attention meant I was only present a fraction of the time. For the most part, my mind was off elsewhere, listening to the hum of the fluorescent bulb or counting raindrops splashing on the sidewalk. The world was filled with so many interesting things to keep me entertained. Monique's serene demeanor invariably helped me find my inner calmness; if only for a moment, I would touch peace. She was so important to me.

The amazing bond we developed in our early years continued to flourish throughout our lives. We had a spiritual sister-soul connection that allowed us to sense when the other was having an 'off' day. Unfailingly, she could always feel (despite being hundreds of miles away) when I was struggling, and she would reach out to me. She just knew. She remained my compass, my guide throughout my life. I would receive random text messages like: *"Joanne, I just have two things to say... I love you unconditionally, and... I love you unconditionally."* Even in the autumn of our lives, Monique was always just a call away. As I had done throughout our childhoods, I'd phone her whenever I needed her advice. Monique would always be there; it was as simple as that. I had no reason to think otherwise.

After suffering through a series of debilitating compressed disks and brittle bone fractures, doctors diagnosed Monique with multiple myeloma, an unyielding cancer of the blood that was gnawing holes in her bones. With the diagnosis came an onslaught of tests, treatments, and painful procedures. Many of Monique's treatments drastically weakened her immune system, leaving her vulnerable to virtually anything. As a result, in-person visits were not an option. She was confined to her own isolated little bubble, one we could not access. For us, my mother and the remaining siblings, this separation from her left us feeling unbearably helpless and far away from her sterile, insulated world. We started weekly FaceTime™ visits, the six of us and Mom, to keep that cord of connection. Those regular chats would become our norm over the next three years.

Monique's illness was unrelenting; through it, she remained fervently optimistic. She undertook trial after trial, and still, this evil nemesis prevailed against all treatments. If anything, it would seem cancer was mocking the medical world as if to say, "Is this really all you've got?"

Our older sister, Diane, told Monique she wished she could take her place for a little while during this grueling journey. As a true fighter, Monique simply replied, "Continue living your life to the fullest and enjoy every opportunity. We can't all be the sick ones. Just keep sharing your life's adventures with me."

Monique was so strong. Stronger than I could have ever imagined. Like an ostrich with its head in the sand, I desperately tried to deny any thought of her impending death, but Monique knew her prognosis. With great loving care, she paved her oppressive journey for us to ease *our* suffering. She introduced us to MAID (Medical Assistance In Dying), an organization devoted to aiding individuals with a doctor's assistance to end their lives, and how she was making the necessary arrangements for herself. Monique hoped we could begin to accept that death would be coming to visit our family.

Although she remained the ultimate warrior with amazing grace and resiliency throughout her arduous challenge, every new medical trial Monique undertook only seemed to leave her weaker. The cancer had started to eat at her jawbone, her ribs, and even her skull. Upon hearing how the cancer had metastasized beyond hope, my brave front collapsed. I crumbled under the weight of my sorrow. With sobs wracking my body, I cursed the skies for daring to take this person away from us, away from *me*. As it became apparent that the end was near, I was inconsolable. By evening, my salty tears had rendered my eyes swollen and my cheeks blustery red. Seeing my state during a video chat, Monique did as she had always done in the past; she chose to comfort me. She texted me a video emphasizing how much she loved me and that *I should not worry.*

It is only with today's eyes that I am aware that the video she sent me was her way of telling me she was going to be okay on the journey. I was so focused on my pain at the time I did not see she was trying to get *me* ready for life without *her.*

Twenty-four hours later, my dear sister Monique lost her battle with Multiple Myeloma. She had fought so valiantly for the last thirty months that despite her blood cell count continually spiraling downward, none of us had been willing to admit she wasn't going to make it, least of all me. My first reaction when I heard Monique had died was a deep, bottomless pain in my heart. A deep sigh allowed all the air to escape my lungs. I was empty. If I am honest, my head knew her death was imminent. But my heart… that was something my heart was unprepared to face.

I would have to learn to breathe on my own without her. I did not know how I would ever be able to do that by myself. I hadn't realized how much I relied on her and what a precious gift she was. Without her, my axis tilted. I found myself sailing in rough seas with no captain to navigate. The helm, my helm, unmanned, was at the mercy of the elements, leaving me without my North Star, tossing me helplessly in all directions. I would have to find a way to navigate my life without her.

The weight. The tremendous weight. For me, grief was akin to walking around in a lead apron all the time, like those worn during X-rays. It wasn't painful; it was heavy, it was uncomfortable, and it felt suffocating. It was oppressive. Invisible small fishing weights were attached to the corners of my mouth, not only preventing a smile but instead forcing a downturned look, letting everyone know the depth of my anguish. More weights were hanging from the outer edges of my eyes, giving me a constant mournful expression. My whole body felt the strain of losing her. Yes, grief is a physical feeling.

With the monumental loss, sadness salivated to creep into my bubble. I was a mess. I knew if I let it, sadness would seep its way into my core and permeate my whole body. I had battled this worthy opponent on several occasions over the years. Although well acquainted, I must admit sadness is not a friend. Truthfully, I despise its presence, yet one can never truly appreciate happiness without having spent time with sadness. I suppose I should perhaps even thank sadness for its all too frequent visits in the past, for it was through sadness that I learned to cherish happiness and acknowledge the abundance of joy in my life.

I knew that my joy could not come out by wrapping myself in a blanket of sadness. Staying in that state would benefit no one, least of all myself. I would have to get a healthier attitude. I had to *choose* joy. My happiness was on me, nobody else. Lucky for me, I have an artesian well of joy inside me. All I needed to do was go within. It is always there waiting for me.

While meditating one night, about six weeks after Monique's death, I was still very much struggling with her absence. I asked her for some form of confirmation, a sign that she was okay. Almost instantly, my whole body was swaddled in a loving caress. Basking in the warmth of the embrace, with tears rolling down my cheeks, I knew I had received my answer; she was fine. *"Merci Monique,"* I whispered. I literally felt joy bubbling in me. I could do as she had taught me; I was strong enough. I could take the helm alone and navigate my life by myself.

Having always been positive, I never needed rose-colored glasses; my vision was already tinted pink. I was born programmed to be joyful. It's simply a fundamental part of my being. Monique reminded me of the abundance of joy and allowed me the confidence to know I would get through her passing. Yes, there was a deep sadness in my bubble, but that was all it was: a feeling, a temporary sensation. I understood that deep, heavy sorrow is but a passing emotion, a brief companion along the journey of grief. Sorrow does not define me, for at my core, *I am joy.*

Monique wanted me to fill my days with joy, curiosity, and ebullient enthusiasm, to embrace life with my arms wide open. My time here is precious and finite. I have been given the gift of life and if I am to honor her, I live in a state of joy for all the blessings in my life, what I have, as well as what I do not have. Her unconditional love continues to give me the strength to persevere. It is on me to remove the noise stuck between my ears and ground myself in infinite peace. I choose every day to live in joy, to be grateful for the tidbits of happiness scattered everywhere. By being present, I find joy, inner peace, and contentment.

Moments of darkness and great hardships are opportunities for growth. They don't feel like a gift, but they are. It's those times in our lives when we can stay in our misery or grow. The choice is up to us. The challenge is to say "Thank You" during these arduous times and accept the obstacle because through it comes growth and the gift of knowing and peace. The sooner we surrender and accept these challenges and obstacles as a gift on our journey, the sooner we heal. Things will always come and go out of our lives: possessions, jobs, and loved ones. We remain constant. Once we learn to live in the now, we find peace. If we can find peace, we can find joy. Living in the present eliminates the fears of tomorrow and the regrets of yesterday. When we live in the *now,* we find the joy within.

Yes, I will always miss Monique, but I know that it is up to me to find joy in my life. It is what she would want for me. Sadness is rear-view mirror stuff. When driving a car, we aren't supposed to be constantly looking in the rear-view mirror; it's only there for reference. Nor is it prudent to only be aware of what is in front. It is imperative that we are conscious of our surroundings. Even though the road is clear, one wouldn't feel safe driving with an unruly passenger. Looking back and looking forward is important, but only as long as we are mindful of what is around at the time. Life is the same way; we aren't supposed to live in the past or worry about the future. If we can learn to be present and live consciously in the now, we will find life gets amazingly easier and calmer. In the present, we can leave the worries of tomorrow and the sadness of yesterday behind.

Right now, right here, that is all we have. The *now* is the gift of today. And at this very moment, we get to choose how we feel. Even in difficult moments, and times of great sorrow, we *still* get to *choose* how we experience those times. Be like the bamboo; bend and sway during life's challenges; don't break. You will be rewarded by the gift of joy that is everywhere around you. We must learn to be happy today, at this moment. When we learn to appreciate all the blessings in our lives right now, it is then that we touch true happiness. We have found bliss. Ultimately, every day is a new chance for you to choose to be happy, to choose to look at the abundance in your life and to consciously choose to live in a state of perpetual joy.

Ignite Action Steps

- **The more you practice gratitude, the more it just multiplies**. Start a gratitude journal and aim to write five things you are grateful for each day. Soon, you will discover just how wonderful your life truly is.

- **Joy is inside you, just waiting for you to unleash it, and every day you have a choice**. What will you choose to do today to spark joy in your life? Smile at the strangers on the sidewalk, give a compliment, or better yet, look in a mirror and remind yourself you are beautiful, strong, and resilient. Recite the alphabet with affirmative adjectives about yourself.

- **Once you learn to look for the positive meaning in any obstacle you face, you are on a path of growth.** Every challenge, every hurdle, is there to teach you a lesson. Pay attention. With greater wisdom, look back at some of your most difficult moments and purposefully find the lesson.

- **When the tsunami waves of sorrow come crashing down again, and they will, stop the crazy thoughts as soon as you notice them.** Take five deep breaths. Go within; find your joy. You have all that you need to get through this, one step at a time.

Joanne Gauthier — Canada
Author, Sower of Joy and Hope
joannecmg
joannegauthier

Karen Whelan

KAREN WHELAN

"When you make the choice to love you, as you, you will discover joy."

My intention is for you to recognize that being here is a gift from the Divine. Your only job is to live your life fully and to do so is to self-permit. *Go, do you!* Let go of the need to be seen and accepted by others. Spring forth from a heart that knows you are here for something great: a quest, your soul's mission. Your Divine mission is for you to wake up to the truth of who you are. To awaken to who you are and discover that profound love within. Being here is your birthright, your inheritance from God.

UNBECOMING TO BECOME GOD'S DESIGN

I was drenched in purity and innocence, playing and twirling around. At eight years old, I was delighted that my black and yellow checkered skirt spun out wide around me. How fairy-like I felt. I remembered he was sitting on an armchair, watching television, when he called me to sit on his lap. I got up and sat there all happy, feeling safe and cozy.

Then, the touching began. My body froze. I felt scared and confused. I wasn't sure why.

After it ended, I pulled up my tights; I went to the bathroom crying, asking, *Why me?* That question haunted me for seven more years, activating the constant punisher, "What's wrong with me?" I spent my days clammed up in fear and hate. The haunting desire to be someone other than myself followed me like a shadow. I remember that day when my inner oceanic bliss washed away — the love of the embodied self — was stolen. In its place, a monstrous hate took over in my mind.

As I grew up, I became a master of self-hate, an expert in Edging God Out (EGO). I hated Karen with such fury, trapped in blaming, hating, resenting, and shame. I had grown up in an environment where I endured abuse, both sexual and physical, a place in which I felt unloved, unlovable, and unwanted. That manifested as wounds of emotional abandonment, wounds that tested my mental and emotional stability.

At the age of fourteen, I ran away with one of my school friends, Sandi, who had gone through a similar experience to mine. We spent that morning sitting on a beach, getting stoned on handmade joints as I listened to her talk about how things changed when she told her family. I confided to her my hatred of myself and my body, an object that had attracted such unwanted attention. My body made me sick, and I wanted to be rid of it.

Amidst my pity, Sandi abruptly said, "Make it stop, then! Only you can do that." Her words cut through the reality I felt I had no control over. Her sharp honesty made the cells in my body shake as if struck by the sound waves of a huge gong, splitting my armored being and forcing me to reclaim my strength.

"How can I? No one cares. Who'd believe me?" I told her. My sense of self had not mattered. I had become an object of gratification for another. I did not exist. To hear suddenly that I had control was transcendental.

On that day, I took a deep breath and finally spoke up about my sexual abuse. I uttered my truth, standing trembling in a social worker's office. I was then taken home to repeat the news to my mother. My story struggled to come out, but the room was filled with my unspoken words. My mother's eyes knew something terrible was about to change her world; I was about to flood it with pain. The burden of "I am the problem" carved its painful message in my heart. My body went cold as I said out loud, shaking, "I am being abused sexually."

I wanted the world to go away as I buried my face into my mother's womb while the social worker, my mother, and my father talked about what came next. My mother threw my father out of the house that day. But he filled our doorway by nighttime, pleading with my mother as he had nowhere to go. My home became saturated in everyone's pain. I felt fragmented, angry at him, and sad for him as I passed by the sitting room (which had become his living space), seeing the uneaten food on the tray outside the door.

Everything became suffocating. I couldn't breathe and couldn't cope with their pain and my pain. Within four months, I was gone and turned into ferociously hating Karen. I attempted suicide, I dropped out of school and became homeless on the street, lost to drugs. I turned my back on the Divine as I felt the Divine had abandoned me. Chaos became the perfect storm to hide from me. During my drug-induced moments, I would stand looking at myself in a mirror, a person with massive pupils pulling weird expressions on her face, despising myself with guilt and shame. I missed my family connections and began to feel and believe that the sun was shining down on them in their world, but in my world, I was living in the shadows, withering in shame.

For the next year and a half, the streets were my home. I knew the drugs would overtake me if I didn't make a change. My way out came from the Divine when I took a chance and desperately marched into a small hotel. I declared to the cleaning manager that although I was only sixteen, I would work extra hard and be a great employee. Despite the holes in my jacket and the offensive smell, she offered me a toothbrush, bucket, and cleaning products, saying, "If you clean this wood panel against the wall, I will consider it." Four hours later, she returned, impressed by my strong will, and gave me the job. That allowed me to sleep at the hotel in the small staff room and took me off the streets to provide warmth, food, and hot water. Being safe meant everything.

After seven months of working there, through a series of Divine signs and coincidences, I found myself on the road to becoming an au pair in France. I was seventeen years old, with a single suitcase, no French skills, and a strong sense of joyful adventure that had been calling me since I was a young child. As I sat on the plane taking off, symbolically, I felt I was un-armoring the shackles of my old life. For the first time, I wanted to step into a new sense of Karen and be someone new in this new opportunity. I was *unbecoming* the self-loathing version of myself, moving toward something more joyous and fulfilling.

It was a terrifying but transformative time living in Gex, France. My au pair mother, Marie-Christine, was loved by the community and described as a gifted healer by other au pairs. But it wasn't until I crashed off my scooter, breaking my finger and cracking my ribs, that I saw that aspect of her. As she lay me down, placing her hands over me, I felt nauseous when suddenly the pain left my body, and my fingers and ribs were healed. Shocked, I looked at her, confused, not understanding how she did that. Marie-Christine only smiled, placed her hand on my heart, and spoke softly, "By hating, you'll fill your body with toxins, and you'll attack yourself. Try to learn forgiveness and it will set your pain free."

As the months went by, her words profoundly impacted me. I carried them around in my heart and spent hours alone, staring out at the horizon, contemplating their *true* meaning until I was moved into action almost a year later. It was as if my soul had popped its head up and said over and over to me, *it's time to write a letter.*

With an open heart and a desire to release, I wrote a letter to my father declaring *I am willing to forgive. I may never forget, but I want this pain to go back to you. I am exhausted from holding onto it. I choose to return it to you.* Posting that letter felt so glorious. I danced down the road. I skipped. I felt light. It was like the world was taken off me. The words, *You did good,* kept singing within me.

That letter, my mother later revealed, became a catalyst for my father to "let the light in." She said, "I don't know what you wrote in your letter, but I can hear him opening the pages and crying every night." With the desire to heal, I shared with my father my struggles and the deep self-hatred I have endured. I spoke of the pain and not understanding why he did what he did to me. Yet, I also share that if I never understood, I was willing to move on and forgive it.

I never thought I would return from France; I had made it my home, fallen in love, and was a few months pregnant with my first child. The liberation I left there and the new acceptance of myself permitted me to feel brave enough to speak to him after all this time. A year after I wrote the letter, I returned from France and finally decided to sit down with my father.

"Why me?" Those words had been shouting inside of me for so long. A dialogue took place between us over the next three months, allowing one soul to recognize the soul of the other. I could see we were both prisoners. We shared the experience of only ever knowing a world of pain, suffering, and lack of love. We both knew nothing of acceptance, wholeness, or joy. I felt a sacred love deep behind my heart in that time and space. As I glanced at him across the table, I knew redemption was the way to pull us both into wholeness. I was setting us both free. In forgiving, I was no longer a hostage to the pain but a host to sacredness in and through me. It was the "hand of God" in action. I could now move forward. But my unbecoming and finding Karen had only just begun.

For the next eleven years, I up-leveled myself. I began therapy, returned to college as a mature student, and welcomed the feeling of being brave and confident. I felt like a phoenix rising amidst my woundedness. To those on the outside looking in, life appeared complete: a stable relationship for fourteen years, ten consecutive years of college, two beautiful children, and a comfortable lifestyle. But there was something deep inside of me that still felt missing. The incomplete feeling would pop its head up, look around, and show dissatisfaction with my lifestyle until I would shove it back down, wishing it away. These feelings intensified, so I rang my friend, asking for an angel card reading and some reiki healing. At the end of the session, she handed me a book, *More Truth Will Set You Free,* by Derek O'Neill. Intrigued, I took the book and left for my holiday with my partner in the Canary Islands, eager to nurture myself and him. I was excited to discover the purpose that was divinely me. I knew there was something more for Karen; I was ready to find it.

On our first day together at the resort, my partner and I sat at a coffee table overlooking the pool. I looked at him, heart pumping with joy as I explained, "My agenda for us spending these few days together is to focus on our love." He looked into my eyes, sadness painted all across his face, and told me, "I can't do this anymore." Frozen in shock, angry and pained, I sat back into my chair, aware I was in a see-through dress wearing only a bikini… feeling exposed and vulnerable. I then saw his hand on the book, *More Truth Will Set You Free*, as he spoke his truth to me. My mind shouted,

That bloody title!

He left the table, and I put on my sunglasses. I kept my face hidden and stared into my coffee, stirring the milk clockwise as tears fell onto the table. After a few minutes, I could calm my upset and sit back in the white metal chair, watching couples holding hands and looking lovingly into each other's eyes. I looked on, deflated, but grew more aware of what was absent from my life.

Then, like a lightning bolt, the words pierced my mind, shifting how I perceived the situation. Deep within my being, the words whispered, *Love is absent; all of this is a mirror reflecting back to you: your lack of love for Karen!* My being straightened with the truth that vibrated through me. As I looked around, I saw that I saw love as being 'out there,' separate from me. I was sitting behind an invisible wall, wishing and craving to be loved, as if love was a thing you had to aim for, work hard for, and acquire from others. All the years of looking outward, I was taking myself further away from home: the embodied self. I was separating from the wisdom within, seeking external validation from others, and needed material objects just to feel like someone in society. I believed I was not lovable, that I was not worthy of love. I had been living my life, responding to love based on this false reality that — *I could not give Karen love; I did not know how.*

I came to realize that if I were to truly know love, I could not just rely on it coming from someone else. I had to become someone who would love Karen independently of another. With this new truth, I opened my beach bag to get my headphones and smiled at that book, announcing to myself, "Okay, I agree more truth does set you free. I want the truth from now on."

I got up, knowing I wanted to spend the day in meditation and contemplation with this clarity. I spent the rest of that day sitting on a blue-painted wooden bench facing the ocean and the Island of Lanzarote. I was sitting in the vibrancy of the world and its bright blue colors, held in the sky and ocean, to the brightness of the white sand and the warm sea breeze kissing my face as it brushed past me. I was fully present in life all around me as I sat contemplating deeper into my inquiry about love.

I remember that I was filled with love at a young age. I was devoted to God. From age seven, I had a little altar over my bed with tiny statues of Mary and Jesus. I would say my prayers every morning and every night. I had a deep faith in God and knew as young as ten that God was present in my life, communicating with me. In the depths of distress during my abuse, I would pray to God and feel the energy of love fill me. Knowing what to do for myself always seemed to come through prayers. But at the age of fourteen, I shut God out, and hate filled the space of love and gratitude.

As I sat on the bench, realizing these new insights, my phone beeped. It was a reply from my 19-year-old son whom I had messaged about the relationship ending. My son's response stunned me: "I know lots of stuff has been happening, even from your work. But see it as God doesn't give you something that you can't handle, so try to let God in more."

I laughed loud and hard; I could not stop laughing at the accuracy of his message. I looked to the sky and mused lovingly, *Okay, God, I am listening. I have shut you out for too long. Now please come home to me. I want to love Karen again, but I need your guidance.*

I reached into my beach bag and pulled out Derek's book. It felt like the book had an energy to it, as if it were to be a guide for me. With this, I closed my eyes, held the book to my heart, and randomly opened to page one hundred and fifteen. My heart exploded as I read the following:

"Sometimes we turn to God when our foundations have been shaken, only to find that He had shaken them. Every day can be like this. You are not the Doer. Even when events labeled disasters are happening, come back to this room, if that is what it takes, to remember how every day can be like this. See, God was a very clever Guy. He hid Himself right in the place that He knew we would never look, in our hearts."

That was a paradigm shift! I could no longer unsee the truth of my old, unlovable pain. I saw my limitations. I saw the feeling that had been poking its head up, again and again, from a hiding place, wondering if it was safe to come out yet. Now, this feeling of worth, joy, and possibility stepped out and stood tall, ready to be recognized.

That moment brought me home deep into the sacred heart space within myself from which the divine mind sees through us and into the world. I made a declaration to never turn my back on myself. The result was a journey into self-love, joy, wonderment, and re-discovering the mystery and magic of Karen. I had lost Karen to the experience of what happened to me, and I had lost my joy with it. Joy is the beauty and innocence of seeing your true essence, allowing us to tap into the wonder of who we are. My seeing became distorted by the wounds within. Yet, I transcended all these limitations and have joy back in my heart. I want you to know that you can transcend any limits in your life and awaken joy and purpose. When you make a choice to love yourself *as you do,* you will discover joy.

IGNITE ACTION STEPS

Here are my best tips for reclaiming inner liberation.

- **Your only job is to self-permit**, to give yourself permission to express yourself in whatever way you want. To self-permit in saying *yes* to life because it's not about what others think. Your story inside of you about what you think others are thinking is a prison cell!

- **Develop Self-love.** This is the component of unshackling your inner limited narratives.

- **Grow a confident self-image**. Remember, nobody can hear your story about yourself, so tell yourself an epic one!

- **Gratitude**: Cultivating a mindset of gratitude helps you move from limitation to expansion. Each day, journal what you are grateful for.

Karen Whelan — Ireland
Psychotherapist, Spiritual Advisor, and Founder of SOULution Therapy
www.soulutiontherapy.com
 dkaren.whelan.393
 the.soulution.therapist

Kari Berridge

KARI BERRIDGE

"Embrace the journey of becoming your best self;
it's the ultimate destination."

I hope that sharing my truth sparks a reflection within you. May it encourage you to confront any hidden secrets, shame, or guilt you may carry and recognize that your past doesn't dictate your future. Mistakes are inevitable; it's the lessons we glean from them and how we handle them that truly matter in our journey toward self-discovery and joy.

BUTTERFLIES

It was a beautiful summer day in Calgary. The sun was shining, and the birds were chirping. I noticed a vibrant red car drive by while out for a leisurely walk, pushing my beautiful 6-month-old daughter in her stroller. The car pulled over and parked. The male driver got out and walked toward us on a mission. He looked at me and asked, "Who is this?" pointing to my daughter.

My palms sweating and my stomach filled with frenzied butterflies, I replied, "I think she may be yours."

His response surprised me. "Are you just wanting money from me? Because I am in a really good relationship right now, and I don't want anything to f*** it up." Ouch, his words stung, and I felt shock, hurt, and numb.

"No, I don't want your money; I just thought you should know."

Feeling stunned and surprised by his reaction, I left the conversation with a cloud of confusion hanging over me. Seeking solace, I headed to my parents' home, where I spent the weekend. With a heavy heart, I confessed to them the truth: I was uncertain about who my daughter's father was. The uncertainty stemmed from persistent betrayals by the man I was living with, which ultimately led me to seek comfort in the arms of my high school sweetheart, a one-time affair.

I could see the concern on my parents' faces. "Don't open up the can of worms if you don't know for sure," was the response I received. They came from a generation where everything was swept under the rug, never to be talked about again. I wasn't sure who the father was, so I adhered to my parent's advice and didn't take any further action. Due to my fear of being judged and ostracized for my desecration, I chose to stay quiet and not pursue the truth of who fathered my daughter.

The secret stayed with me for thirty-five years — buried deep but not forgotten.

Let's rewind to where it all started. I was eighteen, wide-eyed, and fresh to a city three hours north of my hometown of Calgary. It was at a lively country bar where our paths first crossed. He stood out like a beacon in the crowd — tall, ruggedly handsome, with a charm that could rival Garth Brooks himself. It seemed like every girl was vying for his attention, and he effortlessly commanded the room with his easy going demeanor and quick wit. Despite his quiet nature, an undeniable magnetism about him drew me in instantly. Walking up to him for the first time, I had to breathe away the nervous butterflies that were making their way from my stomach to my throat. But he appeared just as charmed by me as I was by him, and in my insecurity, I felt excited he had chosen me out of all the ladies in the room.

The honeymoon phase, however, fizzled out faster than I could have imagined. Around six months into the relationship, I began to witness a darker side of him. His words, once fun and light, turned into cutting knives. He'd hurl insults like grenades, tearing down my already fragile self-esteem. Even though I was battling anorexia and weighed a mere ninety-eight pounds, he'd call me fat. He'd tell me I was ugly and unworthy of love, classic narcissistic behavior that, at the time, I was unaware of. With each hurtful word and snide side-eye, layers of sadness and frustration built up and weighed me down as I wondered how to stop falling short of his expectations. His constant belittling chipped away at whatever self-esteem and self-worth I had until it felt like there was nothing left.

Then came the cheating. It started with his ex-girlfriend, and then there was an incident at a hockey tournament where I foolishly bought into the lie that no women were allowed. The next thing I knew, it was his so-called "best friend." The pattern repeated itself, each betrayal slicing deeper than the last. Each revelation left me shattered, but in my brokenness, I clung to the belief that it was somehow my fault. I convinced myself that if only I could be a better girlfriend and partner, he wouldn't stray. I tried harder, pouring every ounce of my being into salvaging a relationship that was already beyond repair. But no matter how much I gave, it was never enough. The cycle of abuse and betrayal continued, eroding what little remained of me. Yet, despite the inner anguish and the broken trust, I chose to stay despite every hurtful action.

After two years of being together, I hit rock bottom, consumed by a relentless barrage of self-doubt. No matter what I did, I never felt adequate: not attractive, intelligent, or thin enough. This never-ending cycle of perceived imperfection left me craving love and validation like a desert yearning for rain.

It seemed the Universe heard my cries and conveniently brought my high school sweetheart back into my life, though looking back, I have no recollection of how we ended up seeing each other again. I remember how he made me feel: cared about, excited, cherished. Happy butterflies danced in my heart when we were together, and I was wrapped in the feeling I was finally good enough for someone. I realized he had always been the love of my life, feelings that ultimately led us to have a one-time affair in the spring of 1987, and I was barely twenty years old.

I was getting ready for work one day that May when I started to get sick. Not flu-like sick. No, this was different. Off to the doctor I went, and sure enough, I was three months pregnant. Butterflies churned within me. I was sick to my stomach in more ways than one as shock and dread washed over me, making my knees go weak. Right away, I thought, *Oh no, who is the father?*

I quickly mastered the art of burying my emotions and prioritizing others' needs above my own. Raised to believe that showing vulnerability and weakness was unacceptable, I often confused self-blame with accountability. My pregnancy seemed yet another misstep, another burden to shoulder alone. With a child on the way, strength became my lifeline and more needed than ever. I brushed aside my doubts and uncertainties and buried my feelings deep within as I forged ahead with life.

When my daughter was ten months old, I decided to marry the man I'd been with for three tumultuous years. I thought her having a dad was more important than my needs and becoming a father would change his attitude. Unfortunately, despite his charming facade, I often felt worthless and insignificant.

His infidelity continued to plague our marriage, but it wasn't until my daughter was fourteen months old that I reached my breaking point. As I stood before some random woman, a wave of sickness engulfed me, toxic butterflies gnawing at my insides. He had got her pregnant. At that moment, I knew I was right. Finally, I had reached my limit.

After mustering the courage to kick him out of our rental home, I took a pivotal step forward by securing a job. Until then, I had been a devoted stay-at-home mom, but now I was thrust into the unfamiliar territory of being a working single parent. It was a daunting transition that I embraced wholeheartedly as I embarked on this new chapter of my life.

As a newly single mom, I found myself grappling with the challenges of parenthood and my internal battles. Struggling with anorexia and wrestling with undiagnosed postpartum depression, every day felt like an uphill battle. Despite our separation, my daughter continued to have contact with my ex throughout her childhood. However, as she grew older, she distanced herself from him. At eighteen, she decided to sever ties with him completely. His unforgivable behavior and toxic traits proved to be too much for her to bear.

As life came full circle and she started her own family, she felt compelled to reintroduce him into their lives, if only so her children would know their grandfather. It was a decision fraught with apprehension, as she was aware of the kind of man he was. Watching this dynamic unfold from the sidelines filled me with deep remorse. I couldn't shake the nagging feeling that I had made a grave mistake by marrying him, subjecting my daughter to a tumultuous upbringing that she didn't deserve.

The guilt and shame I carried around didn't happen right away; it took its time to fester in my body. Little things started coming up, like the color of her eyes, a dark brown in contrast to mine and her 'dad's,' which were vibrant blue. Her full lips were unlike mine or his but so much like my high school sweetheart's. I had talked myself into the idea that the man I had married was her father, but deep down, I wasn't sure. The feelings kept tugging at me. *How does one expose a lie buried deep for over three decades? How would I, at this point, confess when I still had no proof?* I had looked for my high school sweetheart for over twenty years, through social media and at school reunions, but had never been successful.

Then, in September 2022, nearing my 55th birthday, my world came crashing around me. Unbeknownst to me, my daughter had taken a genealogy test through 23andMe™, and what she discovered would unravel the very fabric of our lives. With a twenty-six percent match, she had found a sister she never knew existed.

When she called me to share her findings, I felt the ground beneath me shift. I had that horrible feeling inside, as if I was about to be sick, as all the butterflies I had kept neatly contained were finally released. As I drove home, tears blurred my vision, and by the time I collapsed onto the floor at my back entrance, I was sobbing uncontrollably. It was a moment of raw vulnerability as I poured out every detail my mind could grasp to my daughter, who was listening without response.

Amidst my emotional turmoil, my daughter uttered the words that shattered my heart into a million pieces: "I need time to process everything." Through my tears, I reassured her that I understood and that I respected her need for space. And with that, our conversation came to an abrupt end.

Little did I know, it would be the last time she would speak to me.

In the wake of this revelation, my daughter made the agonizing decision to sever all ties with me. The beautiful love I had treasured for so long flew away on torn wings. The pain of her rejection cut deeper than any physical wound, leaving me adrift in a sea of regret and sorrow. With the lid ripped off Pandora's secret box, my life turned sharply into the unknown. That fateful night marked the lowest point of my existence, a dark abyss where the notion of continuing seemed unbearable. In a desperate bid to escape the pain, I made the harrowing decision to end my own life. I reached for the bottle of pills tucked away in my nightstand, swallowing a small handful in a haze of despair.

By some stroke of fate or perhaps divine intervention, I survived. The following morning, I awoke to a haze of grogginess, the remnants of my failed attempt clinging to me like a shadow. It was a wake-up call, a stark reminder that despite the darkness that enveloped me, a glimmer of hope flickered somewhere deep within.

In the aftermath of that pivotal moment, I knew that something had to change. Five days later, with trembling hands and a heavy heart, I embarked on a journey of self-discovery — a three-day self-development course that I had signed up for months prior. It was as if the Universe had once again orchestrated the timing precisely, nudging me toward a path of healing and self-love.

Summoning every ounce of strength within me, I set out on the three-hour drive back to my hometown to attend the course. Unsure of what lay ahead, I clung to the flicker of hope that burned within me. Looking back, I am eternally grateful for that decision. It was the first step toward reclaiming my life, seizing joy, and learning to love myself.

During the following year, I threw myself into a whirlwind of self-improvement, enrolling in four intensive 'in-person' programs and devouring twelve online courses provided by an expert in self-development. It was a journey of reckoning, a quest to untangle the web of lies I had woven and to seek forgiveness, not just from others, but from myself.

Like festering wounds, my secrets had simmered within me, poisoning every aspect of my life. They had corroded my health, strained my relationships with loved ones, and robbed me of the happiness and joy I so desperately craved. The weight of shame, guilt, and blame had become unbearable, shackling me to a life half-lived. Each day felt like a charade, a facade carefully constructed to hide the truth lurking beneath the surface. Deep down, I carried a profound sadness within me, knowing that I had settled for less than I deserved. My daughter deserves a father who will cherish and protect her and not continuously betray her trust. But fear held me captive, chaining me to silence. I was terrified of the consequences of revealing the truth, afraid that it would cost me the one thing I held most dear—my daughter. And tragically, my worst fears were realized. But that also meant I had nowhere left to go but up.

During a transformative self-development course, fifty-two strangers faced a challenge: scaling a fourteen-foot plywood wall together with a time constraint. Only four individuals were allowed to help from the top, and once you were over the wall, you could no longer offer assistance. Leaving the last person to scale the wall with just the help of those at the top. As tears welled in my eyes, a wave of realization washed over me. For so long, I had been enveloped in a cloak of loneliness, unaware of the vast support system waiting just beyond my reach. My knees felt weak; I couldn't breathe as a new set of courageous butterflies swirled around inside. It was a revelation, a moment of sheer joy that left me utterly gob-smacked. In that captivating moment, I realized I would never be alone again.

I've come to realize our mistakes do not determine who we are. Our past may be littered with errors and regrets, significant or trivial, but they do not define us. We've all caused pain and made choices we're not proud of. Harboring these burdens silently corrodes us, hindering our potential and stealing our joy. The wrongs we've committed, the secrets we've held, the shame and guilt we've carried, none hold power over our worth or future. After so many years cocooned in self-doubt and grief, I have finally emerged a new woman, capable of seeing the beauty of my own colorful wings.

I made a conscious choice, dedicating myself to becoming the best version of myself. It's been a journey of self-discovery and growth, leading me to write a book, *Cut the Anchor*, aimed at helping others reclaim their joy and find solace in shared experiences. Through honest, raw reflection, I hope to inspire others to embrace their imperfections and recognize that true growth comes from acknowledging our mistakes and striving to improve.

My greatest joy lies in lending an ear to those who may be struggling, reminding them they are not alone in their journey. They are loved unconditionally. We all deserve to live a life surrounded by joy and fulfillment. It's never too late to embrace your true, authentic self. Be willing to put in the work and take the baby steps. Harness those butterflies and use them to fuel your desires and find your strengths. We all have cocooning and transitioning moments before becoming our authentic selves. How we nurture ourselves and love the metamorphosis allows us to emerge and embrace the journey of becoming our best self; it's the ultimate destination.

IGNITE ACTION STEPS

- **Keep a childhood photo handy**, printed or on your phone. When you feel overwhelmed or lost, reassure the child that they are loveable and deserving of joy.

- **Celebrate your daily or weekly wins**, no matter how small they may seem. Write them down so you can see your successes.

- **Dedicate time daily to writing in a gratitude journal**. This helps shift our focus from the negative to the positive and boosts joy.

- **Prioritize moments of mindfulness** by disconnecting from distractions like phones and screens. Consider immersing yourself in nature, whether it's a peaceful walk or simply grounding yourself by touching the earth. These moments bring you back to the present, help center your thoughts, and ultimately foster joy.

Kari Berridge — Canada
Fitness & Wellness Coach, Author
fit2motivate.net
kariberridge
kariberridge
fit2motivatekari

Katarina Amadora

Katarina Amadora

*"Treasure the moments that bring you joy;
they are clues to discovering your purpose."*

I wish to encourage you to take inventory of moments in your life that remain exceptionally vivid. *What emotions were you feeling? What messages do these moments have for you?* If reviewed mindfully, they can lead you to more of what you want and less of what you don't want in your life. What moments sparked joy within you? These may lead you to your purpose.

The Sacred Art of Flirtation

There are moments in your life that stick with you. These tend to be moments that are charged with emotion which colors these memories and makes them so vivid. Sometimes, we may want to forget them because the emotions we felt at the time were challenging. We may suppress these memories or drive them into our shadows. Other memories may be like treasures we hang onto, moments that we bring to mind repeatedly because they sustain us. These moments seem like they are crystallized in time because they provide a link to something special in our past, like a lifeline to a cherished memory. It could be a person, a loved one, or something that gave you a moment of clarity that pointed you in a new direction and gave your life meaning.

Whether these memories spring from a positive or a challenging experience, I believe that they deserve our attention. It is in these moments that we find clues to our destiny. They're like breadcrumbs that can lead to the discovery of your purpose. They can help us recognize patterns in our lives and unifying themes in the world around us. If you tune in to moments that spark joy in your life, they can connect you to something greater than yourself. I believe you can tap into the potential energy these memories carry and use them to manifest a life far greater than you could have imagined.

My story is about my experience of sharing a memory that led me to a surprising discovery about myself, which was different than anything I had imagined. This new understanding led me to choose a path that has brought me so much joy and a sense of purpose that inspires me to be of service to others.

I remember the first time I shared this story. I was in a program training to become a life coach. I was sitting at a long table in a conference room with others in our program. David, the facilitator, asked us to share a story of a moment that impacted us, a particularly vivid memory. He encouraged us to connect with a memory and bring the visceral experience to mind before sharing it. He instructed us to let go of concern about the content and focus on the emotion. The intention was not to teach anything in particular but to connect with a moment that had special significance for us and describe it in a way that transported others *into* that memory. My story had nothing to do with life coaching or what I thought I was training to become. The story that came to mind was a conversation I had in my 20s with a man at least ten years older than me. Something about that conversation struck me so deeply and meaningfully that I have never forgotten it.

Although that conversation had occurred nearly thirty years prior, I could still recall every detail so vividly because it represented an "Ignite" moment that improved my life. The new understanding it engendered shaped many of my memories and interactions from that moment forward. As I told my story, I remember the feeling of stepping back in time. I was there, deeply connected with the thoughts that had gone through my mind. I remember the moments of humor and connection to my younger self as I related the conversation that had been so pivotal for me; the feeling of the smile on my face as I recalled with fondness this man and his influence on my life.

At the end of my story, David said to me, "I have never seen you light up so much in all the time we've spent together. You were incandescent! This is what you should teach!"

I was dumbstruck for a moment. I was training as a health coach. My story was *not* about health or nutrition, medicine, or any of the things that I was learning. It was about flirtation and a pivotal conversation that instilled in me an understanding of flirtation as *attention* without *intention.*

I was still unsure, but something about his feedback felt so right. It made me question how I could use my story as a vehicle to teach others and offer something uniquely my own. Something more than simply regurgitating information that I had learned from someone else. This encouragement gave me the courage to develop an offer, my first workshop, which eventually inspired me to be trained in Tantra, to become a Relationship Coach, and to follow a whole new path.

Enough teasing you… this is my story.

In my early 20s, I was a member of the Society for Creative Anachronism (SCA), a place where people would come together to recreate what it would have been like to live in the Middle Ages. Most of my social life revolved around going to events on the weekends in medieval garb with others who enjoyed immersing themselves in the experience of living in a different time period. We practiced many of the arts and sciences from medieval Europe, and each person developed an identity or a persona with a backstory they would take on within the context of the SCA. My persona was *Katarina Vignéra di Salerni.* I was from the Italian Renaissance period and grew up in Italy in my father's vineyard; however, I attended medical school in Salerno. I chose this because my hobby was winemaking and when I joined, I was in pre-med in college and planned to become a physician. Most of my weekends were spent going to events, and my Thursday evenings, you would find me at fighter's practice, where most of the men and some women would strap on armor and practice medieval combat while the rest of us hung about and socialized with each other.

One of my favorite parts of being in the SCA was going to weekend events, which would usually end in feasting and dancing. My most enduring memories were about the fun of flirting with others in the guise of my persona. My favorite flirting companion was a pirate captain. His name was Captain Lewys Blackmore the Third. I would never have considered dating Lewys. He was at least ten years older than me and two inches shorter! At the ripe old age of twenty-one, dating someone in his early 30s was not something that I would even consider. It didn't matter though, because we had so much fun! Lewys had a way of turning a phrase and making you feel like you were the most beautiful and desirable lady in the room. He was so much fun to flirt with, to dance with, and to laugh with, and I looked forward to our witty banter every chance I got.

For over two years, this witty repartée kept me enthralled to the point that I reconsidered my standards regarding his age. Also, the height difference didn't seem to bother me so much. I started to notice an increasing level of attraction to Lewys. As I did so, I realized that he had *never*, in all our flirtatious exchanges, tried to kiss me or make a pass at me, and I started to wonder why. *Was I not pretty enough? Was I not attractive? Was there something wrong with me?*

I wasn't quite sure what to do with these unfamiliar feelings, but eventually, I decided to take matters into my own hands. After the next event, we found ourselves at the Post Revel (what we called the afterparty). I got up the courage to draw him aside, and I asked him, "Lewys, for two years, we have been flirting outrageously with each other, and yet you have never even tried to kiss me… Is there a reason why?" I waited nervously for his reply, my pulse pounding and butterflies churning in my stomach.

A grin spread over his face, and he replied to me with a mischievous glint in his eye.

"Well, you see, my lady… I have a very particular philosophy about flirtation. Flirtation, as it should be, is about '*attention*, without *intention.*' If I had an intention behind my words, that is like having an ulterior motive. This in itself is also a good and worthy game. However, that game is called '*seduction.*' The problem is that you can never go back once you cross the line from flirtation to seduction. It changes things. So that begs the question, my lady. *Which* game do you want to play?"

I vividly remember that moment, as though it were crystallized in time. As understanding dawned on me, I no longer felt inadequate. I felt blessed to be seen as a worthy player in his game of flirtation, and I had to question my own motives. *What did I truly want? Was it worth risking giving up the most fun I had ever had to cross that bridge? Could I risk giving up my playmate if something went awry?*

I nervously asked him… "I can never go back?"

He replied, "No, it changes things. Once you have crossed that bridge, we can't return to the lighthearted banter of flirtation. Something shifts when you play in the realm of seduction, and you need to know what you want before going there."

I hesitated. I was unsure if I was ready to risk giving up my playmate. As I considered my options, I said nervously, "What if I were just to dip my big toe in the water and see how it feels? If we don't like it, can we pretend it never happened and go back to flirting outrageously tomorrow."

He paused, then he replied, "Well, I suppose *kissing* could be on the table." So… we made out under the table. I was a bit nervous, to be honest. I liked it, but I still wasn't sure if I wanted to cross that bridge fully.

It turned out that this was the first and only night we ever kissed. A number of months later, he surprised us all when he announced that he was getting married. He had fallen in love with his roommate and she was pregnant with his child. They are still together today, happily married with two adult children, and I am still friends with them on Facebook™.

I never forgot that conversation, which has never dimmed in my memory. Relating my story to David years later led me to offer a workshop that was definitely outside my comfort zone called *The Sacred Art of Flirtation*. My first clumsy experience leading this workshop inspired me to enroll in a Tantra Facilitation program. Since then, I have trained in many fields and have a deep understanding of how each can contribute to helping people live happier, healthier, more fulfilling lives. As a newly certified hypnotherapist, I had the good fortune to work with two couples, each of whom referred their partner to me after a transformative session. This experience motivated me to go deeper into the study of Sex and Relationships to develop a niche working with couples, identifying the blocks and patterns that get in the way of having rich and mutually joyful relationships that continue to get better over time. Eventually, this led me to Somatica®, which deepened my understanding of sex, intimacy, attachment patterns, and how we communicate in relationships.

All because I told a story.

It is in the realm of working in the area of sex and relationships that I feel most alive. My work in this area has led to many breakthroughs of my own, the most significant of which was manifesting *the most* amazing partner. Our relationship has up-leveled my life in the most beautiful ways, and it has become the source of more joy than I could ever have imagined. On our fourth date, we attended a show in Santa Cruz called *What is Erotic?* As we left the theater that night, I told him, "I am going to be in that show next year." The following November, we auditioned. Just after our first anniversary, we took the stage with a spoken word piece on what is erotic to me and to us. After the show, we got so many compliments from people who were touched and moved by our performance, and it remains a highlight of our first year together.

I continue to love the experience of leading my *Sacred Art of Flirtation* workshops. In this container, I have the privilege to be able to create a group field where people who enter the room as strangers are led on a journey, connecting first with themselves and then with others. This group field is created so that their energies are woven together, creating moments of insight, laughter, tenderness, and, most importantly, moments of healing. By the end of the workshop, they are usually in a huge cuddle pile of snuggly humans. They leave as friends, sometimes even lovers, who have been transformed in this cauldron, allowing them to truly feel, connect, be vulnerable, and share what was hard for them.

This ability to help others in their relationships has brought me so much joy, and I am so grateful to my teacher, who recognized this light in me. I am grateful that he encouraged me to step outside my comfort zone to offer something that is uniquely mine. I hope you recognize in my story some moment that has sparked joy in your life which has not faded with the passage of time. I encourage you to reflect on that and why the memory is so vivid for you. Sometimes, memories are associated with uncomfortable emotions that tell us to avoid this path so as not to repeat the experience. At other times, they can be moments of love, joy, and treasured connections that tell us, "This is what your soul is calling you to do in this life." When we heed those messages, we can create much more of that which we desire and less of that which we wish to avoid.

Reflect on whether your brightest memories might be a clue to a greater purpose and meaning in your life. When you bring attention to these memories, they become the clues that lead you to your soul's purpose. When you add intentions, they become the rocket fuel that will catapult you to the next level. Putting these two things together will help you cross the bridge from where you are right now to the joy-filled life you desire. Your intentions will shape your life, so *choose* wisely.

IGNITE ACTION STEPS

Take inventory of moments in your life that stand out as exceptionally vivid. Reflect on the predominant emotions in each situation.

1. **If the emotion is challenging, I encourage you to tread lightly**. Consider sharing this memory with a friend or a therapist who can support you in processing the past event and letting go of any meanings that you may have attached to this experience so that you can release them and create a new, more empowering understanding of what happened to you. Reflect on your part in creating the situation, and take stock of how to avoid repeating that painful pattern. Do forgiveness work to forgive yourself and to let go of any negative energy that keeps you stuck. I highly recommend exploring hypnotherapy for any situation or belief that is particularly painful for you.

2. **If, on the other hand, the predominant emotion was positive, reflect on the nature of that interaction. What was the emotion?** What made the memory so vivid for you? Whether the emotion was Joy, Love, Bliss, Contentment, Awe, or something else, ask yourself, *What brought on that emotion? What can you do in your life today and for the rest of your life that can lead you to similar peak experiences? How can you be even more present in your body to feel it all? What clues do you find in these memories that might lead you to a sense of purpose? What can you offer to others based on your unique life experiences?*

3. **Journal on anything that comes up**. Meditate. Give yourself permission to try something new. Step outside your comfort zone. You may find that something in your past experience will lead you to an offering that is uniquely yours. Offer something that no one else can teach because they don't have the same experience you do. If one approach doesn't resonate, try another. Iterate your way to finding *your* unique gift and offering to the world.

Katarina Amadora — United States of America
RTT Hypnotherapist and Somatica® trained Sex and Relationship Coach
www.KatarinaAmadora.com
AmadoraK
katarina_amadora
katarina-amadora-b8118693

Katie Allen and Allison Prince

KATIE ALLEN AND ALLISON PRINCE

"When in doubt, choose joy."

Life can be challenging, and sometimes, the clouds in the mind cover our joy. We're here to tell you that joy is possible. There are time-tested tools to support you in shifting your mindset and uncovering your unique gifts to light up the world. You can overcome obstacles and do hard things. Your challenges will strengthen you and equip you with the tools you need to fly when you are ready to burst out of your cocoon. You, too, can live up to your incredible potential and infuse your life with joy.

THE JOY BUSINESS

There is a story about a man who finds a butterfly cocoon. He notices there is a small opening and that the butterfly will soon emerge. He sits, watching patiently as the butterfly struggles to free itself. After some time, the man decides to help by grabbing a pair of scissors and gently cutting the delicate sheath. The butterfly easily slides out, but its body is swollen, and its wings are shriveled. It does not live up to its potential.

The man did not know the butterfly needed to go through its own struggle so the fluid from its body would be pushed into its wings, and it could then fly. Just as a caterpillar needs to push through the boundaries to transform completely, humans, too, must go through their own metamorphosis. This shift happens not just once but many times through different ages and stages of life.

We undergo this evolutionary process to recognize our strengths, live up to our fullest potential, and remember that we can make the impossible possible. This is our story of two women in pursuit of their dreams, traveling through the many phases of life together. It spans twenty years and shares how we have broken through self-imposed limitations and chosen to focus on joy even in the most difficult of moments.

"The toilets are clogged again, and the back one is overflowing." We felt completely overwhelmed reading the latest text message from our newest front desk staff member, who has only been working with us for a couple of weeks. It was 6 PM on a Tuesday night. Both toilets had been clogged Saturday when our studio was packed with two simultaneous training sessions during the day, as well as a live music event and community potluck in the evening. We thought we had fixed it! Katie was at home, tending to her son, who was home sick from school. Allison was at the studio trying to create a calming and meditative experience for a packed room while the toilets were overflowing. This was the third time in two months since we moved into our new space that our toilets were backed up and out of service, even after we spent nearly $3000 on repairs.

We thought we would be cruising; after seventeen years of hard work, everything would be smooth and easy. How did we get here? *How did we end up signing a seven-year lease on a 130-year-old building?* Well… joy made us do it.

Dedicating our lives to the study of Yoga Therapy and Natural Health was not something that either of us ever planned for. But when you stumble upon ancient wisdom that undeniably transforms you and lights up every fiber of your being, it's hard to resist the call to dive deeper.

Like so many young people in their twenties, we were both finding ourselves. Allison was still determining what she wanted to study when she went to college. It was not until midway through her junior year, when she took a stress management course, that a spark was finally lit. This led her to study kinesiology and eventually into taking a semester of yoga. She took a yoga teacher training after that semester, not to become a yoga teacher, but to better understand why this practice made her feel so good. However, within the first few weeks of the training, she knew without a shadow of a doubt that she had found her path.

Katie has always been fascinated with indigenous healing systems. She spent time in Guatemala studying Mayan linguistics and then pursued a Master's Degree in Public Health at Tulane University. Spending so much time researching and writing papers, her yoga practice is what helped her manage stress: sweating, getting out of her head and into her body. Being part of a supportive community at Wild Lotus Yoga in New Orleans was so impactful for her that she wrote her Master's thesis on yoga's ability to prevent and treat chronic disease.

When we first met in our early twenties, we didn't know we would embark upon the most exciting and challenging journey of our lives together. It would encompass the grandest of dreams and the lowest of lows, built upon a solid foundation of partnership and desire to make the world a better place.

We met working together in a gorgeous 6500-square-foot wellness center. It was perfect for us during our formative years. We were surrounded by healers and wise teachers, always learning, uncovering new passions, and feeling uplifted by our very large community. We had a space to be creative, implement new ideas, and expand our joy. It was the best of times. We developed over 500 hours of training programs; we led retreats to Costa Rica, and we were having a blast with minimal responsibilities. And then it hit us over the head like a ton of bricks. Our beloved home and place of employment for the last seven years was financially unsustainable, and there was the possibility it may not survive.

We were blindsided, although we saw hints over the years that we were not ready to fully recognize. *What were we going to do?* We put every fiber of our being into nurturing this space. As the core team members, we built strong community bonds. It was a place of wellness and personal healing that was beautiful, magical, and meaningful to many people. We couldn't just let this slip away, become fragmented, and dissipate into nothingness. This was our life's work, the place where we matured into adults and built our careers.

One day, we sat on the back steps behind the building and started a conversation about what it would look like to create our own space. We decided to start working on "Plan B" as a backup in case the business was no longer viable. We worked on our business plan for months, which was equally exciting and terrifying, and it was a lot to process.

We were comfortable at the studio we were in. It was our warm cocoon where we felt safe and nurtured. But at the same time, we were at the whim of forces beyond our control. We could have stayed safe in our status quo, or we could look at this as an opportunity to push past our comfort zones, break into a new realm, and put every fiber of our beings into creating a magnificent new reality. After several months, we knew in our hearts and souls that "Plan B" needed to be "Plan A."

At thirty-one years old, we were newly married to our supportive husbands; we had a choice. We could either be the victim of our circumstances and mourn the death of something we loved so much, or we could take life by the reins and be the heroes of our lives. We chose the latter. We chose to stay together, to Ignite a new home for our community, and open our own brick and mortar space; tying ourselves together for the foreseeable future, and assuming all the risk.

In our search to find the perfect space, we first drove around quite aimlessly, fueled by pure excitement and the possibility of creating something uniquely our own. After visiting random strip malls, we were overcome with a sense of confusion and lack of clarity. We decided to pause and get clear on what exactly we were looking for.

We parked the car, pulled out a notebook, and wrote out our studio *Bhavana*. Bhavana is the Sanskrit word for visualization. It's a practice that helps to clarify our values and get specific about what we really want. We listed all the non-negotiable requirements of our new studio, which included the following elements: 2000-3000 square feet, close to a freeway but not too close, large grocery or anchor store, plenty of parking, feels like a retreat center, outdoor dining, coffee shop, juice bar, and a healthy restaurant. It was a large list, and we had the faith that it existed; we just had to find it.

After getting very clear about what we wanted, Katie's mom suggested that we look at Orchard Hills Village Center in Irvine, CA. It was a gorgeous high-end retail center tucked back in the hills. Allison drove into the parking lot and immediately knew we found our new home. It checked off every item on our list, and her bodily tingles confirmed it. The space felt like a retreat, surrounded by olive trees with twinkling white lights. It was perfect.

Nevertheless, the voices of doubt crept in from inside our own heads and well-meaning family members. *Can we really do this? Can we afford this stunning location?* We wondered if it was possible, with our vision of being a donation-based yoga studio like those in Los Angeles or New York, a novel idea for Orange County.

Whenever the fear would surface, we consciously shifted our focus back to our Bhavana, which had evolved into a hundred-page business plan outlining our dreams for the next five years. A wise teacher and therapist, Robert Birnberg, reminds us to focus our attention on the goal, not the obstacles to the goal.

A few months later, we found ourselves sitting in a very fancy conference room surrounded by people in expensive suits. We were about to sign a 100+ page lease with the largest real estate corporation in the county. Neither of us owned business attire, so we were dressed in black pants and sweaters, our version of fancy, as we usually live in yoga pants. It was intimidating, and again, the fears and doubts started to bubble up. *Are we really doing this? Can this really work? Are we signing our lives away?*

At this pivotal moment, we stepped outside for some fresh air to reset. We prayed, calmed our nerves, took some deep breaths, and got clear. We knew deep down that we were meant for more, that we had the potential to create something special that had never existed before. We knew the transmission of joy through sacred space and healing practices is what the world needs, and we'd had the privilege of seeing it every day on the faces of our students. We were doing this for the right reasons, even though it stretched us way beyond our comfort zone. Our intentions were pure. We spent the last year working on our business plan and examining this path from every angle. *This is it. This is go time.* In that moment, we were faced with another choice: to become paralyzed by fear or choose faith. With that intention, we blessed the 100-page lease and said, "Let's do this."

We created the most beautiful space we could envision by saying yes to our dreams. Walking into *Be The Change Yoga*, you immediately felt different. It was like stepping back in time, a retreat amidst the chaos of the modern world. To enter the studios, students floated under the twinkling blue Turkish lanterns in the front windows, hanging vines, finding themselves surrounded by books and healing reminders of how we are meant to live. To enter the two large studios, they would open large wooden temple doors from 1800 Rajasthan with layers of paint amassed over centuries.

The journey of creating the space was magical. We found that when you get clear on the vision (Bhavana) and attune your mind with the frequency of joy, miracles happen, and beautiful things, people, and opportunities flow into your vibrational field. We wondered how we would find ancient relics to make our space feel like a Balinese retreat center. Upon asking, the universe delivered a new friend who imported decor from India, Bali, Thailand, and Morocco. Katie met him at a birthday party in Los Angeles, and he loved our vision so much that he offered us wholesale pricing on everything!

One of our yoga therapy clients owned a large-scale construction company. Even though building out our little yoga studio was too small for their scope of work, he offered to do it for us since we had alleviated his back pain years earlier. He even fronted all the construction costs until we received our tenant improvement funds from the landlord. Thus, we were able to build our sanctuary on a very tight budget with the help of dozens of magnificent humans who lifted us up along the way.

For the next few years, we worked harder than ever, burning the candle on both ends. We compared having a business to having a child and would often say that our yoga studio is our first baby. Our small business required a lot of love and devotion and would often need a hundred percent of our undivided attention. As we were both nearing our mid-thirties, we knew that we wanted to grow our families. We felt as if we were stuck in one phase of life while many of our friends and family members were moving on to having children. Yes, we were doing what we loved… but the expansive pace was unsustainable. As a result, two healthy, strong women like ourselves shockingly had challenges getting pregnant. We learned that this is very common amidst ambitious women powering their way through the world. To achieve our new dream of motherhood, we both had to drastically shift how we lived; we had to slow down, we had to delegate, reduce the energetic output, receive more, and learn to do less.

Anyone who has gone through years of fertility struggles can tell you that it is a very painful experience. Everywhere you go there are constant reminders of what you are missing out on. One can become so hyper focused on what they don't have, that they can't see all of the amazing blessings around them. We each handled grief and loss in our own way, but continued to support one another, focused on gratitude, and never lost faith that we would emerge from this cocoon and ultimately become mothers. Finally after three years, exactly six months apart, our beautiful boys were born and our families were complete. We had it all, a thriving business that we loved and sweet little families that we had longed for. We had finally arrived.

All our hard work and dedication over the last fourteen years had paid off. We had successfully opened the most gorgeous yoga studio and wellness center in Orange County. The energy was magnetic. Classes were full, trainings were packed, and we were the leader for yoga therapy in our region. Beyond our studio, we had implemented programs throughout numerous hospitals and clinics in multiple languages and our graduates were getting hired in clinical settings and changing the healthcare landscape!

Everywhere you looked there were smiling faces as people experienced the alchemy of being transformed through sacred space and lifestyle medicine practices. Every single day we watched people shift and become better versions of themselves. Our days were filled with joy, purpose, and connection. Seeing such transformation in others was magical.

We had dedicated staff and students who helped make our community great. We felt that we had reached the point where we could take a step back and let others steer the ship for a while. We were finding the perfect balance between being business owners and new mothers. Life was sweet. We could finally settle in, nest, spend time with our husbands and baby boys, and enjoy the fruits of so many years of labor.

Little did we know that everything we created and loved so much would be put on life support very soon. There would not be any cruising. For the next four years, every aspect of our being would be tested as we learned to dig deep, double down on our personal practices, stay connected to faith, and ride the waves of destruction and creation that rocked the entire planet and our little world.

In March 2020, as the pandemic was announced, we sat in an empty studio, wondering what we would do next. Still, in shock and denial, we believed the shutdown would only last two weeks, and then we could reopen. As we sat there trying to plan our next steps, the security guard came in and told us we had to leave immediately. So we packed up the necessary items, turned off the lights, and locked the doors to our sacred space.

Our business ended up being shut down for six months. The studio was reopened and closed on three separate occasions. The second time, we both became physically ill from the amount of stress being put upon us. Still, we consider ourselves extremely lucky because many small independent businesses never reopened their doors again. This was the biggest professional challenge we had ever faced. The rules kept changing every few weeks, and made it impossible to make any plans. We lost sixty percent of our student base overnight and had to work harder than ever to keep the remaining students (our guardian angels). We had to teach our classes online from home, where our husbands were also working and trying to keep our very young children quiet. We both receive so many benefits from teaching and enjoy the energy from the group. Teaching online does not have the same effect. Most students had their cameras off, so it felt like we were talking to ourselves while practicing in our makeshift yoga studio in the corner of the bedroom. This was truly one of our lowest points.

It felt as if we were in a little boat being tossed around by turbulent waters with no course, direction, control, or end in sight. Being a new mother is extremely challenging. Being a brick-and-mortar small business owner is challenging. Living through a once-in-a-lifetime pandemic was horrifying. But adding all of these together seemed impossible, a stroke to the system. The channels that carry vital energy *(prana)* and nourishment were severed. Our bright, active, buzzing community no longer existed. In its place was a cold, dark building with no one in it. The lights were out, and replacing the feelings of joy and connection, we found our entire society swimming in a sea of fear, confusion, division, and isolation.

In that critical moment, we chose to re-Ignite and fortify the light within. We decided that our story would not be, "The pandemic ruined our business, stole our joy, and everything that we worked so hard for." Absolutely not. We would grab the reins of our lives and our precious *Be The Change Yoga,* steering it in a new direction for longevity. Closing our business and operating solely online was *not* an option for us. More than ever, people needed physical spaces of connection. They needed to leave their homes and screens and reconnect to themselves and one another, rebuilding the circuitry that led to joy. We were so grateful to have each other. Honestly, the load was far too heavy for one person to carry, and had we not had each other, all of what we built would cease to exist.

To light our inner spark and burn away the clouds of fear, we tripled down on our self-care practices, prioritizing movement, meditation, breathwork, nature, music, and positive relationships. We minimized the negative influences. Over time, clarity returned, and we could steady the stormy waters and see a clear path forward over the horizon.

The decision to leave our space and not renew our lease after ten years was not an easy one. We were extremely attached to what we created — the many wonderful memories — but we knew it was not sustainable. We honestly didn't feel safe being in a high-end retail center after the pandemic. We got creative. Two years before our lease ended, we started 'bhavanizing' a more loveable future. We opened a non-profit arm. We started working with the city and county to explore interesting rental opportunities and land deals. We know that spiritual centers like *Esalen* in Big Sur and *Kripalu* in Massachusetts own their land and thus ensure their longevity. We knew deep down in our hearts that doing this work not only brought us joy, meaning, and purpose but also had a positive impact on our community and beyond. We wanted to find a way to be able to do this great work and continue to ripple out positive change in the community.

We revised our new studio Bhavana, and when our commercial leasing agent gave us a listings report of over 200 properties, there was only one place that stood out. It was a historic building from 1895, zoned as a creative warehouse space. It was easily accessible and centrally located, and everyone in Orange County knew this colorful building. It was more space for much less money. It was dusty, the walls were painted obnoxious colors, and at first, it was extremely hard to visualize *that* as our future home. But we stayed, got to know the space, and the more we meditated upon this old warehouse, the potential beneath this dusty, forgotten place slowly bubbled up, and we could see it. *We just knew.*

We began to draw plans. After seven years of working in someone else's wellness center, and ten years of having our own, we knew exactly what worked and what we would do differently. This was the time to burst out of our latest cocoon and build our forever home exactly the way we dreamed.

Coming out of the pandemic, we realized that what people needed most (aside from vibrant health) is *connection*. For years we watched people walk into our space and leave transformed: calmer, stronger, and more joyful. But then they get into their cars, deal with stress and sensory overload on the freeway, and go back to their busy or not-so-busy, perhaps isolated lives. We had always wished for a gathering space for our community, but opening a cafe was never in the cards and way beyond our skill sets and budget. However, creating a space for the community to spend more time together before and after class, put down their phones, look each other in the eyes, and share a pot of tea was something we were all yearning for. This new space offered us the opportunity to create something magical; to dream big. Thus, *The Tea House* was born.

Since we had been planning this for over two years, we founded our non-profit organization, the *AlcheMē Natural Health Institute*, and we were able to fundraise for the construction of *The Tea House* and community-based pro-gramming. As *The Tea House* plans came to life, we did our best to maximize the space. Katie's dad built us a gorgeous tea bar where people can sit across from our kitchen and we filled the rest of the space with a long seated bench that lined the length of the room across from three tables that could seat up to twenty-five people for lectures, trainings, and workshops. We brought in even more Moroccan and rattan lanterns, and hanging vines and pampa grass covered the entire ceiling. The days we spent designing, building, and pouring every fiber of our being into the new space are the memories we will cherish most. There is nothing more joyful than dreaming big, working toward your goal, and watching it materialize before your eyes, working alongside the people you love the most.

For almost a year, we were still offering all our therapeutic yoga services in the high-end retail location, while simultaneously designing, building, and creating our new home with fingers crossed for a seamless transition. When it was time for the big move, to say goodbye, close the space we had loved and nurtured for ten years and move our community to the new space, we were blown away by the support we received! We had so many people willing to help us move that it only took the team one hour to clear out the old studio! Just like that, it was gone. Ten years of work disappeared in an hour! But luckily, we had something even better to look forward to and take its place.

The support we received continued, and the upswell got even larger. Every day, fifteen to twenty people showed up to help us prepare the new space for our Grand Opening. Jobs ranged from assembling tables and chairs to washing dishes, organizing retail, setting up electronics and networks, sweeping, cleaning, and purging all the stuff we no longer had a need for. It was a very exciting time and an all-hands-on-deck moment that stretched us in ways we could never have imagined. What was most surprising was how much people enjoyed the work and the participation in building something they believed in. We were creating a new reality together. It was hard work but so incredibly joyful.

Our new 3054-sqaure-foot space is a dream. Yes, the old building is high maintenance and quirky, but that has given us all the opportunity to take owner-ship and safeguard our community space. In fact, it feels much more like a cozy home and far from a stale, commercial retail shopping center. We all love being there. We spend our days sharing wisdom that the world needs most right now: how to harmonize our body, mind, and soul, how to look within, study ourselves, uncover our joy, and the unique gifts we are meant to share in this lifetime.

After our classes, we spend time in *The Tea House* and build meaningful relationships. After everyone leaves, we take out our laptops and work before picking up our boys at school. Things are flowing again; everything is as it should be. We feel extremely blessed that we have the great privilege of dedicating our lives to the study and practice of Yoga Therapy, Ayurveda, and natural healing modalities. What we learn makes us better people, ripples out into our families and friends, and uplifts the vibration of our communities. Overcoming these obstacles makes us feel powerful; it's like giving birth; it changes you forever, building confidence and resilience. These are the lives we have always dreamed of, even as they are intertwined with the challenges of being mothers, small business owners, and community advocates.

Despite all the plumbing problems, the small business headaches, and pan-demic challenges galore, we have chosen this path, and we continue to choose it over and over again, year after year. We have chosen to work nights, weekends, drop whatever we are doing when an emergency arises, and wholeheartedly dedicate ourselves to what we have so intentionally created. These challenges are miniscule when looking at the bigger picture. We continue to say yes to our dream and to each other. We continue to look for the joy within the struggle. It challenges and stretches us to our limits, but it's oh-so fun and exciting. We've created our own container for joy, one that expands out and touches thousands of people, and it's always evolving. We are in the joy business, and our shared work in this global community is never done!

Through the transmission of wisdom, we all can uncover our unique gifts, tap into our joy, and cultivate the confidence to pursue our grandest dreams. When we Ignite the twinkling light within our own hearts, it ripples out in an unbroken chain, infusing more joy throughout the world.

Ignite Action Steps

- **When the mind becomes turbulent, find a means to pause and look within**. Closing your eyes and taking a deep breath is an easy way to reset your mind and nervous system toward a more balanced state.

- **Meditate upon the best possible outcome**. Shift your perspective to focus on the goal (Bhavana) and not the obstacle to the goal.

- **Remember what brings you joy**. Make sure that your actions and Bhavana are aligned with the vibration of joy. *What are your unique gifts you would like to share with the world?*

- **Don't give up; the struggle makes you stronger**. When obstacles arise (which they will), remember the bigger picture, double down on your self-care practices, and infuse your mind with faith.

- **Release attachment to the outcome**. Sometimes, the path turns out different than you had imagined; release your grip and allow the miracles to unfold.

Katie Allen and Allison Prince — United States of America
Yoga Therapists, Business Owners, Natural Health Enthusiasts
www.bethechangeyoga.com
bethechangeyoga
bethechangeyogaoc
katie-allen-mph-c-iayt
katieallenyoga

Lady JB Owen

Lady JB Owen

"The joy you get out of life is equal to the joy you put into it."

It is my intention that this story puts a smile on your face and fills your body with a feeling of joy. When you read the words and envision the sentiment shared, I hope you feel a warm sense of delight and happiness. By simply using your imagination and visualization skills, you can actually begin to feel joyfulness. This shows that our minds can stimulate our emotions, and our thoughts can influence our state of being. If my story can spark feelings of joy, then your story can do the same. If we can imagine joy and see it in our mind's eye, we can bring it into creation.

Hold the Vision

I could hear my husband-to-be sleeping beside me as we both lay in bed. His rhythmic breath indicated he was fast asleep, and I smiled, knowing he was well into dreamland, content, and at peace. I, on the other hand, was lying in bed, not asleep, but instead dreaming of our upcoming wedding that was about to take place in just a few short weeks.

I lay there looking up at the ceiling, thinking of all the wedding preparations I needed to do. Yet, at the same time feeling giddy and excited. This was not going to be my first wedding, but it was going to be my best wedding, for I had found the most amazing man who loved and adored both me and my kids.

Peter and I had met only a year before, but our romance was beyond a fairytale and we felt our connection was forged from eons of loving one another during many past lives. We were both in our late forties, and we both had kids: one boy and one girl each. We both were level-headed, practical, and devoted, and had learned enough in our past marriages to make this one treasured and profoundly complete.

Since the moment I first met Peter while traveling in Europe with my two kids, I knew he was the kind of man who would always take care of me. His gentlemanly nature and caring disposition were evident in everything, from holding open the door to carrying the groceries and helping to guide me across the busy cobblestone streets. I remember the first time he put his hand on the small of my back to maneuver me through the traffic, an electric jolt shot up my spine right to the pleasure center of my brain. I felt tingly and flushed like a girl being swept right off her feet.

Although it took six months to solidify our love, we enjoyed a wondrous courtship filled with harmony and gratitude. Of course, life as a blended family with four kids between the ages of nine and seventeen had its challenges. But we took each difficulty in stride, knowing that fate and destiny had brought us *all* together. As a new family of six, we knew we had so much to learn from one another and so much love to enjoy.

When Peter asked me to marry him, it was a moment of pure joy and glee. I hugged him tight, knowing that he was going to be my husband forever, and through him and with him, our life would be grand. In fact, a year before meeting Peter, I had put on my vision board a statement that said, "Life is about to be Grand." It was beside a picture of the Grand Canyon and next to a pair of holding hands. I had been single for a few years and working to manifest the perfect partner. Peter showed up at precisely the moment I had decided that if I was to be single for the rest of my life, I was deeply content. I had done enough work on myself to have found my happy place and meeting Peter was the absolute icing on the cake. It is true when they say the right and perfect person shows up when you stop vigilantly looking, and that what you envision you can create. In our first year together, Peter surprised me by taking me to the Grand Canyon. It was there, amidst the stunning rocks and vast beauty, that he asked me to marry him. Everything about our life felt like a magical dream, a picture-perfect story amidst a fairy tale backdrop of serenity.

That fairytale feeling was what had me awake, staring up at the ceiling, longing to create a wedding that mirrored the feelings we held for one another.

I wanted this wedding to be spectacular and filled with deep sentimentality. Peter and I loved history, chivalry, and a sense of majesty. We admire couples like Mark Antony and Cleopatra, Albert and Queen Victoria, and Lancelot and Guinevere. We wanted to infuse some of their iconic love for one another into our wedding and solidify our union in this lifetime the way we believe we had already done centuries before. After a lot of research and planning, we decided to travel, fulfill our cosmic connection, and get married in Estonia.

Estonia is a country located in northern Europe, surrounded by the Baltic Sea and the Gulf of Finland. It shares borders with Latvia to the south and Russia to the east. The capital city, Tallinn, is known for its idyllic medieval Old Town, which is also a UNESCO World Heritage Site. It has a population of around a million people, rich with diversity yet relatively small compared to other European cities. We chose Estonia due to its stunning architecture, mystical history, and the fact that many of our friends would be there for the annual conference Peter and I attended the year before and where we first met one another. Getting married among the same people who witnessed our love unfolding felt deeply important and uniquely joyful.

Snuggling up next to Peter, I let my mind dream big. I wanted our wedding in a fantastic old church. The kind of church that takes your breath away due to its grand stature and attention to symbolic details. I wanted a harpist playing a romantic tune as I walked up the aisle, plucking away on the strings and performing a song that would bring tears to everyone's eyes. I wanted to arrive in a horse and carriage, with tall majestic horses dressed in all their finery. I envisioned all my friends there, smiling and happy. I could see their faces filled with love and well wishes; warming my heart and blessing our commitment. I wanted the most stunning bouquet that filled the room with the tantalizing aroma of sweet peonies and a lush rose scent. And, of course, in perfect JB fashion, I wanted to be wearing pink! I had been married before wearing white. This time, I wanted to show up as a bride blushing in the most beautiful hue of radiant pink.

With each passing moment, I could see the entire wedding unfolding before me, the people, the church, the carriage, and the kids: my son walking me down the aisle, our two girls as my bridesmaids, and Peter's son as his best man. It was going to be beautiful and grand; everything that represented the marriage we intended to create.

The next morning, when Peter awoke, I lay in bed sharing with him my dream for the wedding. In perfect Peter fashion, he loved all my ideas. He was completely supportive and willing to help execute everything I had conjured up. We spent the next few days making phone calls, researching online, and looking for venues that would help complete our plan. I'll admit it wasn't easy; the time change, language difference, and vastness of my visions were often dismissed and seen as impossible to achieve. Person after person turned me away, saying it wasn't allowed or permitted. Before long, I felt let down that the wedding I dreamed of would have to be revamped and compromised.

I reached out to the conference coordinator to see if they could help. Eager to assist, they shared that they had been venue scouting and had seen a wonderful place that was perfect for a wedding. She explained that it was a stylish, posh venue with pink walls and a pink chandelier. Although it wasn't a church or a grand cathedral, it was on theme with my love of pink. Out of desperation and fear of not finding a place, I told her to book it, and I would pivot and shift on my original wedding plans. We also had no luck with a horse and carriage, peonies were not in season at that time in Estonia, and we had yet to find a harpist for our date. It felt as if my idea was unraveling and too grand to pull off. I outwardly put on a brave face as my fairytale wedding turned into practical decisions and logical compensations we needed to make.

With our kids in tow and our suitcases packed, we flew to Estonia, eager to finally become husband and wife. The first day we arrived, still a bit jet lagged, we all walked to see the 'pink' venue that was only a few blocks from our place. I wanted to ensure it was everything it was described to be and that it met the high expectations every bride has for her nuptials.

As we entered the building, a huge weight of dread hit me like an overweight furniture truck. The walls were not pink but covered in wallpaper adorned with giant green palm leaves. The chandelier was not pink but black ebony. The carpet was purple and thick, like something from the sixties, not the sixteenth century. Tall bistro tables dotted the space, and a wall of mirrors highlighted the bar, filled with liquor bottles from every country and town within a thousand-mile radius. It looked more like a place for a small concert or hip fashion show. *Nothing about it said wedding or pink!*

With all six of us gaping in astonishment, the manager walked up as we had called ahead to inform him we were coming to take a look. In his thick accent, he delightfully explained that they had just finished remodeling and had brought in a designer to spruce up the place. I was speechless and dumbstruck feeling as if I had cotton in my mouth. Unable to respond to his eagerness, I simply nodded as my face reflected my heart-wrenching disappointment. Seeing my sadness and shock, my 13-year-old son bravely stepped up. Shaking the manager's hand, he said in firm honesty, "Thank you for your time, sir, but my mother will not be getting married in this establishment."

Back out on the street, we didn't know if we should laugh or cry. I was proud of my son for knowing me so well and honoring my dream. He was in support of my grand and joyful event and didn't want me to compromise. The kids and Peter hugged me in the middle of the busy sidewalk, assuring me that we'd find a better and more perfect spot.

That began the frantic scouting for a church, hotel, community hall, or any place that would be willing to host a wedding in just two weeks! We went everywhere, but not being a parishioner of the church meant we didn't qualify; not being a local meant we needed to apply and get a permit, which would take months! Problem after problem ensued, and within days, I was in tears thinking of anything we could do to make the wedding take place. We looked at parks and gazebos, even a barn on the outskirts of town! We walked around the entire city looking for anywhere that could host our special event. We considered cutting the guest list and shifting it to two places, one for the ceremony and one for the after-party. We even looked to see if there was an Airbnb™ that would be big enough! My dream wedding was suddenly becoming a fragmented collection of compromises and it-will-just-have-to-be-good-enoughs. All the joy I had around the wedding had been drained from my spirit, and it seemed as if our wedding wouldn't even happen at this pace.

I remember crying one night in worry and defeat. Peter came up to me to reassure me it would all work out. He asked me to stop trying to make just anything work and to tell him what would make me feel happy and bring the joy back into my heart. I reiterated I wanted to get married at a grand church, arrive in a horse and carriage, see all our friends around us, have a harpist playing, and walk up to him wearing pink.

Peter then smiled and said, "If that is what you want, then focus on having exactly that. Don't change your idea to make it easier; don't compromise or give in. If that is the wedding you envision, then let's commit to making that happen."

In one last ditch effort, Peter and I walked through the giant square in the center of town, looking to see if we could find anything suitable. In the center of old Tallinn, there just happens to be a monumental church known as St. Olaf's Church (Oleviste Kirik in Estonian); it is one of the most recognizable symbols of Tallinn's skyline and has a rich history dating back to the twelfth century. It was originally built as a Catholic church dedicated to Saint Olaf, the patron saint of Norway and seafarers. The church is an impressive example of medieval architecture, characterized by its tall spire and Gothic design. At its peak, the spire of St. Olaf's Church reached a height of approximately 159 meters (about 521 feet), making it one of the tallest buildings in the world during the Middle Ages. It has a wonderful set of stairs leading up to the church and looks out onto a massive and impressive cobblestone square with quaint shops and dainty cafes all along the perimeter.

Taking a break from our walk, Peter and I stopped to rest on the church's welcoming steps. Letting the sun fill my eyes, and the warmth of the summer air ease my spirit, I looked around and basqued in the sight of the stunning town square. For a second, I felt a flash, a memory: a vision of Peter and I in that square as two young lovers, holding hands, him in his woolen britches and me in a bonnet and apron. A huge wave flooded my body as if I had been there in that exact spot before, with Peter! It was a joyous feeling to see a flashback and feel as if we had been there in another lifetime, celebrating our love.

I quickly stood up and grabbed Peter's hands, squeezing them tightly. "Would you be willing to marry me right here?" I asked serendipitously.

Right here? He replied, confused.

"Yes, right here on these very steps, next to this huge and beautiful church, with all our friends standing right there in the square, and me arriving on a horse and carriage through that vestibule?"

Sporting a wide grin, Peter looked me in the eyes, lovingly, and agreed he would marry me in that very spot. We ran into the church to immediately speak to the curator. The church had never been asked if someone could get married *outside* on the steps, but they agreed since it technically didn't go against any rules. We then went back out into the square and found one of the drivers operating the horse and carriage rides that guided the tourists around the park. He called his manager, who was willing to contact the city to see if we could get permission to bring the horse and carriage into the square for only ten minutes to deliver a bride to her wedding — they agreed.

We then walked into a music shop just off the square and asked if they knew of a harpist. They did, and within a few minutes, he had her on the phone, and she confirmed she would be there to play for our wedding day!

After that, we crossed the square to enter what had become our favorite restaurant, an old brick building with huge arched windows that served traditional Estonian food. Having become fast friends with the manager, we asked if we could bring all of our guests to the restaurant after the ceremony, and he joyfully agreed. He even went one step further and suggested pink champagne with pink cotton candy on top for each guest when they arrived. I was ecstatic.

The last stop was the flower market on the edge of the square. It was a row of tiny vendors selling fresh flowers brought in from the countryside. I found an old charming lady with the pinkest of pink flowers and asked her to make bouquets for me and the girls. She happily agreed and promised to make them captivating.

What had taken months to solidify was completed in just a few short hours. All the dreaming and wishing came true when we got clear and set our mind to making it happen. I had been willing to compromise and adapt for too long, but even that had not worked out. It wasn't until I was willing to commit to my dream, focus on my desires, believe it was possible, and see it unfolding did it finally materialize. My magical dream wedding came together so quickly when Peter and I had joy and fun connecting with the locals, befriending the people, and allowing the town of Tallinn to support us. Everyone we spoke to that day was willing to make our beautiful wedding joyous and be a part of our special confirmation together.

In my pink wedding dress, riding through the town in a horse-drawn carriage with my two girls beside me, I felt like my dream had come true. People on the street waved as I went by, and I shouted back, "I'm on my way to my wedding!" It brought joy and smiles to their faces. When the carriage pulled up to the church steps, almost 850 people in the square were cheering as they greeted me. As the harp played in the background, my son valiantly put out his arm as I stepped down from the carriage, through the crowd, and up the steps to take the hand of my groom. Every single thing, from the glistening sun to the doves cooing above, was perfect. From the smiling faces of my friends and family to the heart-capturing vows of devotion from my new husband, there was not a dry eye to be seen. Angels shone down on us that day as our love filled the square. Tourists and strangers stopped to witness the love and joy that was pouring out of us, and we committed our lives together. I can honestly say it was a fairytale, a dream, and a perfect memory all rolled up into one. Joy was abundant in everyone who attended, and happiness was cemented in us for all of eternity.

When you put in joy, you create joy; Joy means following your heart. When something seems impossible, it means you need to get clear, more focused, and fully committed to what you want. Don't let others lead you astray or dissuade what you know to be true. Cultivate your ideas, nurture your visions, and hold onto the wishes you have for yourself with all your might. Joy comes from putting joy in. Find ways to work with others and make it enjoyable for them. When you add joy to the equation, not just you but everyone experiences it.

Ignite Action Steps

- **Dream big:** Be willing to have big dreams and big ideas. Take the time to think of something really amazing that you want and then map out every aspect of it to make it come true. When we open our minds to what is possible, our dreams tend to manifest into being. Be willing to see your dreams materialize *before* they happen.

- **Focus:** When you focus on exactly what you want, you tell the Universe what to provide for you. Be clear and precise to ensure results. Stay committed even when it feels hard or difficult. The Universe is testing you to see how important what you want truly is.

- **Commit:** No one said it was going to be easy, so keep pushing forward even after setbacks. Often, a *no* is a *yes* to something bigger and better than what you originally imagined. Someone else's no is simply that, *their no*. I like to think of no as a *new option* or *next opportunity*.

Lady JB Owen — Canada
Founder & CEO of Ignite Publishing™, Speaker, Author,
Humanitarian, Philanthropist and Knighted Lady
jb@igniteyou.life
jbowen.website
LadyJBOwen
*jb_owen_*
ladyjbowen
jb-owen

IGNITE
Joy

Leona Wallace

LEONA WALLACE

"The key to joy is being playful."

This is a story designed to show you the key ingredients I have found to spark that inner sense of joy. It is a story that brings a smile to my face and joy into my heart whenever I replay it, invoking cherished emotions my body remembers and can experience all over again by just thinking of the story. Emotions are so powerful; they stay stored in our bodies and can be re-ignited instantly. I wish for you to feel those sensations inside of you so that at any time, you can invoke the feelings of joy and delight to get you back on track to your dreams.

PUDDLES IN FLORENCE

The aromas of fresh croissants and baguettes always made my mouth water. *Oui, Bonjour. Comment ca va?* My French was improving, and I had only been living in Paris for a year. I was exploring how I could expand my personal image and my coaching business. It was clear that I was required to do some public relations. Yet, the reality of living in Paris and how it secluded me from my new business growth was quickly apparent. I was feeling despair and lost in the city of millions. *How could anyone find me, and if they couldn't, how could I help them?* Lingering questions that were always in my mind and heart.

It had taken every ounce of courage to move my life to Paris and start anew. But this isn't a story about courage or faith; it is one of joy, and at that moment, I wasn't feeling much happiness.

I was certainly making an effort to live my best life, that was for sure. Growing up mainly in North America, I had it drilled into my consciousness that the only way I was going to succeed was by hard work and persistence. It was never enough. I couldn't get success fast enough. At that time, success meant something different to me than it does now. It was about how much I could make. *How many things I could buy and experience with that money I made? How should I look and show up to the world? The more successful, the better because then I could have everything my heart desired.* I had been so busy creating and pushing that I forgot about the stopping and receiving part, one of the most crucial parts of creation. *Joy* wasn't a part of my vocabulary.

As I was sitting in my tiny, tiny apartment in Paris, I had the feeling of being lost and invisible. It was all foreign to me, and I was looking at everything incorrectly. You have to understand that Paris and I had a love-hate relationship. Having worked in the late eighties in the fashion industry in Europe, Paris had left a nasty taste in my mouth that I was still navigating through. When I worked in Paris, I coordinated fashion shows and networked with the 'who's who' of the fashion world. It was a very fast-paced industry surrounded by temptations and slimy individuals. I had many times seen girls come in all bright and hopeful and leave completely soulless from the work they had been doing. Still, deciding to leave the industry at the time was devastating. I left my fashion fantasies on the table and came out the other side with low self-confidence and a fragile view of the world. Paris wasn't what it was hyped up to be.

I found it strange that, when you are open to receiving miracles, they can come from nowhere. Years later, as I revisited these memories of low self-worth, I decided to journal and connect with my heart to see what I wanted to experience next. The message I received was that it *is time to be truly visible to your authentic self.* I stayed with this idea as I had my hand on my heart. This was not a mindful message; it was a message being received through my *higher self* from a *higher source*, pulling me in. I distinctly knew my inner self, calling from another dimension and beckoning me to listen. I stayed in that energy and just felt the power of the message.

I don't know how long I sat there, but I do remember coming out of it from a 'ping' on my phone. A friend forwarded me an email with the subject line "Looking To Become More Visible?" It was an opportunity for a photo shoot in Florence, Italy.

What, Florence? My favorite place on the planet connected to some amazing dreams that hadn't happened… *yet*. Of course, it was a YES before I read the details or replied to the email. The offer was a last-minute chance to fly to Florence for a photo shoot with a lady whose experience screamed authenticity. I loved all of her photos. I wondered if she could capture the feminine essence in me. I was feeling so lost, and this was precisely what I needed. I signed up right away, grabbing the one-and-only available spot. *I was in*!

Days later, I found myself on a short plane ride to Florence, where I would have my photoshoot. How did I feel? *Sick to my stomach.* I had self-doubts. I had the voices in my head. *Who do you think you are? You can't do this! You are too old for this. Remember who you are, Leona, a small-town girl with hopeless dreams.* I had so much self-doubt and so many limiting beliefs bubbling up to the surface. I took a breath, practiced my breathing, and removed the dragons of doubt as I heard the captain announce our arrival.

There she was below, Florence, enticing me to open up my dreams and think bigger. As a little girl, I fantasized about ending up in Italy, along the Mediterranean, living a romantic life of renovating a villa, writing my book, and having tons of family around me as I lived happily ever after. I could feel that little girl who lived inside of me coming back to life, excited for this next adventure.

I landed and quickly approached my private driver, who would take me to the hotel. I loved everything about the city. The Renaissance architecture had the allure of romanticism. The sounds of the locals in the streets selling their handmade items. Oh, the smells—the smells of leather in the marketplace, the bakeries surrounding the plaza. All of it made me feel at home, even though everything was foreign. My excitement kept growing despite the fact I was still a little frightened. Showing up as an older woman with more curves and lines of experience expressed on my face brought in waves of self-doubt again. Along with the questions from others, "Who the hell do you think you are?" The internal battle of proclaiming yes to this elaborate experience would open up another level of desire. *What is next for Leona?*

I always tell my clients that opportunities are like opening up the cupboard and seeing that one wrapped gift on the top shelf. Feeling as if it was the only gift and hesitating to open it up, in case that was the only one you'd ever receive. Yet once you were brave enough to reach for it and open it, you saw more gifts to experience. Every time you said *yes* to one gift, more gifts would appear. This willingness to be vulnerable and show up for myself was that first gift. Another gift would appear if I trusted the process and said yes to my heart's desire. Here I was in Florence, about to experience a dream of a lifetime. A beautiful fashion photo shoot!

As the driver rounded the corner to my hotel, my heart skipped a beat. There was the Palazzo Vecchio. The hustle and bustle of the hundreds of tourists always made my heart sing. The Palazzo Vecchio is the old city hall in Florence. It overlooks the Piazza della Signoria, which holds a copy of Michelangelo's David statue and the gallery of statues in the adjacent Loggia dei Lanzi. These landmarks, found in so many romantic Italian movies, brought me back in time and made my heart sing even more. This place was genuinely majestic and, at night, would glow bright enough to light the city.

Finally, we arrived at the hotel, and it was everything I could imagine and more. Long velvet curtains, renaissance paintings, and decadent furniture adorned the room. The allure of ancient Italy's magic tantalized every emotion within me. I felt my body more at ease with this whole experience. I planned out the next day and immersed myself in what was about to unfold.

I began to unpack and lay my things out for the next day. I was considering my evening dinner plans when suddenly, I heard a long crash. I went to the window and saw the sky filled with dark, ominous clouds, looking as if they would unleash a storm to be reckoned with. Hmm. I would need to reconsider my walk through the Piazza. Not to be discouraged, room service would be in order.

It was a dark and stormy night in so many ways besides the weather. I tossed and turned all night, my head filled with doubts. I wondered if the storm was a sign, whether I should have come all this way to say yes to such a dreamy dream. I told myself, *This is what happens when you say yes to something so frivolous.* As I brushed away the conflict, I tapped into my inner knowingness and calmed myself down. I sat up and decided to eliminate these emotions, knowing they were only signs of my resistance to what was about to happen. It was obvious to me that this experience was more than just a photo shoot in Italy. It was about opening up my heart's desires that I had left behind as a young girl and permitting myself to do this now. It was like the gift in the closet. Once I said yes, there would be so much more on the other side. I must breathe into this resistance.

I opened up the shutters and embraced the storm. I stood gazing out at the darkness and repeated to myself; I *am worthy of this experience and so much more.* Over and over again, I said the words until I began to feel the emotion of what I was repeating. *I am worthy of this experience.* I felt this bright light coming from my heart. It began to expand as I breathed it in and opened up to feeling it more. I stayed with this for a while as I calmed my entire body. I took this lightness back to bed with me, with the shutters wide open. I fell asleep quickly and slept like a baby.

When I awoke, the sun was shining on my face. I smiled and said to myself, "Today, you will fully embrace this opportunity and the gifts it may bring." I would allow myself to open up all of my senses and immerse myself in this day without expectations. After some journaling and inner reflection, I did some stretches and breathwork to center myself and receive the unexpected miracles. Something definitely had shifted in me. I felt great; even though it was extremely wet outside, it wasn't raining anymore. It was time to receive the gifts!

The 'glam squad' arrived armed for the day: hair, makeup, and sample photographs. Dressed as if she had just arrived from California, the photographer had years of experience with these kinds of photoshoots, blending in her charismatic and laid-back attitude. She was all about capturing the essence of the woman. She made me feel comfortable with light-hearted conversation, asking me more questions about myself. She laid out the plan for the day and how we would travel to iconic places that she had scoped out, listing famous locations I loved.

The makeup artist did an amazing job of bringing out my beauty, making me feel even more confident and assured. Before we left the hotel, I put on my first outfit. This dress had found me when I was visiting California. It was a peachy orange and I loved the soft feminine nature of how it flowed and swayed, capturing the playfulness of me. Off we headed to the first location, chauffeured in a black car while drinking champagne. *Of course!* It was a complete experience. We could see it was filled with massive puddles as we approached the local park. Getting out of the car, I had goosebumps. I saw an opportunity, and I wanted to grab it. *This is your chance, Leona!*

The photographer watched as I removed my very nice shoes and headed toward a giant puddle. I could tell she was feeling me. I lifted my dress to my knees and started to dance around in the puddle as if I were that little girl again, giving her permission to play. I splashed and spun around. The camera clicked away as I played, and I could feel walls falling around me. I felt freedom. I felt complete joy! I didn't care; I just let go. The more I danced and played, the more I felt joy ignite within me. It was as if all of the shackles had been released. The moment was wonderful.

As we continued to the next location, I was feeling much more at ease. We headed up toward the Palace entrance and found a place to change my outfit;

this time, a teal green jumpsuit. I pretty much leaped out of the car when I saw the lion's heads at the entrance. I had to. I just had to. I went over to them, played with the statues, kissed them, and allowed them to tell me secrets. I was having fun, totally immersed in the *now*. I noticed that the crowds were gathering to see what was going on. The photographer gave me directions and the beauty expert touched me up. I was lost in the whole experience and completely bathed in joy. As we were finishing at the location, I noticed the crowds had grown larger and were all applauding and yelling, "Brava Bella!"

Oh wow! I was in my element. I loved everything: the environment, the experience, and the attention. Yes, I was eating it up! I could feel myself at ease, wanting more. I had no fear, only the knowledge that the gifts would get better. *Leona had found her stride.*

We headed off to our final location. At that point, I had changed into something a little more elevated. My Italian lingerie set, a long green military jacket, and my new Louis Vuitton shoes. Oh yes, I was so ready. This location is what they call a piazza. A famous square with many cafes, beautiful architecture, and many people. As I left the black car, I could feel myself hesitating a bit. The self-doubt was trying to creep back in. I took a deep breath and placed my hand on my heart, feeling the joy I had ignited already on this amazing day. I heard myself say, "Have you had enough, Leona?" I shook it off and decided to step into the excitement and visibility. *You've got this, Leona! Let's do it!*

I strutted out into the center of the cobblestone street for the world to see me. I let go of my fears and reservations and tapped into that joy I was feeling earlier. I allowed the light to unleash the woman inside, wanting to be seen for who she really was. My photographer so graciously guided me through the experience, and I was immersed in it. *Feeling it. Embracing it. Loving it!* As the day continued, I grew into more of the woman I knew I always was. I felt my confidence increase and my love for myself grow.

We decided to end the day at a famous and luxurious restaurant where we indulged in decadent Italian cuisine. All of my senses had been expanded and awakened to a new level. I could see the power in my newfound *YES!* This was not just a photoshoot but an experience that allowed me to Ignite and accept myself. I was ever so grateful for the precious gifts and gems I experienced throughout the day. I returned to the hotel with sparks of new ideas and inspirations of how I could create something similar for other ladies. This day truly was the catalyst for what would be the next layer of the work I decided to create for other women around the world. I knew my purpose had evolved to providing a self-empowering and heart-healing haven that would become a place for others to find their own personal Divine Beauty™.

I would love for you to say yes to those gifts and treasures just waiting for you to unwrap. Stepping into your truest heart desire is the gateway to joy and finding the beauty in you. Life can be filled with storms and rain clouds, but that means there is always a puddle to play. *It's already in you; find your joy and play.*

IGNITE ACTION STEPS

- **Get intentionally connected to your heart every day**. Make it a practice to physically touch your heart, feel it, embrace it, and listen to it. Then, just breathe for a few moments. *Really* connect.

- **As you keep your hand on your heart**, ask these three questions.
  - What type of person do I *desire* to *be* today?
  - What is the *one* thing I desire to *enjoy* today?
  - What is the *one* thing I will *do* today to bring me closer to prosperity?

- **Allow your heartfelt answers to guide you** in creating your daily intentions. By doing so, you will be closer to invoking more joy.

Leona Wallace — Canada
Speaker, Author, Teacher, CEO of Awaken The Beauty Coaching and
The Beehive Community
www.AwakenTheBeauty.com
Angelinmotion
lovegoddessleona
LeonaWallace
ladyleonawallace

Liliana Avila Roque

Liliana Avila Roque

"We are Divine Light Beings, living short Human Experiences."

May you find a place of peace within you as you build your spiritual practice. May you enhance your communication with your loved ones, once they have crossed over to the other side of the veil. Every soul has decided to come to planet Earth, one of the nicest planets in the Universe to live their own unique experience. Very few tickets were available, make sure you take advantage of the trip!

Walk Me to the Gate

Like the touch of the ocean breeze on one's face, I navigated life very smoothly as a deeply psychic child. However, when I was in my late twenties, I turned off those abilities, like shutting off the light in a room and letting the darkness and silence fill up the space. I was going through a difficult relationship. I activated my internal 'airplane mode' and disconnected from Source. Later, in my forties, the thought of losing my elderly father began to frighten me, breaking my heart into a thousand pieces. That moved me to open up once again and prepare myself to say goodbye when the time came.

That Thursday morning, the traffic in Mexico City was insane. After my business meeting, I was about to head back to my office in the south of the city. However, deep in my heart, something told me to stop by and see my dad. So I did.

I arrived at his house and went up to the second floor. I silently entered his bedroom and watched him sleeping peacefully with a profound and endearing tranquility. My father, Mario, an eighty-four-year-old kind man, was sleeping like a baby but snoring like a bear. He was sitting in his rocking chair, holding the newspaper he enjoyed reading so much. The midday sun caressed his skin, and his white cheeks were rosy. There was a profound stillness in the room. I sat on the bed and enjoyed the moment. I stayed sitting there until an inner voice told me that that moment was going to be the last time I would see my dad in perfect health, with so much peace and light. After a while, I wiped a couple of tears from my eyes and gently woke him up by moving his foot with mine. He slowly opened his eyes and looked at me with great joy on his face. I could feel how much he loved me, how he had loved me during this lifetime, and many others.

"What a pleasant surprise!" he exclaimed. "What are you doing here, Güerita, my blonde sweetheart?" he continued. I told him I felt like dropping by to say hello. He was delighted. At that moment, one of the most relevant and love-filled conversations we ever had began. It was the beginning of a farewell with total awareness. He asked me in detail about my thoughts regarding death, which I prefer to call *transition*. We talked about the 'veil' separating different dimensions, the welcoming from Archangel Azrael, and our Guides on the other side. We discussed past lives, a concept he didn't believe in, and he discreetly furrowed his brow.

For a couple of months, he had been expressing a lot of interest in all these topics, making me wonder if he was getting ready to depart. At that moment, I asked him to please say goodbye to me when he decided to leave, to let me know beforehand. He gave me his word he would. We hugged, and we continued chatting. At the end of our conversation, he said, "You know, I feel calm because I know you will accompany me." I didn't exactly know what that meant, but I said, "Yes, of course! I will accompany you!"

I got into my car and watched him walk down the street and chat with his neighbor through my rear-view mirror. I placed both hands on the steering wheel and told myself, "Of course, I want to accompany him. The only thing is that I don't want to die myself!" I burst into a nervous laugh. I drove away feeling calm because I knew that my dad's passing wouldn't catch me off guard. After all, I was going to accompany him.

The weekend passed without incident. However, I received a call on Monday night that made my heart race. "Your dad is very unwell," said my mom with an inconsolable voice. "Your siblings are on their way." Sons, daughters-in-law, and grandchildren all arrived immediately. We thought that was the moment of departure. But it wasn't. That Monday night was the beginning of an eighteen-day journey that would lead us to the magic of the intangible, to tap into other dimensions, and to be surprised by synchronicities. It was a journey to the spiritual world and a beautiful soul's journey to a different plane.

My brother Alejandro, a great anesthesiologist, transformed the TV room into a cozy hospital room. With an oxygen tank, two nurses on 24/7 shifts, and a great team of doctors led by his son, my dad was surrounded by love, and all his needs were met. His health deteriorated rapidly from one day to the next while the magic of spirituality became present. He continued to be the great Teacher he always was. Our spiritual gifts laid the groundwork for the farewell and a new relationship in different dimensional realms.

On day four, I was comfortably seated in the blue armchair at the foot of my dad's bed. My laptop was on my lap, and my mind was absorbed in office tasks. The stress of responding to each email had me disconnected from what was happening around me. Sitting on the bed, my dad was eating flavored gelatin the nurse was giving him. Between one email and another, I heard my dad's voice in my mind. *How strange!* I thought. *I can hear what my dad is thinking.* I looked at him, and we both smiled. I continued with my emails. Again, I heard him. He told me he felt nauseous with every bite the nurse gave him. I couldn't believe it! "Please, you feed me instead." I heard him say in my mind. As I looked at my dad, he began telling the nurse that he didn't want any more jelly. She stood up, placed the plate and spoon on the tray, and headed to the kitchen. My dad called me to his side. I approached him, and he whispered, "Güerita, please give me the jelly from now on. When the nurse does it, I feel deeply disgusted and don't want to hurt her feelings."

I couldn't believe it! I could hear my dad's thoughts! He was sharing his thoughts with me. As many of my spiritual teachers had pointed out, from that moment on, I would quiet my mind, turn off my ego, and listen only to my intuition. I would let the energy flow to receive all the spiritual gifts that the Universe had destined for my dad and me.

The following Friday, we spent the afternoon together, and by evening, we had rearranged the blue armchair so I could lie down. It was a bit uncomfortable to sleep in, so I decided to listen to music, put some lavender in the diffuser, and go into meditation. My dad was still very uncomfortable, constantly complaining in a very soft tone of voice. I took some crystals and asked if I could place them on his chest at the level of his heart. He said yes and smiled gratefully. I then began to give him an energy healing to help him relax. After about ten minutes, he entered a deep sleep.

I took the opportunity to lie on the armchair and sleep. I started dreaming. In my dream, we had arrived at the airport. My mom, siblings, and I accompanied my dad to the airline counter for check-in. He was embarking on a very important journey. The four of us said goodbye to him in the spacious airport hallway. There were many people, it was very busy. We walked with my dad toward the security area to begin his journey, and then, for some reason, he turned back. He told us, "It's not time yet. My flight is not ready to depart." I woke up immediately and knew that although the end was near, there was still a little time before we had to say goodbye.

That weekend, sadness began to fill my heart. Whenever this happened, I remembered my spiritual teacher's words: "Go to the God that resides within you." After several breaths of going within and contacting the God within me, a great peace flooded me, and the sadness and anxiety disappeared. I could observe that my psychic abilities were opening more and more precisely. Taking all those courses and preparing myself over the years made me feel great inner peace.

Around day nine, I was sitting in front of my dad's bed. The house was in absolute silence. The nurse was chatting with my mom in the kitchen. The diffuser filled the room with a relaxing scent of bergamot. I placed some crystals and quartz on the bedside table, lit a candle, and played soothing music. I was enjoying a profound peace when I had the intuition to get up and approach my dad. I stood beside him and placed my forehead right above his. To my surprise, I heard my dad's thoughts clearly! He said, "Güerita, other lives do exist! I've seen it! Do you want us to live another life together?" I immediately responded, "Por supuesto! Of course, I want to live another life with you!"

On day eighteen, the sun shone in all its splendor as I arrived at my parents' house. I entered through the maple wood door and ran up the stairs to find my dad very weak. I spent the whole day with him. He slept most of the time without engaging in any conversation.

At night, I returned to my house. Exhausted, I was getting ready to sleep. Intuition invited me to meditate, but I was too tired to do so. I curled up on my bed. Just as I was about to close my eyes, I saw a pink orb float behind my back and rise toward the ceiling, going out through the window. I heard my dad's voice clearly in my mind, saying, "Güerita, ya es hora." It was time.

Two seconds later, my phone rang. It was Alejandro telling me that the moment had arrived. I slowly got out of bed, aware of every small movement, put on my jeans and jacket, and headed to my car. That short drive from my home to my parent's house was a moment of blissful reflection on everything that had happened during the last eighteen days.

I ran up the stairs, listening to the pounding of my heart. I remembered my dad's words, telling me that I would accompany him. However, I didn't know what would happen or what I was supposed to do. Yet I felt no fear. I had the intuition to lie down beside him. I asked my mom and siblings if they minded, and lovingly, they said no.

I laid down and held his hand. The family continued to whisper in his ear, reminding him how much we loved him. The early morning hours were cold, so I covered my legs with a blanket. Suddenly, sleep overcame me, and without realizing it, I heard my dad say, "It is time. Walk me to the gate." I found myself walking through a black void, which was warm and safe. We were holding hands with great excitement, and at that moment, I felt his joy in my heart. At a distance, I saw the silhouette of some people, but I couldn't distinguish their faces because their whole bodies emanated a very bright and beautiful golden illumination. I understood that I was in the tunnel mentioned by people who have had near-death experiences.

Suddenly, I was filled with fear. It wasn't my intention to cross to the other side of the veil with him. *I am not ready to die yet.* I turned to my left and looked deeply into my dad's eyes. I thanked him for everything and let go of his hand, knowing we had reached the gate together. Then, instantly, I saw myself entering through my Crown Chakra and back into my body, as Alejandro said, "That was his last breath." But I replied, "No, there's another one left." I was still seeing him walk towards those beings of Light. He hadn't reached them yet. Once I saw them embrace him, his last breath exhaled. Then, I said aloud, "Now, he has crossed over."

At that moment, I realized that my dad had transcended. That my dad had died. And I was fine. I was going to be okay. He was starting a great journey. The most important journey of all is the journey back *Home*. Knowing my dad had died and I was okay was incredible. I had been so afraid of losing him over the years that I couldn't believe the peace and tranquility I had in my heart.

Wearing black pants, a white blouse, comfortable shoes, and a couple of quartz crystals in my pockets, it was important to me to feel comfortable during the funeral. The coffin was surrounded by flowers, mostly white. My nephew Nicolás, only six years old, rested his forehead on the coffin and cheerfully looked for different flowers and leaves to place on the box. Then I heard my dad joke, "Even in death, I must take care of Nicolás!" I couldn't believe it! He was still making jokes and entertaining Nicolás by asking him to collect different flowers and leaves, a game my siblings and I often played with my dad when we were little. Right before my eyes, new and different ways of communication were opening. I could hear things I had never noticed before and felt a knowingness guiding my steps. Later, I would discover that whether in dreams, through synchronicities, or a song on the radio, I would continue to be in contact with my dad.

An important date was approaching: my father's birthday. Only a few months had gone by without him being physically present. My mom, being very Catholic, wanted to organize a mass. However, my son, Santiago, came up with a more fun idea. "Let's go to the casino. Grandpa Tutu loved it!" We all thought it was an excellent idea. So, all the family who were of legal age gathered at my dad's favorite casino in the south part of Mexico City. Upon arrival, the first thing I saw on the entrance rack was a cream-colored hat with a black ribbon around it, identical to the one my dad used to wear. *I see you've already arrived, Tutu,* I said in my mind as a great joy and excitement filled my heart.

Our first stop was the roulette wheel. To our surprise, the first number that came up on the roulette wheel was twenty-two. My Dad's nickname was Tutu, or two two, and the dealer's name was Mario, my Dad's name! This croupier, Mario, was incredibly assigned to our table all night, whatever game we played. I had to smile as it was evident my dad continued to play and make himself present at every moment! It was so much fun!

The months passed, and I began to miss my father's physical presence. One night, during my meditation, before falling asleep, I asked Archangel Azrael to arrange a meeting with my dad and to help me remember. I dreamed I was walking alongside an angel, a being of light. He asked me to keep my eyes closed as we moved forward. We stopped, and he said, "Now you can open your eyes." I noticed that we were in a very long hallway with curved walls. Everything was pristine white. On my left side, there were some classrooms. The windows at the bottom of the wall were also curved. I squatted down to look through the window and saw my dad and my uncle Joaquín, who had passed many years before him. I didn't see the teacher, but there were several empty benches. My uncle Joaquín didn't notice my presence. However, my dad turned and saw me. Suddenly, he was standing right in front of me. He was radiant, very happy, and filled with light. Surprised, he said, "Güerita, what are you doing here?" I replied, "I miss you so much and they let me come to see you." I asked him, "How are you?" He said, "VERY WELL! I'm very happy! This place is amazing!" My eyes filled with tears from the overwhelming emotion of seeing him. That loving feeling stayed with me for the next weeks to come.

Dreams, synchronicities, and funny comments continue up to this day. I have discovered that my spiritual practice has led me to open these new channels of communication. I see that when a loved one moves to another country, we use video calls and apps to help us stay in touch. I use meditation and clear intentions to connect with my father, who is also living an experience in another realm. After following my intuition and recovering my psychic abilities, I feel like I turned the light on in that dark room. I have turned my inner Airplane Mode off. I am no longer afraid of people's passing. I have seen with my eyes and felt with my heart the peace of walking to the gate and the joy that souls have when they finally cross to the other side of the veil. I would love to share that by connecting with your Guides and loved ones you will IGNITE JOY in your life!

IGNITE ACTION STEPS

Through your daily spiritual practice, find a place of peace within yourself. Sit comfortably, close your eyes, and pay attention to your breath. Set the intention to connect with your Guides.

- **Guided Writing.** Write at the top of the page: *Dear Spirit, what do you want me to know today?* Start writing down everything that comes to your mind. Your Guides will communicate with you. They will give you the answers to your questions.

- **Dreams Journal.** Writing your dreams will help you remember them. Many messages from your Guides come during your dream state. Be open to receiving.

- **Protect yourself.** Surround yourself in a bubble of golden light. Intentionally set the intention that *you are always in the right place, at the right time, for the right reason, and with the right people.*

Liliana Avila Roque — Mexico
Mechanical & Industrial Engineer, Founder and
CEO at AVILA International Education Consultancy
www.avilaeducacion.com
avilaeducacion

Lydia Burchell

LYDIA BURCHELL

"Moments of joy are the way to greater things within us."

I hope you, the reader, will learn that even in the most stressful situations, taking time to stop, breathe, and connect with nature can create a new direction, a new connection to self, and something bigger than each of us. The messages and clues are all around us; we just need to stop, connect, observe, and listen. When we allow nature to joyously embrace us, we can discover the sense of belonging and self-worth that can help us frame our past and, more importantly, shape our future.

THE PRINCESS IN THE CASTLE

As I slid into the front seat of my steely-blue Honda, the whole back seat was taken up with items for my cat: litter box, kennel, and blankets galore so he would have plenty of places to hide. I had tried to make it as comfortable as possible but my cat hated the car. My husband and I had sold most of our belongings, and the rest were being shipped. There was no plan to return. This was meant to be a one-way trip. It was the biggest event I had ever faced. I looked up to see a tear trickle down my Dad's cheek. We both knew this was it. My leaving on a journey across Canada, 8,000 kilometers, from Nova Scotia to British Columbia meant the end of us seeing each other daily as we had done for more than thirty years. My heart was breaking. It was hard to breathe.

Tears were something I had never seen from my father. He was a tall, stoic, hardworking man known for his kindness, solidness, and gentle laughter. I knew him as my protector, my guide, my quiet hero. I had grown up as a tomboy, building boats, fishing, and being the boy he never had. I loved our daily trips to the newspaper store, just the two of us, and he would buy me candy. I was never that close to my mother but the bond with my father was unbreakable. We had a quiet knowing. We were always there for each other.

My choice to leave our quiet seaside village was a big deal. Few ever left or ventured far. They instead stayed, making that their home for life. Many of my friends only left on holiday and generations had lived in the same area. Some never actually thought I would leave; the rest were convinced I would return.

For me, though, the decision to leave had been reached through much consideration. I had been laid off from my job, and the economy was not great. My husband, at the time, had managed to secure a role in management on the West Coast. He also had family there. After many hours, even years of discussion, we finally decided to move. I knew the news was painful for my father, yet he told me that I had to go live my life. I also felt it was time to expand, and staying in my hometown meant I would be stifled and unable to grow. I needed to see beyond the horizon. There was always something within me that wanted something more.

My first job was in a clothing store, and I would love to try and model new garments. Each outfit was a new experience, and I would thrill myself by putting together fashion combinations like those you might see on professional models. I envisioned myself in big spaces, doing big things beyond the norms of our small, small town. I yearned for change and to do something exciting and full of adventure. I was surrounded by people who wanted the *familiar* while I wanted the *unknown*. I felt I had outgrown our tiny village, and life was inviting me to experience more.

I had been feeling the pull for something different in every part of my life as I grew into adulthood, including the world of romance. The guys I grew up with often worked so they could party on the weekends. But one man, a little older than me, had left our town at a young age and lived out west. When he returned, he carried himself with a flair that was different from the guys I knew.

This man wanted to take me out to the movies and for nice dinners and sweep me off my feet. Eventually, I married him.

On the outside, our relationship looked amazing. We were very social. We appeared to have lots of fun together. What wasn't known was I was living a dual life. Many people had no idea about the not-so-subtle abuse, the smashing of glass at my feet, the throwing of the remote control that just missed my head. I had left and gone into hiding eight times in the year before. Anger was at the center of our household, and letting anyone know of my struggles meant deep shame and embarrassment I wasn't willing to share.

However, he had given a few reasons to welcome a shift in our environment. My husband had finally taken anger management classes and promised things would be different. I thought moving across the country would be a new chance for us both, a new chance for joy to emerge.

As we drove, I was in awe, passing through the Great Lakes, the golden wheat fields, the Rocky Mountains, the jade-coloured lakes, and massive snow-capped peaks. I watched through a window as these testaments to nature's power and magnificence moved in and out of my view. Finally, we arrived in White Rock, a nugget of a city atop a hill on the Canada-United States border. It was small, quaint, and much larger than the town I grew up in.

I felt fantastic. I was keen to get to know my sister-in-law. She showed me around and helped me settle in. A few weeks after arriving, I looked in the local newspaper hoping to find ways to meet new people and make connections. I found an ad with a request for volunteers at a women's center. It had a clothing exchange that pulled me in, taking me back to my first job and love of sharing fashion. It was a place to help women find support when facing challenges in their relationships or sanctuary and guidance in navigating and even leaving abusive situations.

The following Monday, I arrived at the Women's Place center on the second floor of an old brick building. I drew in a long breath and opened the creaky door. *Who am I to be coming here?* I thought to myself. I felt like I didn't belong and it wasn't my place to involve myself in the lives of people I didn't know. In Nova Scotia there had not been anything like this center for women in need of help. I truly did not know what I was walking into or how I would be of service. I had just traveled more than 8,000 kilometers from one side of the country to the other. My home, my people, were so far away. I was still in the same country but felt like a stranger, a guest.

I entered the main meeting room and gave the woman at the registration desk my name. I sat quietly on a folding chair on the edge of the large dark space where women were gathering. Laughter spread across the many feminine faces of counselors, volunteers, and program organizers. I was hopeful this would be the place I would make new friends.

A leader in the group introduced herself and welcomed us. She spoke about what the center offered women: *access to government resources, legal assistance, employment, assistance with children, and emotional support and counseling for those coping with difficult circumstances.*

Then the leader said she had a story she wanted to read to us. She held a white piece of paper, one side printed with the words she would share. It was the story of a beautiful young princess. A man had promised her a dream life: a wonderful castle in a fantastic land where she would have whatever she needed. She didn't know he would be taking her away from everyone and everything she knew. He took her away from her family and friends so he could control her. At first, she was happy living in a spectacular castle, but her joy turned to sorrow over time as she could not see her loved ones, whom she dearly missed. She was not allowed to come and go as she pleased. Her freedom was slowly squeezed away.

As the woman read the story, I could feel my throat closing. I tried to hold back the tears. Finally, I could no longer stand it. I slipped out of the room and ran to the restroom. There, I sobbed. My body felt weak. My mind raced. The story felt like what *I was living.* I had hidden the bitter truth from everyone. I thought the new destination would be a fresh start, but I was more isolated, separated from those who loved me, away from my supporters and safety net. My husband's anger was resurfacing. We had made plans to move across this vast country to a new job, new hope, and a great adventure, but instead, things were getting worse.

There was a gentle knock on the restroom door. The leader who was sharing the story asked if she could come in, and I reluctantly said yes.

At first, it was difficult to share the reason for my tears. I felt so much shame and guilt. I felt I shouldn't let people see this side of my life, this unbearable situation. I was the princess, isolated and alone, controlled and restricted. I just hadn't realized it until that moment.

As I told her my story, she said, "You know, I think you should join this program rather than volunteer for it."

Within a few months of participating in their program, I was feeling a possible shift on the horizon. I was learning I had value and that I did not need to put up with any kind of abuse. I went back to Nova Scotia for my Dad's 65th birthday, yet I became very ill during my time there. When I flew back to White Rock, still ravaged by illness, my husband demanded I had to return to work because of the money I had spent on the flights. I knew then I needed to leave.

I had started saving and putting money aside in preparation for leaving him. One night, sleeping in the spare room, he stood towering over me, growling like a bear, threatening me after a night of drinking. I knew the time had come. Despite not having the money to pay rent somewhere else, I was determined to go. A friend helped me find a transition house. There was no turning back, and I wanted to be free.

The next morning, I escaped the confines of that relationship. Slipping out of the house with only my purse, I found my way to the home of a woman from the women's center. She had gone through a similar experience and had a wealth of information to support me. It was the beginning of yet another new life, a life of being solo. Living in a transition house felt like a double-sided blessing. No family. No friends. No familiar resources. I was a stranger in a new world and it was scary as hell. Yet, the only thing I had to focus on was me. Slowly, day by day, I stepped into a new life, no longer controlled. I found new connections and possibilities. A freer version of me.

It took a while for me to find my footing, confidence, personal compass, and value I felt for myself. One year later, on a gray, overcast day, two friends and I drove across the border and up a long, winding road to take a hike on Mount Baker. Autumn was just beginning in the rugged northwest. As I sat on a hard rock, I noticed snowflakes dancing in the air. Beyond the snowflakes was a towering mountain top. This was a sacred space, only accessible from July to September. It was a piece of paradise above the treeline, the rest of the year it was covered in snow. I saw a valley with a flowing river at the bottom as I looked around. To my left was a white glaciered dome. The sheer vastness of the mountains was breathtaking. I realized I was sitting amongst some of the most spectacular nature I had ever seen. I felt an epiphany wave through my entire body. *I then knew something bigger than me had created all this.* I was drawn to the energy that dwelled atop that mountain. The power of nature awakened me. The feeling of joy wrapped me in its arms. It was a sensation of pure bliss. I felt alive with a sense of freedom that things were never going to be the same again. That day, I stepped into the version of who I was meant to be.

Before, when I had been under my father and husband's watch, my life was centered on giving to other people and meeting their needs and expectations. But now I knew there was something more important and vast that was sheltering me and surrounding me. I could release myself and let go of the ties that held me back. I could rest in serving myself, cradled in the power of nature and her Creator.

The shift from that day was immense. It was a new beginning. I stepped into spirituality, connecting to a Higher Power. I went on a learning quest. I read so many books. I would spend hours in a small local metaphysical bookstore attached to a cafe across from the beach. It had crystals and card decks, candles, and positive quotes adorning the walls. The energy of that place was incredible. I had a thirst to understand and appease my curiosity. There, I felt safe, my sanctuary for years, my place of solace and regrowth.

As nature embraced me and opened my heart to a sense of joy and belonging, I grew to see my self-worth. As time created distance from the painful experiences, and joy took the place of fear and grief, I was able to look back and reflect on the journey I had taken and the role my ex-husband had played in it. I could remember the good I had seen in him while knowing his presence could no longer serve my future life. I could also take responsibility for my role in my past. Across my huge healing journey, I realized ours was a very codependent relationship and that it takes two to keep an unhealthy connection going. I had been very insecure, which could have been the root of my desire for adventure and my reluctance to find it myself. Because of him, I finally moved away from that small town. Despite the pain he caused, and in part because of it, he was the catalyst for the greatest journey of self-discovery. A journey I could have never dreamed of.

Now, filled with joy, I deliberately spend more time outdoors. I love going to the beach. There is a healing energy in listening to the waves crashing. All my troubles seem to slip away when my feet walk upon the sand. On other days, I love to escape into the forest. Camera in hand, I often step into the magical gallery of the trees, the trickling of the stream, and the lush smell of the air. Nature is a work of art. I see the joy and magic in the small flowers and greenery all around me. Nature is always putting on a show and I want to keep a piece of those experiences with me as I go forward loving life.

On my journey, I have learned that even in the most stressful situations, taking time to stop, breathe, and connect with nature can create a new direction and connection to self and something bigger than us. As we stop, connect, observe, and listen with an open heart we will discover the messages and clues that are all around us. Moments of joy are always possible and there for the taking. When you value yourself with love and care, you live your life filled with passion, purpose, and joy.

IGNITE ACTION STEPS

- **Stop.** When stress sets in, we often want to power through and keep going. It is more energizing to stop, take some time to recalibrate, and step out of our current environment.

- **Breathe.** The most immediate way to connect with nature is through your breath. Take a few long, deep breaths and exhale slowly. Do this a few times until you can feel your body relaxing.

- **Connect.** Connecting with nature is a great way to energize yourself. Stepping into the forest or planting your feet in the beach's sand are excellent ways to rejuvenate yourself. If you don't have time to get into nature, connect with an indoor plant, or better yet, keep an aquarium.

For more stressful situations, get an elevated view of what is present for you. Imagine lifting yourself to a height that allows you to get a more macro view from above. *What do you see? What needs to happen? What will you do next?* If you are a nature lover, don't forget your camera. Taking photos of nature is a wonderful way to relax and tap into your creativity.

Lydia Burchell — Canada
Speaker, Author, Coach, Facilitator, Distinguished Toastmaster
lydiaburchell.com
lydia.burchellstrand
burchelllydia

MELISSA A. CORRION

*"Create your own identity and awaken, transform,
and bask in the joy of being your true, authentic self."*

My intention with this story and my life mission is to help adoptees and other trauma survivors awaken and understand that they are *not* their trauma. It is often rooted in what happened to them in their childhood and the many generations before them. I want you to know that it is possible to become your *own* mother and re-parent yourself. I want you to know that forgiveness is for us. It allows us to move forward in our lives and become our true, authentic selves.

THE ADOPTION BLUEPRINT

I lost my mom the day I was born. The only thing I ever knew was taken away from me. The smell of her body, the sound of her soothing voice that gave me comfort, and the love and safety of her being were all stripped from me at birth. What a horrific way to come into the world. Immediately, I suffered an injury which is called the 'mother wound.'

I was relinquished at birth by my mother and then again by the mother I would spend the other part of my life with. My birth mother didn't die; she left me. I was given up for adoption. Taken away from the person who had carried me for nine months in their womb. Given to a foster family of complete strangers for three weeks. Then, off to another house that would be my permanent home. Or so the story goes. The mother wound trauma my little body endured in my first few weeks of life was enough for a whole lifetime. This was the beginning of my life of adoption trauma and 'dis-ease' in my body.

For as long as I can remember, adoption was like a flashing neon sign over my head. I have no recollection of being told of my adoption, just that I was always 'the adopted child.' My parents had always wanted a little girl. They had a hard time conceiving their two other biological children, both boys, so they adopted me. My mother made sure to tell everyone that she met that I was her "adopted daughter." I just yearned to be called her daughter Melissa; no need for the 'adopted' label. Such a distinction felt like a heavy burden I never asked for. Her classifying me seemed to be all about her making herself look good to others and feel good about herself.

I thought my biggest hurdle was being relinquished at birth, but the weight of carrying that flashing adoption sign stripped me of my identity. I also carried that weight on my physical body, manifesting as emotional eating. Nothing was ever enough, including food. Being relinquished at birth, I never felt like I had enough of anything. Being rejected from my only safety at birth was a mother wound trauma that stuck with me for life. It left me feeling unworthy and undeserving of a joyful life full of love and happiness. What compounded the pain was the lack of nurturing care I felt from my adoptive mother.

Growing up, I was taught that outward appearances mattered the most. Our house was spotless, you could see the vacuum marks on the carpet. I couldn't sit on certain furniture without being yelled at. There was rarely harmony in the house even though it was immaculate. My adoptive parents fought all the time and I spent many hours hiding out in nature or by myself in my room.

My mother defined herself by her physical appearance. She was very petite and thin. Her long, black hair was always curled, her makeup done just right, and she dressed to the nines when we were out in public. She watched what she ate, refusing to gain a single pound because that was shameful and disgusting. I was always ridiculed for my eating habits and my weight, not only by my mother but other family members and my peers. Reflecting back, I am sure shaming was part of the blueprint she learned as a child in her own home. Words had an effect on my self-esteem and worth throughout my life. Being the 'adopted heavy girl' meant I struggled trying to find a happy, joy-filled life.

We were avid churchgoers and always dressed up for church. I remember loving to hear the organ belt out the hymns in church while singing. The loud sound of music has always been an outlet for me to release some stress and fill my heart and soul with joyous excitement. It was repetitive and reliable. It made me feel safe and closer to God. I needed that as a child swirling with adoption trauma.

My mother loved to sew, so all my clothes were homemade. Of all my friends, my mother ensured I had the best clothes for my Barbies and dolls. I would have longed to learn to sew like my mother, a skill that would have been valuable throughout life, yet there was never that type of bonding with her. She could never give herself to me; she *gave* me material things instead. Just not her emotional love, which is what I needed and longed for my whole life, especially as an adoptee. I felt much closer to my dad. I was his little girl. He was the silent, quiet type who agreed with everything to keep the peace in the house. He didn't stand up for himself much, which would have benefited me as a child, but that wasn't in his blueprint either.

The trouble as an adoptee was I didn't know the blueprint I was born with, just the one I was given by the family that raised me. Not knowing where I came from and how that DNA affects me is something I have struggled with. I wasn't allowed to have that information. Growing up, I always wondered, *Where do I come from? Who do I look like? Who am I really? What is my identity?* I felt shame being told by people that I didn't look like my family. It's only in the recent past that I have found my biological parents, and it turned out that I have a half-sister that I communicate with, which is a blessing.

I have learned self-love since it was never shown throughout my life. My emotional needs were never met: anger, sadness, grief, or fear. My mother couldn't handle that, as she wasn't able to show her own emotions to her parents. So, I learned to stuff all those emotions inside me, too. More weight to carry as a child. I insulated those feelings with food so they couldn't hurt me, trying to create safety from within. I believed that I wasn't good enough because I was given away to be raised by strangers. My body has lived in fight or flight since conception, looking for the love I never received from two different mothers. Giving love to myself surely was not in my original blueprint; however, I have re-coded it into my new blueprint by rewiring my brain.

The one place you could always find me as a kid was outside. It was my safe playground. I played in the ditches alongside our house with a big stick, pretending that it was a fishing pole, looking for frogs and toads or whatever I could pull up. The smell of the lilacs would waft up my nose as I played outside in the hot summer sun. I would ride my bike with my friends around the neighborhood until the street lights came on. We would run back and forth to each other's pool, doing cannonballs and swimming like a fish until our skin shriveled. I could never get enough of the water or sun; it was my peace and serenity. It was the calm in my storm of life.

I learned to find love and joy in nature and with my cats, communicating with animals from a young age. My mother didn't like cats, yet we always had them running around the house. I knew there was a Higher Power working in my favor there. My cats were my safety and solitude. I would wrap them up in blankets and push them around in my stroller. I always talked to the birds and many other creatures when they were singing outside. That is how I learned to be compassionate and loving from nature and animals. It was a different kind of connection with them; it was safe and comforting, with no fear or flashing signs to carry. Nature and animals were my guiding life force, and still are today. They bring a calming feeling to my body, like laying in a hammock with a warm, cozy blanket looking up at the sun or stars. Maybe this is what my mothers's womb felt like. Maybe that's why I felt so safe in that space.

The older I got the more destructive life became. I took my adopted blueprint with me as I didn't know my other heritage or any other way of living. I watched my mother always have physical issues with her body, which I ended up with myself. When you stuff all the emotional feelings into your body by using alcohol, drugs, food, or whatever your addiction or outlet is, they eventually become a physical dis-ease or illness in the body. I wasn't kind to my body, the body I didn't even know I existed in. I didn't know how to feel emotional pain. I learned to feel through physical pain instead, like my mother. It was always being suppressed. All those traumas since birth were tucked away, stored deep inside me. The physical pain continued to get worse through the years, and my body paid dearly. The older I got, the more dis-ease and illness set in: auto-immune, fibromyalgia, chronic post-traumatic stress syndrome, and more.

My mother didn't teach me healthy self-care or how to make myself a priority. I never felt the joy of being loved by her, no matter how many degrees I achieved or what I accomplished. I was never enough. I do believe she loved me; she just didn't know how to show it emotionally or show affection to me. Nurturing wasn't in her blueprint. My anger grew the more I had to suppress my emotions and the more I rejected myself and my needs. I never believed I was worthy or deserved to be happy and live a life of joy and love until the day came when it was time to say goodbye to her.

She passed away early one warm spring morning. The sun was just coming up, peaking through the trees. The morning dew was still fresh on the grass, and the birds were chirping loudly. Oddly enough, the smell of lilacs was in the air, just like when I was a kid. Her room was full of bright, beautiful flowers and colorful balloons. As I said a quiet farewell to her lifeless body, I saw the blue hummingbird pecking in the bird feeder outside the window. I felt a tingle, a sense of rejuvenation and empowerment, slowly wash over me. A weight lifted off of me, and at that moment, the flashing sign went dim and fell away. *I was free!*

That was my defining moment. I vowed that I was no longer going to be defined by that adoption sign anymore. I am adopted; that is just a fact. I am no longer willing to be identified as "the adopted daughter." I am so much more than that. It was time for me to step into myself. Time for me to awaken-transform-align with my true authentic self. I knew I would make it through this adoption mother wound trauma. I would embrace the fact I was strong, important, and deserving of complete love. I decided to change my lifestyle, mindset, and old patterns so that I would not live the rest of my life with physical issues and end up with a terminal illness or disease like she did.

I have gained an awareness of why my parents couldn't show me their emotional side, which has helped with my healing journey. It wasn't in the blueprint given to them growing up. When you aren't shown that blueprint for expressing your emotions and self-love, the cycle continues with every generation until someone decides it's time to break it. That person was me and I took responsibility to ensure that my life and my children's lives would be filled with joy and play, excitement and enthusiasm, along with understanding, acceptance, and unconditional love.

I now get to change my family's trajectory by learning how to give that love to myself that I so longed for and not stuff down all those emotional traumas I have endured throughout my life. I can stop the same traumas and patterns from repeating themselves in my family by allowing love and forgiveness, and demonstrating that to my children, myself, and those around me.

While I was a child, I had grasped joy in my own little ways with my animals and playing out in nature. Now I embrace joy fully with both arms. I have learned to Ignite joy from within myself, finding that joy from the precious things in life. Smelling the beautiful flowers, hearing the birds sing, pushing my cats in their stroller, and allowing myself to just *be* without judgment. I have prioritized myself with a daily routine filled with self-care and self-love. I have built a strong foundation from the ground up. I incorporate movement and nutritious food, journaling, meditation, breath work, inner-child-like play, and shamanic drumming to bring in calmness, which helps keep my body and mind out of fight or flight.

My joy-filled life is about living in the present moment and not from my pain point, which was robbing me of my present *and* the future. It is about knowing I am worthy and enough of all this life has to offer, accepting myself just as I am. I have gained an awareness of where my food addiction came from, and now I get up and dance or go outside in nature and ground my feet into Mother Earth instead of stuffing my emotions with food.

Through prayer, shamanic journeying, biofeedback, reiki, and other holistic modalities on my healing journey over the past twelve years, I see the bigger picture of my childhood experiences. As a shamanic healing facilitator, I help others heal from their traumas and empower them to Ignite their own joy from within, from the little things they appreciate in life. Healing the mother wound has had such an impact on my life, and I am committed to helping others do the same so that everyone knows that they don't have to have a sign above their heads that says anything less than they are worthy…amazing…perfect… loved… and *Bad Ass*!

Many of us carry the heavy burden of a label we never asked for, carrying it like a neon sign over our heads. It can cause us to question who we are and wonder who truly cares for us. We learn from the words and the actions of those who came before us, sometimes falling into the cycle of repeated trauma starting from a time when we were too young to know any better. But as adults, we have all the power when we release ourselves of the adopted blueprints that limit us from pulling the plug on that sign. Once you set yourself free, you can create your identity, awaken, transform, and bask in the joy of being your true, authentic self.

Ignite Action Steps

- **Pray to God daily and give all your cares and worries to him**. He is here to guide us on our earthly journey every step of the way. Give thanks and gratitude to God for all the blessings in our life.

- **Work with a healing facilitator to get to the root of the 'mother wound' injury and solve it**. Allow someone to help you find the positive amidst the challenges.

- **Stay in a positive flow of energy**. Get outside in nature, barefoot in the grass, with the sunlight beaming on you. Feel Mother Earth giving you her love by pulling you into the earth and grounding you into a calm state of being

- **Look at yourself every day in the mirror** and tell yourself how perfectly imperfect you are. Tell the person in the mirror they are worthy, powerful, and deserve all the love and joy in the world. Use *I am* statements. *I am worthy, I am unstoppable, I am beautiful, I am love, I am courageous*, etc.

- **Light up your inner child by honoring them with play** and kid-like activities that fill your soul with joy and happiness. Get a support stuffed animal or whatever your heart desires that brings you back to your childhood, where you felt that love within your heart.

- **Listen to your favorite music** that empowers you and makes you feel alive and full of love and light. Get up, move, dance, or do whatever makes your body feel good. Movement releases pent-up stress. Music and dance will raise your vibration and bring calmness and joy within.

Melissa A. Corrion — United States of America
Shaman, Biofeedback Practitioner, Animal Communicator
www.lionheartalignment.com
Melissa Corrion
melissacorrion
lionheartalignment

Melody J. Carberry

Melody J. Carberry

"Sometimes, a little shift in your outlook can shift your entire outcome."

My intention is to spark a little joy in your everyday life. I hope that you will see what may be waiting for you just outside of your current experience, perhaps even open your heart to it. It takes a little glimpse of something that you cannot *unsee* or *unfeel* to awaken your senses. Embrace the value of surrounding yourself with people who cheer you on and open you up to new possibilities. Sometimes, a little shift in your *outlook* can shift your entire *outcome*. Your light *is* destined to shine brighter.

The Dress Club

We all know people who seem to be happy all the time. As a child, I wondered, *Do they have a secret? What could possibly allow them to have this innate ability?* Their joy seemed like a superpower. Everyone wants to be closer to them because it feels so good to be in their company. They leave things better than they came to them, something I appreciated. It didn't matter if it was a job, a position, or a group of friends. They were always leading with their heart. That created a spark of joy in me to do better and be that person who always made others feel better. Their kindness ignited an exhilaration like I could take on anything.

As much as I loved being consciously kind, I was always very quiet when I was younger. I didn't talk much but often felt a sense of joy inside. Those who know me now would find it hard to believe that I was ever quiet, but I was. I was a child who talked less and listened more. I learned that joy did not come from something I did, nor felt like pride from an accomplishment. That feeling was a warm little light inside, one I hoped shone brighter than some of my experiences growing up. Things weren't always perfect, but I knew I would be okay. A survivalist at heart, if you will.

I believe that sense of joy came from having strong women in my life like my Grandmother Lena. I loved the times my three siblings and I had with her, whether she came to town to care for us or we got the adventure of staying on the farm with her and Grandpa. I have always said she is the wisest woman I ever knew (she *was* a Grandma, after all). Always sweet and kind, never boastful, and rarely a harsh word. I only ever saw her upset a few times. That might have been when she caught us 'city kids' jumping off the barn roof into hay bales or eating the veggies right out of the garden as if we were devouring a four-course meal. She was often in the garden collecting something or other to cook for the evening meal or add to the root cellar. With her lovely dark hair always in place, she would wear pants under her dresses. That was the proper thing to do as a dress wearer who had gardening to do. One time she helped redo my whole bedroom, sewing these lovely curtains and bedding to match. It was the first time I ever felt the sense that something was just for me. I felt so important and valued. I still feel her kindness with me to this day.

Another Loving woman in my lineage was my mom, Marge, who is known to everyone in our circle as Grandma Marge. She always has a smile on her face and is the kindest person. Always asking how everyone is and never misses a birthday or anniversary, making sure that each of us has a hug and a kind word spoken to them. My Mom has been an inspiring example of dedication to my siblings and me. She also knew the value of friendships, of which she had many. Other ladies often sat around the living room or outside around a campfire during the camping season. Hearing the laughter when they gathered was always uplifting, inspiring me to want the same experiences in my life. *I want friendships like that.* Knowing the bonds of women gathering and what that feeling may have been for them, I can only imagine the joy that was being sparked in those moments.

I believe people come into your life for a reason, a season, or a lifetime. When the reason is fulfilled, you may not always keep in touch. Those who arrive for a season may be part of your world for a short period while your kids attend school together or are enrolled in the same sport. Perhaps you work together or share a common group of people for a while. At some point, change happens, and you drift apart. Then, there are the lifers that move in and take up residence in your life and heart. Their presence is never too much; you talk all day or several times a day, and your husbands can't imagine what you could possibly have left to say after the fourth or fifth call on the same day. There are no words for having a connection like this: someone who is *your person*, loves you, holds space for you, and challenges you when needed.

My lifer was Tracey, the kind of person who loved hard and was fiercely dedicated to her family. Her family became mine and mine hers. She radiated joy; she was the epitome of joyfulness. Even her middle name and her Mom's name was *Joy*. I knew Tracey was special and we just *got* each other. I would start a sentence, and she would finish it, and vice versa. Sometimes, no words were needed between us; just a look said it all. Many times, we were accused of sharing the same brain. (It felt more like we were sharing our souls.) We cherished what we had, laughed a lot, and made sure that if there was fun, we were amidst it all.

Tracey and I had such a splendid time together we wanted to spread it around, so we joined a Dress Club, a group of local women including a florist, an esthetician, and even a lady from my hometown. The club was a vibrant mix of all ages and backgrounds, pulled together by laughter and connection. Tracey and I knew a few of the ladies, so we fit in seamlessly. It was our first experience doing anything like this; it was a genuine way to spend time. We would gather for a potluck meal and conversation, enjoying getting to know one other. It was the gift of a season with these amazing women.

Then, my life shifted. My husband-to-be, Al, and I were moving for new work opportunities, and Tracy was staying put. Despite being miles apart, Tracey and I continued planning our weddings and starting our families via multiple daily phone calls. We always knew we would one day find another group of kindred spirits and perhaps rekindle a Dress Club. Distance meant nothing to us other than more "road trips." We were one and the same, a single soul dwelling in two bodies.

Tracy and I had so many beautiful moments together, rare and precious as if we had won the friendship lottery. Side by side through it all, we met who would become our husbands and planned our days of wedded bliss in time. Such an honor to be part of those new beginnings. Starting our family, we were blessed with our firstborn, Jessica. Less than a year had passed, and I was expecting our son, Christopher, while Tracey was expecting her daughter, Brenna. We were best friends with big bellies, and being pregnant together was pure joy. Brenna was born in July, and Chris was born in October; we were so in love with our littles. Life was good.

As our future unfolded, I learned that my lifetime with Tracey would not be as long as we had dreamed. We had so many more life events and great road trips to experience. Our memory banks always seemed full, and we were happy to welcome whatever was next. Then, the unsettling diagnosis: Tracey had breast cancer. *How could this be?* It felt like I had no air in my lungs; it was impossible to catch my breath. *It must be a mistake.* Tracey and her husband, Blake, had just started the beautiful family they practiced so hard for. No time was wasted. Surgery, then chemo and radiation, all became part of her daily routine. The treatments were overwhelming and, at times, brought her to her knees. Tracey was a warrior in life, and this situation was no different. I felt useless yet hopeful. We lived less than an hour and a half away at the time of her diagnosis and treatment, and I knew we needed to move back so we could be closer to her. We would raise our littles together; we had promised each other.

The next summer, I was seven months pregnant with our last son, Nicholas, when we finally made the move. Despite her treatment and happiness for the distraction, Tracey was instrumental in finding the perfect home for our ever-expanding family. It was a good move for so many reasons. We focused on love and excitement around every holiday. Any excuse for a party! Whether an egg hunt at Easter or a birthday party, every ounce was poured in. Even on the dark days, we had so much to be grateful for. Tracey was finally feeling better; we felt we were moving on from that season. So we hoped.

On an extraordinary sunny morning, Tracey's final breath was taken late in June. Al and I got the call to bring Blake to the hospital. Tracey had chosen her moment. There was a tiny window of time when no family member was in the room with her. Graciously, a dear friend would be at her bedside. Brenna, her sweet little cherub, not even three years old, knew her Mommy would not be coming home. She told her Auntie that morning when she got up that her Mom came for a visit to say goodbye. A moment of divinity that anchored what Tracey wanted most in life: to be a Mother.

I was beyond numb; no words or emotions could express the depth of this loss. Always able to find my way, believing that whenever a door closes, a window opens. Yet this time, I couldn't find the window. Tracey's passing was a really heavy door that had slammed with such force it shook me to my core. Everything had shifted; there was no time to grieve with the business of our young families. This beautiful connection I had most cherished was now this gaping hole in my heart. We *promised* we would do this together, which now meant something different. On those days, I didn't want to get out of bed. I would lean on others while others would lean on me. I was barely getting by at times and only by putting one foot in front of another. I was acutely aware that my salvation was largely in the hearts of our children, something I never took for granted.

I sought the guidance I needed through a grief counselor who assisted me in finding my way. I caught my breath, noticing that my light was still there. It was time to let some healing in for all of us. Tracey's family, my family, and most of all, Blake and Brenna. Dance started for our girls, and soccer for our boys. Then school began. The next thing I knew, I was finding myself amongst a herd of Moms and teachers, and I became a lunchroom supervisor. The world seemed to be in color again. I loved being at the school. I did scrapbooking with other moms in Mrs. Blades' class for our local Hockey Team. I needed to be busy; my family needed me to be okay. Once again, I could feel the pull of women coming together.

A conversation began one day with a few of us moms standing in the schoolyard. I felt the familiar calling of "The Dress Club." I longed for that connection with a group of women raising their families just like me. This perfect moment regarding a new girl gang sparked a joy I craved to rekindle. A time of renewal and possibility, I could feel the warmth of Tracey there with me, encouraging me to lean in. *Let your light shine*, I heard as though she was whispering in my ear.

The Divine Divas began with a desire for connection and the spark of light Igniting. Six of us lived right on the same crescent. With such anticipation, we couldn't wait to start; these excited and willing participants would certainly give reason to celebrate. We were delighted to spend one evening a month together as we decided what we wanted to accomplish. *What did each of us want to get from this new gang?* The intentions were set to do the kind of things we might not do on our own and make it fun. It was the perfect fit for me.

With ten women in total, each Diva would host one month of the year, and we would take the two summer months off. September of 2002 was the beginning of something truly divine. Every month we each eagerly gave $25 to the host Diva. She would then have $250 precious dollars to spend on whatever she chose. What a gift this was as a Mom. We rarely spent this sort of money on ourselves; there was a certain guilt attached to self-indulgence. The rule was that no bills were paid or groceries bought, but rather a permissive *something* just for yourself. Like a new outfit, a pair of shoes, or, in my case, when I was the chosen Diva, a new bed set complete with pillow shams, decorative matching pillows, and a bed skirt. The whole package. Gorgeous and decadent with gold and green, adorned with my favorite color, purple. The bed set reminded me of the delight I felt when my grandmother and I had made my room so lovely years before. Appreciating the elegance, I had never spent that kind of money on something that gave me such a thrill. I realize I shared the bed with my husband, but that prettiness was just for me. Making my bed became so much more of an exquisite indulgence, knowing it was purchased by my first Diva Dollars.

We have taken pleasure in a tremendous amount of things over the years, checking off many bucket list items. Each month, the Diva hosting would come up with an activity, anything from rock climbing to drum circles, archery, Glamping (glamorous camping), murder mystery nights, and recording *Man! I Feel Like a Diva*, our spin on Shania Twain's incredible song *Man! I Feel like a Woman*. (I want to say we gave Shania a run for her money, but her career is safely intact.) We had this little hole-in-the-wall recording studio in our city that let us sing our hearts out. Before that night, we had no idea it even existed. The mission was to delight in doing things that we may not normally do. We loved to gather, enjoying signature dishes and drinking whatever our favorite whistle-wetter was. The whole point was to be present, lift each other up, celebrate each other, and leave the night better than we came to it. Sometimes till the wee hours of the morning and most often till our stomachs ached from laughter. I love our energy, how we always put our best selves in, and our whole hearts' love for our gang. One of my favorite activities with the Divas was volunteering for our local Ronald McDonald House™. It truly was a feeling like no other when you feed a family, so all they have to do is care for their sick child. That experience gifted us with a feeling of community and connection.

Feeling the abundance of joy is overwhelming when I think about the tremendous gifts we are to each other. Sometimes it was a challenge to show up as our best selves (as well as being okay if we weren't). Either way, we lovingly held space for whichever version showed up. We have celebrated and supported one another through all of them. We gave graciously with whatever was needed, knowing that the language of the heart is simple. After almost twenty-two years together, there is no sign of a *best-before date*. Whether we took a poll or used the process of elimination on dates, we were committed. Otherwise, my FOMO (Fear of Missing Out) would get the best of me. I treasure those beauties with gratitude for all that has been shared, gifted, and freely given. Thankfully, no accounts are kept, and no repayment plans are expected. We pay in Love, food, elbow grease, and the common thread of friendship.

Not long after the Divine Divas began, The Desperate Divas were formed, all because our daughters played ringette together, a game like hockey but tougher. We were delighted in being together so much we decided to make it official and get into a relationship beyond the rink. Among gathering for meals out, we celebrate our Christmas get-together at the Little Red Barn, owned by one of our very own Desperate Divas. We feasted amongst all the laughter, then settled in for a good round of 'Secret Santa,' better known by us as the "shit gift" exchange. There are still some gifts that surface that we all try to avoid, yet these often bring the biggest howls of laughter. Both groups of divas have many similarities, and they are willingly tied together by these beautiful friendships.

Many beautiful souls have filled my cup in so many ways. Such as the women I worked alongside for almost nine years at Strategic Hearing. Even though we each had offices, I cherished our time around the table each lunch hour. Experiencing that camaraderie was such a blessing. The next group, The Inappropriates, began around a table at a fundraiser. Our founding member, our Head Inappropriate, invited each of us to join. Our collective group gathers for road trips, delighting in great shopping, food, or any new local business to support. Like so many others, these beauties are pillars of the community. Their kindred souls keep spreading joy. They share a language of unspoken willingness that nourishes my soul. As you can see, it isn't always an official club. You may find yourself in the middle of something magic right where you are, surrounded by like-minded women mirroring the same desire for connection and community.

This lifetime has shown me the importance of surrounding yourself with people who cheer you on, raise you up, and allow you to shine. This may be your family, siblings, coworkers, a partner, or maybe your friends. I encourage you to get some girlfriends that you think will offer inspiration or a safe space. Join them, or better yet, start your own Women's Club. I promise you won't be sorry. Tracey taught me the importance of friendship and so much more. Even though she is not physically here with us, we all carry her light in a way that still honors her presence. Find what sparks you and let your light be a beacon to those who cannot *unsee* or *unfeel* your joy.

Ignite Action Steps

J Join a group of women already together or create one. Show up authentically for each other. Be committed; they may need you as much as you need them.

O Offer your time, offer a hand, offer your friendship. You will never regret it.

Y Why because you deserve it. Let your light shine so bright that it becomes a beacon for others should they need to rekindle their own light.

Melody J. Carberry – Canada
Author, Speaker, Reiki Healer, Hairstylist, Director of Op, VP Dirt Werx Ltd
msha.ke/melodycarberry
Melody Carberry
@melodycarberry

Nicole Shewaga

N ICOLE S HEWAGA

"To free yourself, you must explore yourself."

I hope that the story of my relentless pursuit of freedom inspires you to follow your heart and uncover the newest, truest version of yourself. I wish for you to find the *"you"* that explores your passions and pursues joy. Join me in becoming the creators of a life beyond our wildest dreams.

A P RISONER

Change your life or die. Those were the only two options I saw for myself. Death felt like the path of least resistance. I was desperate for help, for someone to witness the shell of a human I'd become and show me the way out. My mind was consumed by shame. My body was feeble from ache. Every part of me hurt. I lay on the floor, collapsed in a heap of skin and bones; my mouth felt like sandpaper. I had been putting drugs up my nose for so long that it no longer worked. I lay there and sobbed as the hopelessness pinned me to the cold linoleum floor. I was a prisoner to opiates, a slave to the next high, chained by the weight of their hold on me.

There was one glimmer of hope, though, one shining light that I couldn't ignore: my 1-year-old daughter. For the first time, I felt a love stronger than my hatred for myself. I couldn't quit using drugs for me, but I would do it for her. She needed me, and I had to figure out how to be the mother that she deserved.

There were two central themes that paved the way for my opiate addiction: my relationship with my biological father and my undiagnosed neurodivergence. My parents divorced when I was four because of my dad's addiction. Not long after, he crashed his Mustang into a tree head-on. My 2-year-old sister and I were both in the vehicle. My sister's injuries were minimal: a broken nose and some black eyes. I was in the front seat with no car seat. I was scalped by the force of the dashboard from my eyebrows to several inches into my hairline. I broke my left shin bone and fractured my lower back. The accident gave me lifelong chronic pain and a nervous system programmed to freeze during traumatic events.

After the accident, my dad spiraled deeper, abandoning us for over ten years in his crack addiction. I formed a subconscious belief about how men show up in relationships. My father was inconsistent and emotionally unavailable. He hurt me and abandoned me. That belief would dictate how my romantic relationships played out for many years to come. I formed the belief that I must be unlovable if my own dad could leave me. This abandonment wound fueled my drive for perfectionism. *Work to become lovable.* I became obsessed with being the best: an A student, Athlete of the Year, competitive sports champion, and academic award winner. I existed in mediocrity as I collected accomplishments, an under-achieving overachiever who only sought challenges I knew I could defeat. Failure wasn't an option. No one would love me if I failed.

My drive to achieve was made even harder because I did not know my brain was wired to work differently. I spent my life unaware of my ADHD, Sensory Processing Sensitivity (SPS), and Rejection Sensitive Dysphoria (RSD). I experienced everything, my senses, emotions, failure, and rejection, with greater intensity than most. I was a highly sensitive child, and it was known early on that this was not good. My emotions were big and that was overwhelming to people. I was often told I shouldn't feel the way I did, that I was overreacting. My neurodivergence screamed, *"You can't trust yourself! Your emotions aren't valid!"* I learned that I didn't know how to be normal. Things I did unconsciously were seen as strange or corrected as poor behavior. I was notorious for fidgeting, tapping, talking to myself, and talking too much. I didn't know the right way to be. I trained myself to observe others, anticipate their expectations of me, and become that. I was a prisoner to my programming.

The lack of self-worth and trust in myself created problems in my teens. Depression hit first, and anxiety shortly after. I had no awareness of how bad my mental health was. I didn't know that it wasn't normal to fantasize about your own death. I didn't know that most people don't imagine driving full speed into a telephone pole while they drive to work. Playing a part to appease everyone caused a deep disconnect from myself, and I began to rebel. I started drinking at fourteen and using hard drugs at seventeen to numb my pain. I used MDMA for the first time after I found out my boyfriend cheated on me. I was introduced to cocaine by a different boyfriend, who showered me with praise for the 'gangster line' I railed back my first time. He was so proud of me. And that validation was the *love* I craved. Partying became a source of pleasure and a break from the dullness of trying to be perfect. Eventually, my life became a combination of grind and let loose. I worked full-time, went to university full-time, and partied full-time. My wild party lifestyle wasn't hidden, but no one saw it as a problem because I was still achieving more than most. Turns out I was just really good at being a drug addict.

As you can imagine, my beliefs and programming caused many problems in my relationships with men. At eighteen, I began dating a string of drug dealers. My mom called it Bad Boy Syndrome. I liked dating drug dealers because of the status I thought it gave me. It was also very convenient, considering how much I liked drugs. The drug dealers I dated would lie, cheat, and have narcissistic tendencies; they were inconsistent, emotionally unavailable men who would hurt me and abandon me. Just like my dad. I was a prisoner to my lack of self-worth. I was desperate to be loved.

I was twenty-one when I met 'the Angel'. He seemed like a dream come true, the perfect blend of bad boy and good guy. Our connection was deep but quickly turned to chaos. He didn't commit for the first year, bouncing back and forth between myself and many other women. We danced between our disorganized attachment styles. His anxiousness showed up in the form of jealousy and control, triggering my detachment and avoidance. Then, we would switch roles. We had three major break-ups over six years, stemming from constant cheating and betrayals. After the third breakup, I was certain I was done.

After a couple of months of grieving, I was excited to be single. I dove back into the party lifestyle, drinking and doing *all* the drugs. One night, I was asked by a friend if I knew anyone who wanted to buy a large quantity of oxycontin for a low price. Yes, I definitely knew someone who was interested. That person was me. Oxy, a magic pill that took away all my physical and emotional pain. It felt like I was floating on a cloud while getting a soft, warm hug from the inside out. Within two months, I was physically dependent on this opiate.

Six months into my opiate addiction, I found out I was five months pregnant. The shock of the positive pregnancy test drained my body of sensation. I stared blankly at a wall for four hours. I felt my baby kick for the first time that same day, like an alien sliding an elbow across my insides. Fear and excitement swirled through me like a tornado. I was spinning, but I loved her immediately. I knew she was a girl. A psychic had told me two years prior, and I could feel her. I was in a haze, but our connection was instant. I could feel the depths of love I had for the new life I contained in my body.

I wish I could tell you that my addiction ended there. It did not. I quit everything but Oxy. I justified this to myself by reading online that it was dangerous to go through withdrawal while pregnant and that some mothers continue opiate prescriptions through pregnancy. I tapered my dosage so that I wouldn't have a baby addicted to drugs, consumed by the fear of what effects my substance use might have on my baby. I'm not sure how I got so lucky, but the universe blessed me with a healthy baby girl.

The first year of my daughter's life was a downhill spiral. The post-partum depression hit quickly. By the end of the year, I had gone from using 40 to 400 mg of Oxy a day. I also started using cocaine daily to keep myself balanced. Thoughts about where I would get my next pill consumed me. Two years of physical and mental torture brought me to that day: a pile of skin and bones on the cold linoleum floor, begging for death or a savior.

The Angel showed up right when I needed him. He saw my suffering; the only one I trusted would have the emotional stability to handle the news. I confessed my addiction, and he jumped into action immediately. His strong intellect and wide network made him the guy who could solve any problem. He helped me tell my family. He connected me with a mental health and addiction nurse who planned my taper and detox. I had no choice but to get back together with him. I owed it to him to love him. He saved my life.

I was committed to getting better for my daughter, so I intuitively designed my own recovery plan rather than leaving her to go to rehab. I detoxed at home and started therapy. I explored every form of treatment I had access to. From trauma therapy to hypnotherapy, somatic therapy to psilocybin therapy, bodywork to energy work. I was desperate to learn how to feel good, and I was willing to explore any and all options. The science-based approaches, the woo-woo spiritual methods, and everything in between. I spent much of my personal time researching trauma, addiction, the mind-body connection, and anything else I thought might help me understand myself better.

Each method of healing taught me something important about myself. For four years, I did the work but kept experiencing a plateau. I was a prisoner to my mental illnesses. I would work with a new therapist, learn some things, feel a bit better, and then sink into apathy. I know now that we must cross paths with many healers and teachers to find ourselves. Sometimes, we must hear something fifty times in fifty different ways before we can process it meaningfully. Each healer has unique gifts and wisdom from which we can gain insight. I had to explore myself from every angle.

I started experiencing a noticeable transformation after working with my favorite therapist and chiropractor. They taught me how to be *in* my body and feel energetically, which changed everything for me. I didn't even know what being in my body meant. I didn't realize that the car accident and my chronic pain from my childhood caused me to be stuck in 'freeze mode' most of the time. I had very minimal awareness of the sensations in my body and often felt nothing at all. That disassociation, combined with my ADHD, caused me to live solely from the thoughts in my head. My choices and decisions came from my analytical mind and my emotional responses from a place of threat. I was stuck in a state of survival because I was disconnected from my body, my emotions, and, most importantly, from myself. Following my ADHD diagnosis, I started on prescribed medication, which gave me the mental space and emotional regulation to truly examine the root of my unhappiness and free myself from the dispassion of a life on autopilot.

Unfortunately, part of freeing myself meant leaving my relationship with the Angel. For over six months, my heart was pulled in many directions. This man saved my life. He did everything in his power to facilitate my recovery. He loved me and my daughter deeply. Together, we created a life of comfort and stability. He was my savior, but at the same time, I felt like a prisoner, suffocated by possessive love. He would say he never had expectations of me, but the harsh stabs of criticism told me otherwise. My personal interests felt minimized and unsupported. My body couldn't forgive the years of betrayal and humiliation. We tried therapy, but couples counseling doesn't work when one person thinks they're only there to fix the other. I knew the relationship was over once I understood that we weren't growing together.

I began to recognize that my needs *are* important, and I'm worthy of having them met. All of the external validation in the world would never make me feel loved until I believed I was loveable. I learned to trust that I am the only person who truly knows what's right for me, even when what's right for me doesn't align with the expectations of others. I had to learn that my emotions are valid and mine to manage; I'm not responsible for how others feel. I understood my feelings as a signal guiding me to alignment with my heart. I got to a place where I trusted myself and felt worthy enough to make a decision that I knew in my heart was right for me, regardless of how everyone else felt about it. I chose *me* from a place of unconditional love for the first time.

Twenty-four hours after I ended my relationship, I experienced what's known in the spiritual world as a Kundalini Awakening. I had come home from work feeling barely human, collapsing onto my bed face-first. I lay there for a few seconds, processing how heavy my body felt sinking into the bed. A realization struck me as a bolt of energy shot through the top of my head and down my spine. I was overcome with an electric feeling of pleasure. It rose from my tailbone, up my spine, into my brain, and flooded my entire body like a full-body orgasm. I had no idea what was happening, but intuitively, I started breathing long, slow, deep breaths. With each breath, the sensation of pleasure is built. The outbreaths caused an overwhelming pulse in my head I describe as a braingasm, and the built-up pleasure surged through my body. It continued to build, an electric ecstasy coursing through me until I couldn't take it anymore. The experience of bliss so intense without climax was too much. I sat up, shook my head, and the pleasure dissipated. I remained stunned for a moment, and then the feeling of joy rose through me, and a smile stretched across my face. *I'm finally free!*

My world changed completely after that experience. The feeling of liberation was exhilarating. I felt like I was freed from the chains of a hundred lifetimes. I started to experience the world through a new lens. The beauty of nature that surrounded me was astonishing. I noticed things for the first time, even about where I'd lived my whole life. I suddenly noticed the bright red berries and smooth green leaves that grew on the Arbutus trees. My eyes were awakened by the orange glow of a summer sunset, lighting the tree's bark in a way that made it appear neon. I watched the glistening sun dance upon the water of the Pacific Ocean. It was the first time in my life that I appreciated and felt the magic and gratitude for the vast beauty surrounding me. *This is the most joy I've ever experienced* was a thought that flooded my being numerous times over the six months as I began to rediscover myself.

There were several notable changes, but the most important one I gained was my understanding of human behavior. I could recognize the fears and patterns behind misaligned behaviors in myself and others. I evolved from a shame-filled sack of bones to someone who sees and feels beauty all around us. I learned that I could never become the best version of myself if I only did it for my daughter. I had to be willing to love myself as much as I love her. I had to unwind my old beliefs, recognize my values, and trust myself by connecting with my body and emotions. I learned that the more I explore myself, the more I free myself.

Today, I make choices that are aligned with my heart. I explore my passions and pursue fun. I ride waves of emotion with welcoming acceptance as I allow myself to *feel* through them. My self-awareness grows exponentially as I choose to be the creator of my life rather than a prisoner of my past.

Each day, I am motivated to explore and experience playfulness. My purpose is becoming clear. I feel the most liberated I've ever felt, and I can say I have truly immersed myself in joy.

When you begin to connect to your body and emotions, you meet yourself energetically, and a whole new world opens up for you. A world where you are empowered and motivated to grow. One where the idea of change becomes thrilling with potential. When you allow your emotions and energy to move through you, your nervous system begins to regulate, your triggers soften, and life around you begins to flow. By prioritizing a mindset of joy and gratitude, your highest path is lit up for you in a way that can't be ignored. Inspiration, creativity, and purpose show up, and if you follow those callings, you have the opportunity to create a life beyond your wildest dreams.

Ignite Action Steps:

- **Observe and explore your thoughts** to recognize the patterns and beliefs that are impacting the life you're creating. Ask yourself, *What truths, lies, and feelings are coming up in my life?* Then, ask, *What wound is being triggered?*

- **Sit with your difficult emotions** until they've moved through you, and you return to a neutral state. You must feel it to heal it, or the pain and discomfort will resurface. Allow your emotions to move through your body without resistance, and the core wound that's been triggered will begin to heal.

- **Practice being in your body**. Bring awareness to the sensations you feel when you're experiencing challenging emotions. Going within is how you get to know yourself energetically. Let your body guide you to discovering how you truly feel and who you're *meant* to be.

Nicole Shewaga — Canada
Freedom Seeker, Truth Teller,
Perspective Shifter, Explorer of Consciousness, Girl Mom
www.dalestales.ca
allmedale@dalestales.ca
dalestales333
dalestales333

Shirley Jones

Shirley Jones

"Detachment plus self-acceptance, amplified by gratitude, leads to joy."

I would like for people who read this to know themselves through the power of their life story. As you code your inner GPS for the journey, you will find yourself traveling through the realm of conflict. But if you keep driving, putting in the work, and trusting the promptings of your heart, your destination will be a throne of splendor. I believe that change is possible and that magic *can* and *does* happen. There are spiritual formulas that will help you achieve joyful success. Such success is defined by your relationship with God, yourself, the people around you, and the entire human race. Joy is about being in unity and peace with yourself and calibrating the vision you have for your life and those around you.

Finding Heaven After Hell; Trusting the GPS

I stood in the security line of the Montreal airport as the agent pulled from my backpack what they seemed to believe might be a weapon of mass destruction. "You can't take this with you on the plane," they stated sternly. The offending item was a bottle of very expensive baby lotion smelling of lavender. I had brought it in order to practice my daily ritual of rubbing my body with moisturizer, an act of personal self-love. I often treated myself as a baby, and my trip was all about going into reset mode!

That incident alerted me to the possibility of a dramatic shift in my perspective and understanding of myself. My initial reaction was to feel upset, flooded by cortisone, the stress hormone. The bottle of lotion had been my daily soother for so long that I stressed about how I would survive without it. I felt the pull of my long-standing tendency to take control of my circumstances. Yet, my inner GPS had been coded toward love, and that is where I knew I was headed. Getting to the plane was more important, so I avoided triggering a panic attack, released the reins of control, and just requested the backpack. They could do what they wanted with the lotion. It was time to let go of that old story.

A feeling of freedom flooded my body, and an inner courage bubbled up as I spotted a Victoria's Secret® store on my right. I had never dared to go into this kind of shop before as I had always been taking care of my more 'inner child' self. I now sensed that the woman in me was rising. Having released the baby moisturizer, something pulled me into the store as if I were being magnetized. I did a quick upgrade on my system and chose a plunging black bra with matching panties, then grabbed a pair of red ones. Two bottles of lotion, one *Coconut Passion,* one *Love Spell*, and a bright red lip gloss completed my purchase. It felt great to step into my womanhood.

Suddenly, hearing my name over the loudspeaker, I ran to the front desk, where a tall, Black security guard asked me if I had forgotten anything. Of course! In a senior moment, I had left my computer behind in the security area. Gratefully, I grabbed my precious possession as he told me that it was truly a miracle that he'd connected the computer to me in the crowd of hundreds of passengers. "Madame Jones," he said, "You have no idea how hard it was to find you." I'll never know the lengths he went to. I remembered him because I had told him that he had a 'great vibe' while I was going through security. This unusual comment must have made an impression. With my computer in hand, I was on my way to my true destination, Barbados, and love.

The road my inner GPS put me on had been long and arduous. I experienced a loss of identity at fourteen years of age when my family name, Jones, was abruptly taken away by my stepfather and mother. They had announced that I was to be known as Shirley Shore. Being stripped of my name broke my spirit, making me believe I had no control or say in my life. I fell into such a depressive state that I started smoking and drinking. My life spiraled downhill from there. I experienced sexual violence at the age of sixteen. Those events, as well as other previous traumas, caused me to suffer from Stockholm Syndrome, where I formed a trauma bond with my abuser. I married him in 1976, and we had three sons and two daughters together.

We did the best we could in our relationship with what we knew. As I reflect on my journey of forgiveness for my former husband I can admit he was an excellent provider. However, I did not feel like I was in a partnership and was constantly anxious about sharing a home with him. It's unfortunate that many relationships start out on the wrong foot like this, with a lack of understanding of what consent means. For years, sex was an aggression I felt perpetrated against me, though I mislabeled it as love. It wasn't until 1985 that I fought for my right to decide when and how I wanted to have sex. I became a member of the Baha'i Faith because of the central principle of equality between men and women. The use of violence is prohibited, so once I understood that I stood my ground and started to take my first steps out of *Hell*, letting my inner GPS guide me toward Heaven instead.

I raised my children and endured that marriage for thirty-six years, as my inner guidance directed me to stay the course. I didn't want to do to my children what had been done to me as a child, making them bear witness to a violent divorce. I had no control as a child, but I was taking control in my own way by remaining there, on the outskirts of *Hell*, to give my children stability and security. But once they were grown, I had nothing left to anchor me to where I was. It was not home anymore, and I needed to find my way toward a different destination. I made the choice to leave, at last, and programmed my inner GPS to head out toward real love. I was determined to trust the process and to follow the signposts provided to me.

Through ten years of independent living, I learned to become my own best friend, finding myself more and more along the way. The transformation of my energy made it easier to see where I was headed next, following the Goals, Purpose, and Strength within me.

The culmination of my energetic shift included a vision of a whole new beginning for myself, my own business as a Story Alchemist, and having a loving partner. A few months before my 66th birthday, I rewarded my years of hard work with a trip to Barbados. I had dreamed of going there since I was a young girl, smelling the salty air emanating from my aunt and uncle's suitcases as they traveled to the island twice a year. How I longed to go to such a magical place and now I was on my way.

I left Montreal with new lotion and undergarments, a new mindset, and complete confidence in my inner guidance system. Eager and unaware of what would unfold, I landed on the beautiful island of my dreams. My host met me and escorted me to his home, where I had rented a room to enjoy my nine days in Barbados. As soon as I set eyes on him, my whole world shook in a constellation of gratitude.

We were destined, in spite of physical markers or painful histories. Me a 65-year-old Caucasian woman with a story of hellish proportions. He a 55-year-old Bajan native to Barbados, his skin color as rich as chocolate with his ancestral roots embedded in a history marked by the devastation of slavery. I learned he was an incredible man, a pillar of his community. He had a stellar record of service and many warm and loving friendships with people. I didn't know it at the time, but our two worlds were about to Ignite.

Our energy came together in a divine flow. His interest in me became noticeable and genuine quite quickly. He asked me if I wanted to get married again after knowing him for just a couple of hours. And I said *yes!* However, I stated that I was very particular. I explained that I wanted a friend first and foremost. He nodded his assent. Definitely, friendship is essential, it is the bedrock of all relationships. It is the highest form of relatedness because it's completely voluntary.

The first evening of my arrival, he guided me down the path to the ocean. I was on his left-hand side, and it was dark; I couldn't see very well. As we came closer to the beach, I took a step to the left, and my feet went out from underneath me. Unbeknownst to me, a canal was created to move water overflows through the town. Mercifully, it was only about a foot deep. Falling forward on my face, slamming my chest into the beach sand, I was thankfully unharmed. At the moment of impact, it dawned on me that this was a sign from God and that I must pay close attention. Yet, I felt a close hand of support and nurturing care from my guide. I deduced that the Creator was telling me that this was something to pay attention to, to take notice of. As we watched the waves wash up on shore, I surrendered to the path that God had laid forth for me and wondered what this man's role would bring to my life.

As time passed, over the course of nine days, we noticed the harmony and unity in our movements. We cooked together; he taught me recipes from his tradition, like delicious coucou, a bread laced with okra and based in cornmeal. We gobbled it up with breadfruit salad and barracuda. We did ordinary things: swimming in the ocean, walking into town, going to church. I was falling in love with him and the setting, the people, and the energy.

I wondered where this friendship would go and if it was written in the stars. All I knew was that by his side, I bloomed like a thirsty rose watered with a shower of grace. In the presence of this man, I felt like a grown-ass woman, not a crickety old lady or a little girl. He charged me up spiritually. He demonstrated attentiveness, intelligence, and intuition and was very protective.

I felt so much fun enjoying the sensation of love, the emanation of the roots of relatedness, and the steady heartbeat of the universe as it opened up the portals of possibility. I was conscious of the road I traveled to find him and, more importantly, myself. I was ready and strong enough to face the future, even if it was uncertain. *Who knows where this is going to go?* All I know is that Love has winged its way towards me and perched on my shoulder. No doubt it will be challenging from time to time; so be it. Such is life. I'll take it all in my stride, practicing my formula for joy, detachment, plus self-acceptance, amplified by *gratitude*.

The formula for joy and inner peace begins by allowing ourselves to detach from our past and learn how to forgive ourselves and everyone in our story. This leads us to activate more self-acceptance. When we feel a deeper acceptance of ourselves, the recipe for success is amplified and begins to bubble with gratitude and emanate self-love. In a state of self-love, we become our authentic selves, who we truly are. Then, we mirror the love that we desire to manifest. Letting go of an old habit made way for a whole new state of being, at one with myself… and now, with someone new.

In the discovery of newfound love, internally and externally, I was awakened to the gratitude of my past. I wouldn't have the capacity to appreciate the Heaven I found without having traveled the path from Hell. I am grateful to my former husband and the spiritual musculature I developed during our time together. Finding compassion and forgiveness was invaluable in my journey toward my new Heaven on earth. Because of that marriage, I have five beautiful, talented, amazing children and grandchildren. I am grateful for them and the joy they allowed me to feel as a mother, even in the moments when I miss them as they live their own adult lives. In the process of moving forward, while reflecting back, I feel that I am truly on a new aligned path, living according to my newly defined Goals, Purpose, and Strength.

I have found joyful success, discovering how relational all of life is. Through my relationship with God, with being my own best friend, and then my friendship with the other members of my human family I resonate at a higher frequency, dissolving my past and creating a joyful future. Human consciousness *is* one. We are drops of one ocean and waves of one sea. As I swam at the Barbados beach, I became more and more aware that we are reflected in the faces of the people we meet. In our endless diversity, we mirror each other. If we study them, the currents of the water help us understand that we must be flexible and have a unity consciousness to solve the world's problems.

There is a current in Spirit. It is clear to me that there is a design in which we live, and it develops our capacities. Whenever anything happens, we learn from it and take a step towards our personal vision of Heaven.

I see the pattern God designed for me to develop into a woman who has the eyes of her empathy open wide to people's hearts and senses their vibration. Who listens attentively and reflects what she hears, who can distill the murmurings deep within their soul to its essence.

I do not know what the future holds for this new love I have found, but what I do know is that regardless of whether it is with myself or another person, I am dedicated to focusing my attention on what is going on inside my heart. I know that being in integrity with myself is the most important action I can take.

I hope that these words have touched your heart. All relationships can be healed, and all relationships matter. We are all connected with God`s indissoluble bond. We are One. All I know for sure is that now I am in the flow of Heaven's energy after living through what I no longer call hell, but the divine guidance during the course of my life. I am following this vibration of love, detachment, gratitude, self-acceptance, and ultimately *heavenly* joy!

When you realize the difference between the frequencies of heaven and hell, you must decide to tune into the frequency you prefer. This requires self-discipline, and this is the power of your GPS. Dial into your Goals, Purpose, and Strength. Find the love you have within you. Be willing to take a trip of a lifetime because when you do, you step into a life of joy and magnificence.

IGNITE ACTION STEPS

- **Keep your first attention on yourself**; as the airplane security plan goes, put on your oxygen mask first.

- **Keep a journal** and write down the stepping stones of your life. This will inform you about what your memories are, and you can harvest the lessons. Just keep asking yourself: *What did I learn?*

- **Decide on a way to heal yourself** by doing a practice like twelve steps, yoga, meditation, gratitude, and/or energy healing. Get a Coach.

- **Attract yourself to people who are attentive and caring** and with whom you can be yourself. Your tribe is a reflection of you, so be intentional.

- **Surround yourself with people of every color**, because they have a perspective and diversity that is important and valuable to us. We need to be humble and willing to learn and grow. We must dismantle our prejudices and let go of racist behavior, learn how to be a true friend, and see what matters from within. All hearts are the same color.

- **Shift your vibration** by practicing gratitude every single day, writing it down, and saying it out loud. It is very powerful, and you can learn to practice it in every moment. Gratitude is like a scrub brush and a hot, soapy water bucket. With it, you can clean off the mirror of your heart of all limiting beliefs and step into unity consciousness, where we are one with ourselves and with those around us.

Shirley Jones — Canada
Story Alchemist
www.mystoryalchemist.com
shirley.jones.99
shirleyjones.ca
shirleyjones999
shirleyjones.ca

Stacey Tompkins

Stacey Tompkins

"Your life is worth the fight!"

When going through hard times, it can be a challenge not to get stuck in the depth of the emotions that each struggle brings. My intention in sharing my story is to remind the reader that when life throws you unexpected curveballs, you ultimately get to choose how you will let them affect you. Giving up is not an option! I believe that when you give up, you can easily lose sight of what could be. Instead, when you choose to fight and persevere, doors will open that you didn't know existed, and the life you dream of will then be possible. Joy comes in life when we are aware enough not to take the little things for granted. Embracing happiness and choosing forgiveness can transform how you heal and live your life.

A Dream Interrupted

I had it all planned out. A new baby to love and bond over, new memories, a sibling for my stepson, and an opportunity to bring a child into this world. I pictured holding my new baby so close that their heart would beat alongside mine, knowing that the little life in my arms depended on me. I imagined chasing my toddler around the backyard as they giggled and squealed with joy. Adding to our family was something my husband and I both dreamed about.

Getting pregnant was years in the making. After all the doctor's appointments, surgery, and fertility treatments, I was finally expecting. I knew a new baby would bring us all joy and connection and add so much life and love to our family! Together, we would build a life and enjoy the simple joys, like movies, bedtime stories, sunny days outside, and walks in the forest. I was beyond ready for all of the new experiences and excited for this next phase of my life to begin!

Nine months quickly passed by; it was time to have a baby, and I thought I was as prepared as possible. Being a nurse, I learned about labor and delivery in school and witnessed it firsthand. I found it astounding how a woman's body not only can grow life inside but also has the ability to transform, shape, and contract to deliver life into this world. I knew childbirth could be so many things — raw, beautiful, intimate, painful, joyful, and challenging — and I was ready to experience it all! The plan was to have a delivery as natural as possible and let my body do what it needed to do. I was excited to take on natural labor and show my husband what I was made of. I felt good, was in great shape, and thought I was mentally prepared for what was to come. I was determined that the delivery of my baby was going to be relatively "normal." I had it all planned out.

I went into labor at midnight; the contractions came hard and heavy. I remember my husband pulling the car over so I could vomit on the way to the hospital, something I would do again when we arrived. Every two minutes for the next ten hours, I would experience pain unlike anything I had ever felt before. I had what you would call back labor. Essentially, this means the baby is faced the wrong way, sunny side up, and the back of the baby's head and shoulders push down on the Mom's spinal nerves during every contraction. The pain was excruciating!

I remember early in the night lying on my side, grunting and hollering like an animal in pain while I shook and death-gripped the rail of the hospital bed. None of the traditional labor techniques worked. There was no conscious emotion; my body had the reins. At some point, I was convinced to try the bathtub; just getting there was a challenge, but the water gave me relief. I positioned myself on my knees to let gravity do its job. I was stubborn and determined to do it my way, and with the help of my husband at my side, I was convinced that *I got this*. When each painful contraction hit, I reached to grab the side rails, rose from my knees, and thrust my hips forward to offset the agony. I was so in the zone of labor to realize what was happening or how I might be hurting myself. The nurses checked on me intermittently, but it wasn't in me to receive any help or direction. Eventually, I was so exhausted that I lay fully submerged on my left side. But my body did not give me any rest, and the contractions continued. Every two minutes for the next four to five hours, I hyperextended my left side and contorted my body as I reached up to the grab bars and simply tried to cope.

When morning came, it was time to see how much my labor had progressed. I very slowly got out of the tub and was escorted back to my room. I had nothing left and finally agreed to receive something for the pain to get me through. The final stages were so hard! Soon after that, my body was ready, and that baby was coming whether I was ready or not. As I grunted and pushed through each contraction, I watched the doctor and nurses discuss my progress at the foot of the bed. They looked at me with intermittent encouragement and concern on their faces. The doctor coached me through each contraction and urged me to push hard, but eventually, it felt like there was so much pressure, and my baby wasn't moving through the birth canal. The doctor told me that I needed to open my hips more, but I couldn't! I remember yelling at him, "I can't!" because my hips felt locked into place. But he kept encouraging me, and I felt the urgency in his tone. I worried that my baby wasn't okay or that I would be rushed into surgery, so I forced my legs open and consequently felt a "pop" in my hip. *Hmmm.* I would worry about that later. Finally, my baby was able to turn her body inside of me and was welcomed into the world. *I made it. We made it.* I had a healthy, beautiful baby girl. She was perfect in every little way.

We spent the next twenty-four hours at the hospital. I quickly realized that getting out of bed was extremely hard. My groin, legs, and pelvis were incredibly sore, and I could hardly walk! I was grateful that my husband and friends were there to escort me back and forth the short distance to the bathroom. I struggled to get out of bed; moving my body ached, and it took so long to do anything. I thought this immobility was normal; I had just given birth to a baby, after all. I was eventually discharged with a healthy baby, and as far as the nurses were concerned, I was okay as well. My mobility and the pain related to my movements were never assessed. I only suspected something was wrong when I attempted to walk to the nursing station, and I only made it to the room next door. I thought I just pulled some ligaments and dismissed it, assuming it would be fine in time. My husband grabbed a wheelchair, and the three of us headed home.

I was beyond excited and blessed to be a new mom; I was in love with everything my daughter brought to my world. I was thrilled to experience all of her 'firsts' with her. She was a happy baby who ate, slept well, and was an absolute joy to be around. I chose to be intentional with my time and to focus on all the amazing little moments with her; this got me through. I chose happiness over focusing on the misery that my pain brought. But I was tired. Really tired. I didn't yet realize it, but I had acquired injuries that would probably affect me in one way or another for the rest of my life.

At our two-week check-up, I consulted my doctor about the pain. At the time, we both thought that all I needed was a little bit of physiotherapy to fix me up. I was anxious to feel normal and wanted my mobility back so I could enjoy this new phase of life with my family. So, I religiously went to appointments. For the first year, my daughter and I were in and out of physio two times a week. We got good at feeding on the go, and she became my little appointment buddy. I would lay on the bed and nurse while the physio machines worked on my leg; it was quite the adventure. I did what I could for that first year to aid in my healing. I tried acupuncture for inflammation and massage to calm the muscles, but even with all the therapies, the relief was temporary, and nothing fully worked.

At the time, I felt relentless pain for twenty out of twenty-four hours a day. I was coping, but it was a struggle. When my daughter slept at night, I would toss and turn because, no matter how I lay, I was in pain. For the first two months, my thigh would randomly go into muscle spasms that would have me bolting out of bed and pacing the hallways in the middle of the night. Lying on my left side was impossible due to the deep gnawing aches it created, and shooting sensations plagued me when I tried to sit still during the day. Sleep deprivation and the constant awareness of pain were also emotionally draining. I felt robbed of the "new mom experience." Spots along my left pelvis, hip, and leg were constantly irritated by what felt like a "pop" or "snap" of the ligaments and tendons rolling over each other. The smallest movements would cause this to happen and set off a cascade of inflammation and agony! When I climbed stairs, I would feel tears in my groin. Any long-distance walking wasn't an option.

I had to say "no" to lots of activities with family or friends, and it crushed me to do so. The isolation and disconnect got heavier and heavier to carry. I felt the constant pull of sorrow, asking, *Why me?* I didn't let the injury destroy me, but for moments, I felt alone, unable, and exhausted. Even when support-ive friends and family surrounded me, I felt very alone. I didn't want to make my pain their problem and did not want to burden them with how constant the agony was.

I loved being a mom and was beyond in love with the baby girl in my arms; our connection was exactly as I imagined it would be. She brought so much joy and love into my world, and being her Mom was such a blessing. But I felt cheated by the injuries I sustained, and the daily agony took over some of the dreams I had for all of us. It didn't feel fair that though I was prepared, my body still let me down!

I'm stubborn, and I've never been one to take lots of medications. Because I was breastfeeding, this also made treating the pain difficult. Ice packs, tensor bandages, and essential oils became my best friend. There were many nights that I would tensor an ice pack to my leg to numb the pain so I could sleep completely. Ice burns were a regular occurrence but were worth it because they helped. Eventually, I gave in and made do with over-the-counter medications. I took as much as I could, but at times, they, too, weren't enough. Month after month, I went to all the medical appointments that I could, but sadly, it wasn't helping, and when one part of my injury would get better, another would flare up. I knew in my heart something was seriously wrong and that I needed to do what I could to get my body back.

I researched constantly to see what might be wrong with me. I thought that if I knew, maybe I could find a way to fix it. With each new idea I discovered, my doctor would agree to order new tests. MRIs of my hip showed nothing, ultrasounds came back normal, and the tests suggested there was nothing wrong with me. Yet, after a year of constant treatments, I still couldn't walk for more than two blocks, I couldn't sleep on my left hip, and I continued to suffer relentlessly. I grieved the body I used to have. I grieved being able to be active with my family: hiking, playing sports, and traveling were things that brought us close. I missed sleeping without pain. The fear of making my pain worse dictated my life and my choices, and I consciously fought to compartmentalize my emotions. Who I was able to be and what I could do had changed; I missed who I was! But worst of all, I had a dream of healing and having another baby. The reality of adding to our family was sadly becoming further and further from my reach, and this devastated me. I knew I couldn't risk the chance of being more debilitated from another pregnancy. I was already maxed out on my ability to keep it all together!

After a year, the realization finally hit that this pain wasn't going away any time soon. Moving forward, I had some decisions to make. *How was I going to let this affect my life? Would I let this injury permanently debilitate me? Or would I choose, despite it, to have the life that I dreamed of and be the mom, wife, and person I wanted to be?* As I moved through these questions and reflected on the life I wanted to live, I knew I didn't want this injury to hold me back. The suffering wouldn't continue to hold power over my life; I was! It was then that I knew it was up to me to choose optimism and live life the best I could despite my injury; giving up wasn't an option!

I was determined to live in life's 'little moments' and the joy they brought. I chose to focus on what I could do instead of what I couldn't and to not take things for granted. I allowed myself to feel the heavy emotions intermittently but decided I wasn't going to let the weight of everything define my life or who I was going to be. I slowly… very slowly, began the journey to healing. I started to learn what aggravated my injury but also what helped. I did everything I could to support myself and became the first line of defense against a never-ending cycle of pain. As a family, we were able to adjust our expectations to how we could spend time together so activities wouldn't hurt me. I leaned on God, my wonderful husband, and my loved ones for strength and intentionally created opportunities for growth, joy, and love in my life. This meant allowing my heart to swell with pride and joy as I watched my children learn and grow, feeling the love and connection as I read bedtime stories, melting to 'couch cuddles' and long, comforting hugs. I felt the satisfaction of cooking delicious meals, enjoyed laughter with family and friends, celebrated winning when we played games and cherished the love and banter that we had with one another.

As a family, we planned adventures where we went camping and did hikes that I could do. Mother nature brought connection, nurtured me, and healed my soul. The sun warmed and energized every cell in my body. The paths we walked on gave me a feeling of calm as the smells of dirt, dew, and trees tantalized my senses. Rivers and waterfalls washed away my worries as we spent hours throwing rocks into the water. I cherished all of these times! My marriage also weathered the storm, and though I wasn't physically the same anymore, we were able to find ways to connect and still chose to love each other fiercely. I pursued a love of photography and entrepreneurship and changed jobs so life could be what I wanted it to be. Knowing I would only have one baby, it became a priority to ensure that I had time to take in every moment of being a Mom that I could. Even though I was in pain every day, life did not stop, and I embraced it!

I also continued to be relentless in my journey to healing. Finally, in year two, I saw a neurologist and learned of nerve damage to explain some of the pain, and eventually, a bone scan identified problems in my pelvis. But it wasn't even close to all the answers. I was still tormented daily and grasped at whatever hope I had left. I was willing to try anything and everything and spent a small fortune doing so. I wanted my body back! After three years passed, I made one final appointment where I pleaded with my doctor to see what else I could do. It was then, at the age of thirty-one, that I was told that I would have to live with chronic pain and disability for the rest of my life. There was nothing more my doctor could do (other than medications). I was devastated!

The fight was hard, and at that moment, I wasn't okay! My life was supposed to be starting, and I wasn't prepared to have a lifetime disability. For a while, I felt sorry for myself, but then I used my anger to propel the determination I needed to carry on. God willing, I would find the help I needed! Instead of dwelling on it, I doubled down on my mindset to not have my injury define my life. I once again continued to focus on all the things that brought joy to my world and carried on with the healing journey.

Slowly, through perseverance, I started to heal. Because I never gave up, I finally met a team of chiropractors and a naturopathic practitioner who truly cared and helped my injury. It gave me hope, and I slowly found other people who were also willing and capable of helping. Since then, I have undergone so many adjustments to realign my pelvis and spine, soft tissue work, injection therapies, strength training, and various muscle and joint therapies. With the help of these amazing people and my ongoing learning, trial and error, I finally understood the extent of my injuries and how I could help them.

I learned that I most likely partially dislocated my hip and pubic joint when it "popped" during delivery, and the ligaments and tendons in my legs were likely hyper-stretched and micro-torn when I was in the tub. Because of that, I have scar tissue, and my joints won't always stay in place. My muscles constantly spasm to compensate. My nerve injuries affected everything and took forever to heal! I now understand how my body is connected and how treating one aspect will help another. I learned that when trauma is involved in an injury, it is also important to process and forgive the emotions that the injury holds. Through all that learning, I have slowly been able to heal and put my body back together.

Now, eleven years later, I can honestly say I am living life to the very fullest, and I have been for quite a while. Though I still have days with pain and suffer flair-ups that set me back, there aren't many things that I can't do anymore. Once upon a time, I would have thought I would never move in the ways that I do now. But, for the last five years, I have been able to be active again, doing what I love. I get to dance hip-hop a couple of days a week and share a dance studio with my daughter. Dance is very freeing and brings so much joy to my life. I continue to soak up the great outdoors, and traveling has been possible once again. Finally, I can sit for long car or plane rides without relentless pain. When I work as a nurse or a photographer, I can move fast and freely, push wheelchairs, and chase children. I no longer have to worry anymore about how long it will take to walk somewhere, and the pain rarely distracts me from what I have to get done. Finally, I feel free!

I could have given up, but I didn't! I am proud of what I have overcome. I am not 100% better by any means, and I don't know if I ever will be. Life is truly good, and I believe that what I have been through has given me a deeper perspective on what other people face in life. The experience has made me better because I don't take the small things for granted; life continues to be filled with richness and joy. I am enjoying all of it! The dream I am living today may be different than what I planned, but I most certainly am living my best life, and I am grateful for it all. It is only up from here.

Life will always give us challenges; it is how we approach those challenges that determines the success we have. In life, we are often told, *no, it's impossible*, but if you believe it is and persevere, anything can happen. Sometimes, we can not do it alone; it is important to find your tribe that will support, uplift, and invest in helping you. With the determination you have inside, you are capable of doing anything you set your mind to. So fill your life with joy and follow your dreams. The little moments in life are worth everything.

IGNITE ACTION STEPS

- **Be relentless in your journey to healing**; when you hit one roadblock, turn around and try a different road.

- **Choose joy, an optimistic mindset, and practice gratitude**. Even when life is getting you down, if you write out what you are grateful for and choose to think about what is good in your world, you and those around you will reap the benefits.

- **Each therapeutic medium you try can be a stepping stone** into healing. Research what might help and give it a chance to help you. Try more than one appointment before you give in. Sometimes, what you least expect to help will make a big difference.

- **Give yourself permission to feel the emotions of the healing process** and find balance in the perseverance to get better. Find outlets to discuss the emotions you feel and allow the feelings to flow. It's okay to be done *trying* at times, sometimes our minds and bodies also need a rest from the fight. Once you feel rested, more healing work can be done.

- **Surround yourself with people who uplift you**, support and encourage you. Seek out people who are willing to listen and think outside of the box to help.

Stacey Tompkins — Canada
Licensed Practical Nurse, Professional Photographer, Mom and Wife
www.staceytompkinsphotography.com
 Stacey Tompkins Photography
 Stacey.Tompkins.Photography

Stacie McCracken Callan

STACIE MCCRACKEN CALLAN

*"When Joy and pain collide, the universe is about to deliver
a blessing. Be patient..."*

If I could deliver wishes, dreams, or miracles, my purpose would be fulfilled. Since only one can award such blessings, I will merely share my many stories in hopes that my trials, tribulations, and comebacks can inspire others to keep pressing through. My promise to God is that I will always do good even when no one is looking and will continue to help those around me, even when I can't help myself. In sharing this personal story, I hope anyone struggling to navigate their own rocky storm should be brave and focus on the best possible outcome to stay strong, be conscious of their faith, and believe in the unseen. My wish is for the readers of this book to finally find the joy within.

YOU ALWAYS HAVE A CHOICE

The year of hell: 2020. For me, it was as if humanity got completely knocked off its axis. In the beginning of 2020, life was good. I had spent nearly a decade building not one but two successful businesses. I was married, my four daughters were doing well, we traveled as a family, and I was knocking things off my bucket list one by one. From the outside looking in, my life was like a dream. I had experienced miracles and had been blessed many times. I had lived more in forty years than most have in a lifetime.

In the blink of an eye, it all came crashing down. Like a domino effect of torment, my life began to unravel. It was like the universe had said, "Oh, wait a minute. We forgot this one over here. She's had an extended period of happiness."

I remember the deep uncertainty like it was yesterday. The news started to hint towards a massive pandemic that could leave our country devastated. A "shutdown" would occur. That was five days prior to my state's apocalyptic closure, which was like something from a movie. Everything was closed. I'm not just talking about businesses closing their doors and everyone wearing a mask. I am talking about no people on the sidewalks, no cars, or deers walking across the main streets in our biggest cities. It was as if all human forms ceased to exist.

I recall what we all felt. *"Is this doomsday? Is the world ending?"* My businesses were forcefully shut down; the accounts dwindled by the second, and the fear of losing everything I'd ever built heavily weighed on my mind. At that moment, I made the choice to see this as a gift. Amidst the fear, I did my best to stay positive for my family. I stopped watching the overzealous, repetitive, negative news. I started to read and exercise. I had created a 'chart of hope' for my family and taped it to the kitchen pantry door. It was an estimated countdown to when we thought things would return to "normal." Every morning, we would mark an X on the countdown, and then we would go on to plan a fun-themed dinner for the evening. We even hosted our own dinner parties and murder-mystery nights. We played games together for the first time in years. As a type A personality and one who was used to burning the candle on both ends, I needed to focus my energy on my family and their well-being.

I found Joy in that time with my family. A joy that hadn't been there in years from all the rushing about I was doing – four girls, twelve sports teams, two businesses, investment properties, employees, and the "rat race." Now we were all together, laughing, sharing stories, loving one another. My God gave me a gift in that moment. He gave me that feeling of family one last time before they all would leave the nest. Despite the struggles and uncertainty, the pandemic finally showed me how to let my faith be bigger than my fears. A lesson often preached about but rarely practiced. A lesson that I now fully understand. When your hands are tied, and there appears to be no way out, bow your head and lean on God. I found joy in the middle of my fears, making it much easier to lean into my faith.

Months later, as business resumed, a new norm had crazed my real estate company. The world as I had known it was forever gone. We were running harder and faster than ever before. In an area where an average agent would typically sell one to three million a year in sales, myself and another from my team were busting out nearly fifty million in roughly six months. It was pure mayhem! We were exhausted, to put it lightly. People were irritable, unkind, and just plain shitty to one another. I had found pride in the relationships I built in my twenty-plus years in the industry. I was always good at letting go of a tense negotiation and giving the other side the benefit of the doubt that they were just doing what was right for their client. Now, I was turning into everyone else. I was irritable and short with people; I found myself saying things I would never have said… Or felt. We were all tired, making us the worst versions of ourselves. The tension ran high; my body hurt every day; I felt what anxiety was like for the first time… boy does that suck! Running on little to no sleep, stomach issues, migraines, joint pain, and a slew of other health issues sank in. The more that piled up, the more angry I became. It cost me. It cost me good people, my peace of mind, and time that I couldn't get back. I wasn't the only one suffering; the global shutdown also affected my children; their childhood was stolen. They lost their traditions. No prom, no formal graduation, no grad dance. No blissful childhood memories were left for them, just the residual of fear.

Despite all the negativity that was swirling in the world, little did I know that a blessing was secretly falling upon us. As the world reopened, the real estate industry skyrocketed, and people wanted their lives back and were more eager than ever to make a move. Our bank accounts not only bounced back, they catapulted! With the additional funds, I could take my kids to Europe, put ample amounts into their college funds, and even build a wine cellar that year. Looking back on the memories of those trips, having watched my eldest navigate her college years, and the peace, serenity, and stillness that I embrace every time that I sip a glass of wine in "the Grotto" (my wine cellar)… Each sacrifice was not in vain because, in the end, it *did* bring me a form of joy. We managed to thrive as a family through a seemingly impossible time. As I moved my second eldest into college for her first year, it was with a heavy but proud heart that we said our goodbyes amidst cherished memories.

Exactly five days later, my world would change forever. I was standing on the dock at my cottage when a call came in. "Sadie was in a bad accident, and you need to meet the ambulance at the hospital." The worst pain, fear, and panic any parent can endure is the possibility of losing a child. As I sit here today, I can still recall the immense fear that ran through my body at that moment. With very few details, I truly felt as though my daughter might die. To describe that feeling is nearly impossible. Imagine the worst physical pain coupled with your saddest moment and multiply it by a billion, and even then, it doesn't come close to reaching the level of terrifying worry a parent can feel. It is more like an out-of-body experience, one I struggle to describe.

Upon getting the call, I remember visualizing the most horrific automobile accident imaginable. I made the assumption that she was in a car accident, and that was when my mind ran wild. My sweet, sweet girl is lying somewhere in terrible pain with no help. It was every parent's worst nightmare.

I would later learn Sadie and her friend, due to their school's COVID-19 restrictions, decided to come home for the weekend. The girls had returned to town and decided to visit the animals on Sadie's father's farm. The two of them had taken the all-terrain vehicle (side-by-side) up to visit the animals, a drive that she had driven a hundred times. That day was different. When leaving the farm, Sadie gave the gas pedal hell, which is typical for teenagers. Not knowing that the town had just graded the dirt road, she hit a corner and completely lost control. As the ATV started to tip, the girls' "best day" became a nightmare. Emily was left in the ditch with a severe concussion and a fractured pelvis. Sadie was inevitably dragged down the road with the ATV and was found some distance from Emily. She was face down in the dirt and awoke to a horrible pain in her ankle. Thankfully, the shock she was in numbed her brain from the reality that was right in front of her and about to unfold. Sadie's leg looked like one of a soldier's during the war; a huge hole was gapping in her lower leg. The girls lay there for more than an hour before anyone found them.

In the minutes following the call, my heart didn't just sink; I think that the devil himself ripped it from my chest. A pain ensued throughout me; not a physical pain but an emotional anguish that carried the weight of the universe. To me, my little girl was gone. As I ran through the kitchen, frantically grabbing my keys, it was as if a lightning bolt of consciousness jolted through my body. I was reminded that my mindset is my biggest tool. I knew that the outcome was grim and that the only thing I could do was to change my mindset and, hence, change the outcome. I felt as if she was not going to make it, and I had a choice to make. I dropped to my knees and began to pray. I asked God not to take her. I used my strong intuition, belief, and inner knowing to change my fearful thoughts. I knew I only had mere moments to shift the trajectory of what was playing out in my mind. I used manifestation to reset the narrative of the horrible story I envisioned. I focused on what I wanted, not what I feared. I began to pray and continued to repeat, *She's going to be alive. Please don't take her.* I will never forget the feeling in my soul when I got in the car to head to the hospital. I pleaded with God that amongst all of the 'bad seeds,' the world *needed* more Sadies. She's a rare one, with a kind heart and a pure soul.

Upon reaching the hospital, we were told that because the kids were now eighteen, we wouldn't be allowed inside the ER, given the COVID-19 restrictions. "Are you f**king kidding me?" They were going to have to arrest me; there was no way I was not seeing my daughter. The inevitable moment arrived as I stood in the parking lot waiting for the doctors. The doctors came outside and asked who Sadie's parents were. With a heightened level of fear and frustration, I spoke up. They then proceeded to say that only one parent could come into the hospital as Sadie was being transported to a larger facility where a trauma, ortho, and plastics team would be awaiting her arrival.

Without hesitation, I rushed in to see her and quickly made arrangements to head south. The other hospital had to make an exception for me to be able to enter with Sadie. The determining factor was that even though she was eighteen, she would have life-altering decisions that were just too difficult to make on her own.

In an instant, the workaholic inside me had evaporated, something I never thought would happen. After years of working eighty-hour weeks, running myself ragged, and determined never to leave a task incomplete… suddenly none of it mattered. The choice was easy. Without hesitation, I sent a message to my staff and agents. I told them I wouldn't be coming in on Monday and that I didn't know when or if I would be back, and frankly, I didn't care whether I ever returned. Nothing else mattered at that moment but my daughter. I now know that, as with Sadie, my own life lessons were unfolding.

The first days at the hospital were indescribable. I listened throughout the night and into the following day as my child cried out in pain for nearly twenty-seven hours straight. She lay there with a gaping hole in her leg and blood all over her head, face, and clothing. There were not enough ERs open and not enough staff to accommodate her. So, they put her in a room and waited. With every agonizing moment that passed, my mind, once again, raced with the worst possible outcomes. She was nearly guaranteed to endure brain damage, and the realization she could lose her lower leg was a very real possibility. I went to the head nurse station and demanded, threatened, and pleaded for them to transport her to another hospital. They merely looked up at me and ignored me. It was the most helpless feeling of my life. Anger and fear consumed me.

As days grew into weeks, I remember trying to hold up a facade that everything would be alright, that she would walk out of there with both legs. I recall trying to make her laugh by dancing around the room in the middle of the night to help elevate the pain and every waking hour that came with it. Neither of us had any sleep and very little food; we were falling through the cracks. So, just like our pandemic 'hope countdown,' I created charts on the wall to give Sadie some hope about how far she was progressing. All the while, I was scared as hell of a different fate. Despite my exhaustion and fears, I chose to show her as much joy as I could muster, which I knew would help her through her own moments of doubt.

I later discovered that on the night of the accident, there were so many severe cases that they had no choice but to prioritize based on who would die and who would live. That was why we were made to wait so long. Although Sadie could suffer life-altering consequences, it was clear to the hospital staff she was not going to die. My prayers had worked. Those long nights in the hospital, looking at the top of the church steeple with the lake in the backdrop, praying endlessly were not wasted. Despite my anger in those moments, I am utterly grateful for the outcome. Sadie endured so much pain, so many surgeries, and a lifelong lesson. But she is alive and well; she kept her leg and has a hell of a scar that comes with an amazing story — a story about one young lady's perseverance and one mother's very large lesson learned.

On the day we left that hospital, I praised the Lord above, knowing that there was a massive lesson to be learned from this event. One that I knew would come but couldn't begin to wrap my brain around it at the time. Quite a bit of time passed before I understood the lessons of that tragic day. The instant changes and sacrifices that were made during that event have since created joy in my life. Something that would have never come to fruition had I not been forced to walk away from my businesses. When the pain of that accident ensued, who knew that it was to bring me joy in going from nearly eighty hours a week down to less than forty? When joy and pain collided, the universe most certainly delivered me a blessing. My mind has become less entangled by the daily tasks; I sleep more and spend quality time with my kids. I learned to shift my priorities and remember what matters most.

The takeaway is that we all have battles we need to fight. It is our choice in how we navigate them that makes the difference. When you are at your lowest, you can choose to rise above and pray. I had to fight desperately for what we call "inner peace," and in doing so, I've found joy. Incorporating praying, reading books, exercising, and meditating into your daily routine can create positive improvement in your daily problems. Although no one's life is problem-free, these actions can certainly decrease the anxiety, fear, and negativity that can lead one to spiral.

It wasn't easy, but I chose to find myself — not to find myself again but to "find my new self," the woman who had to emerge from those battles. What I discovered is that finding joy is learning to have faith — faith in God, faith in yourself, faith in the Universe. It's not just saying that you have faith; it's the act of believing it to be true and allowing it to guide your choices.

When life took me by the throat a dozen different times, I learned the true meaning of joy. It was all that I had left to hold onto when things were at their worst, and low and behold… that joy was delivered. My faith in God proved He always came through for me, bringing me back to joy. Faith is *knowing* that when that next bad time arises, he will always be there; *always*. As I endured these life lessons, it became easier and easier to feel and understand faith at a different level. It wasn't until I looked back and could reflect upon these profound moments that I realized the good that had come from them. At these junctures, I was able to discover the true meaning of faith and joy combined. You see, the two go hand in hand. The true meaning of faith is that when the bad times hit, you believe in your soul that you will get through it. Each time I witnessed these events unfold, I was less phased by their impact and able to reach the state of joy more quickly.

After practicing, studying, and reading dozens of spiritual teachings and books… I knew that the outcome that day would have been life-altering if not for that moment of prayer. Some would beg to differ, but if you know… you know.

Remember, faith is blind but you shouldn't need to see the proof in order to believe. Thankfully, I rely wholeheartedly on the unseen now. And therefore, I have found my joy. It's not sweating the small stuff that used to eat me alive. I understand it takes many of us time to learn this lesson, and when we do, what a gift! I'd have given anything to learn this lesson sooner.

The underlying message here is this: life is going to test you. You will fall on hard times, and they will be awful. It won't be easy, but close your eyes and imagine the best possible outcome, and remember that you are the only one who can bring true happiness upon yourself. But above all else, we must remember Henri Nouwen's wise words that, "Joy does not simply happen to us. We have to choose joy and keep choosing it every day." My wish for all of the readers of this book is for you to finally find your joy.

IGNITE ACTION STEPS

- **Take the gift.** Don't forget to notice the small things. They are so important to finding your joy. Gabrielle Berstein's book *The Universe Has Your Back* was very helpful in reminding me of all the beautiful signs and moments delivered to us daily.

- **Practice kindness.** Make it a point to be who God intended you to be, not what the others are doing around you. Be kind, even when the universe doesn't feel so kind to you.

- **Hardships don't last.** In the middle of your most trying moments, give yourself grace. Hold tight to a positive outcome and take even the smallest of blessings as a lesson.

- **The most obvious…. PRAY.** Prayer is one of the best ways to heal and find joy.

Stacie McCracken Callan — United States of America
Broker, Business Coach, CEO of The Stacie Callan Group
and Century 21 MRC,
www.mrcvt.com, www.scgvt.com
TheStacieCallanGroup
C21vermont Century 21 MRC

IGNITE
Joy

Tanya Dow

TANYA DOW

*"Show up as your most authentic self,
open to the abundance and beauty the Universe has in store for you."*

It is my intention that this story spark a fire inside of you. May it ignite a flame to give you the strength to call back your power and love yourself enough to know you are truly worthy of having all that life has to offer. I wish for my words of vulnerability to allow you to find your voice if you have lost it. Be fearless; do not allow anyone or anything to dim your light.

MUDDY WATERS

STUCK. That was a constant feeling for me. Like being trapped in thick mud that is clinging so tightly to my legs and I am unable to break free. Every effort I would make to move would only result in me sinking deeper and deeper. I was stuck in a physically and emotionally destructive marriage that I had allowed to have complete power over me. I was always apprehensive about expressing my real feelings or voicing an opinion out of fear of another public argument in front of family and friends. I knew any type of conflict would send him into a downward spiral of cocaine and whisky and result in him being 'missing in action' for sometimes weeks on end. I would never know when or if he would return. If and when money would go missing. I never knew who would show up on my doorstep, how many erratic phone calls I would receive from him, or if anyone I loved would be hurt along the way. During those tumultuous times, I would ask myself, in tears, "How did I end up here?" "Where did I go wrong?"

The emotional chaos differed from how I grew up — in a loving home with my parents and two younger brothers. I spent much of my childhood at my grandparents' farm fishing out of the dugout, riding the quad, building forts in the trees, and being in the garden barefoot with Grandma. We lived in a small community of around fourteen hundred people, so everyone knew one another. I had many friends and was involved in sports and activities. I was 'successful' at everything I did. I won awards, had good grades, and always tried to be involved. I was a leader, and my peers listened to me.

In grade ten, my teacher asked the class to consider our future aspirations. We were then given the assignment to write an essay about them. I imagined going to university and becoming a lawyer. I was married, but we had no kids. I traveled, helped people, and was accomplished. My future self was a strong and thriving woman. She could stand on her own two feet if needed but also had a partner who loved her. I had no reason to think that my life would unfold any other way. I worked hard, and I achieved everything I set my mind to with some level of success. Little did I know that the partner I was about to choose had other plans for me.

Years earlier, as a young teenager, my girlfriends, boyfriend, and I attended a party at this guy's house in the neighboring town. I didn't know who he was. I knew he was older than me; I recalled seeing him with my friend's brother. When our group arrived, the two-story house was so packed we had to swim through the crowd just to get anywhere. My friends began to drag me up the stairs where all the girls were hanging out. I was hesitant to leave my boyfriend, who hadn't found his friends yet. I didn't want him standing in the corner alone. As I was pulled upstairs by my persistent friend, I heard, "Hey, Blondie!" over the loud music. I looked down into the kitchen, trying to see who spoke. "You better be in my bedroom in ten minutes when I get up there." I surveyed the room frantically to find out who the over-confident jerk yelling at me was. He was standing in the corner of the kitchen, shaggy brown hair with faint blonde streaks in it. He wore a backward hat, silver chain, and a tight green shirt that showcased his muscular physique and tattooed arm. We locked eyes as he repeated himself, smiling at me with this mysterious, sly, charming look. "Naked," he added. It was as if the music was muted, and the whole kitchen was watching; I could feel a hundred sets of eyes on me. And there, directly across the room, was my boyfriend. He had heard the whole thing.

I didn't go to that guy's room that night, but something about his confidence and alluring personality intrigued me and made me want to talk to him. Months later, my boyfriend and I broke up. That guy got my number through our social circles, and we began talking and dating. After almost four years, he decided we would spend New Year's in Las Vegas. He rented us a luxury car, and we took a day trip to the Grand Canyon. I was catching vibes that something was up but pushed it to the back of my mind because it wasn't out of character for him to make extravagant plans.

He ended up proposing to me. My heart began to beat faster than normal, and a rush of heat overtook me. It was an unsettling euphoria; I felt my excitement at odds with some deep reservations. I said yes because I felt I couldn't say no. I called my parents that night. My mom began to cry over the phone. "I hope you are happy, Tani," she said. I began to cry as I hung up, and he questioned if my mom had made me upset. "No. I am happy and excited to start planning," I assured him, convincing him and myself it was joy that I felt. He had this questionable power over me. I didn't see it then, but my light became fainter and fainter. When we went to bed that night, I rolled over, staring at the large ring on my finger as a single tear ran down my cheek.

Early in our marriage, I was feeling pressure from him and his family to have a baby. All of our 'couple' friends were getting pregnant and starting their families. I wasn't ready. I wanted a career, adventure, and experiences. Having a kid didn't fit into that equation. I was twenty-three years old, we had just gotten married, and I had only recently graduated from university with a Bachelor of Secondary Education. I was working for my dad at an oil and gas company while I waited for my teaching license to be approved. To a bystander, it would have appeared that I was in denial about my chosen circumstances, but I consciously knew my relationship was unhealthy. So, if I had control over anything, it would be whether I brought an innocent life into my mess.

As my feet continued sinking deeper into the mud, I became more unsettled about the idea of getting pregnant. He believed we were moving forward with trying for a child, and I did a good job of side-stepping the conversation. I couldn't bring myself to tell him the truth. Then, one day, it all erupted when he discovered I was still taking my birth control. He was furious that I had deceived him. Regardless of whether I was ready, his insecurities made him believe me not wanting to have a baby was equivalent to telling him I didn't love him. He kicked me out of the house, leaving me no choice but to go to my parents. Instead of feeling sadness, relief poured over me as I wondered, *Is our marriage really over? Am I actually moving forward to solid ground?*

He hit rock bottom after we had been living apart for about a month. He promised to get sober and do marriage counseling with me, but I ended up doing more sessions alone. I believe that after a few meetings, my counselor became aware of the amplitude of my situation, the manipulation, and the abuse, and that was why she suggested I meet with her one-on-one. My sessions shifted and became more about me and what I needed from my relationship rather than taking the blame for his addiction or being the one to *fix* all of our problems. It was reassuring to affirm what I knew all along, deep down inside. All of the screaming matches that led to holes in the walls of our home… *were not my fault.* The thousands of dollars he spent on drugs and alcohol, knowing no other way to cope with our disagreements… *were not my fault.* The bruises that appeared on my body from being grabbed or pushed to the ground, the awful name-calling that sabotaged my self-esteem and self-worth, and the false accusations of being unfaithful… *were not my fault.*

Three months had passed when I began to see hopeful signs that made me believe he could change. I got a glimpse of the guy I had fallen in love with. I let my guard down, and I moved back into our home. Another year passed and things were going surprisingly well, so I decided that I didn't need counseling anymore. I put my rose-colored glasses back on and redirected my focus back to my marriage. He had found a well-paying, consistent job and had also rediscovered his passion for fitness. We enjoyed going to the gym together on the nights his work didn't require him to be out of town, and we escaped life together with motorcycle rides at sunset. Life appeared to be going well.

Then I found out I was pregnant. I can remember walking out of the bathroom to the living room. He sat on the couch, patiently waiting for the pregnancy test result. I began to cry, and a familiar feeling entered my body: heat and a fast heartbeat, excitement and doubt. I felt myself sinking into muddy waters, *stuck* again. Like before, he questioned why I was crying. Again, I reassured him. I told him I felt joy despite being a little scared to be a mom. He assured me that things were 'better now' and that I would be a great mom.

Nine months flew by, and before I knew it, my son was born in March 2016. This guy I had married was so proud. My heart was whole with trust in him and hope for our future together. He wanted a son to carry on the family name, to bond with on a level he never experienced with his own dad. I truly believe he loved my son, but his sickness wouldn't allow him to be a father, husband, or life partner.

Despite a physically traumatic birthing experience that left me feeling sore and helpless, my motherly instincts kicked in, and my main focus became my baby. Soon, it was time for our family to leave the hospital and head home. He returned to work after a few days, and I became a stay-at-home mom. It seemed like yesterday I was that teenage girl sitting in class writing about my future. Being a mom was not one of my aspirations. Now, here I was, caring for a newborn. As I began to bond and connect with my baby, my love and dedication to him grew stronger and stronger. That undeniable feeling of unconditional love only a mom knows for her child is exactly how I felt.

Two months passed, and I was trying my best to learn the new balance of being both a wife and a mom. Finding that balance was hard as he constantly fought for my attention over our child. He was so used to having my undivided time, not comprehending how exhausted I was after finally getting the baby to bed. I didn't want to stay up and watch TV, and I most certainly didn't want to be intimate. I was still recovering from the birth, and I was not loving my postpartum body. But he believed that being sexually intimate meant that we loved one another. I could tell him over and over that I loved him, but his reassurance of my love was sex. Now that we had a new baby, it felt more crucial than ever that I comply with his needs to keep him happy, even on the nights my mind and body told me "no." In those moments, the feeling of rage would consume me. A feeling so strong I would envision throwing him off of me, but within seconds, that powerful feeling would shift to sadness, and then I would wake up the next morning feeling sheer disappointment in myself.

One evening, he made a sudden choice to disappear for two weeks, under the understanding that he was going out to get some ice cream. During that time, I went through so many emotions… panic, sadness, anger, fear, guilt, and shame. To this day, I still don't know what set him off, but I guess that's addiction. Addiction doesn't care about anything other than the entity it has power over. When he finally showed up at our house, my parents were there. They offered him rehab. While he was away, they would take care of everything, including myself and my son. We all just wanted him to get better. He declined. He said he had gotten sober alone before, and he would do it again.

That was the wrong answer. His refusal was my confirmation that our marriage was over, that he was choosing his addiction over our life together. I asked him to stay in a hotel until I could collect my things and move out of the house. He agreed and then left. I had a million emotions flooding my body as the night grew dark. I cradled my son to sleep, thinking about my next steps and our future. A few hours passed, and I crawled into bed, so exhausted I could hear my heartbeat in my ears. I lay there just about to close my eyes when I heard *beep, beep, beep.* It was my front door keypad.

My heart began to race; I lay there for what seemed like a lifetime. Then I jumped out of bed and darted for my son's bedroom. My soon-to-be ex-husband came around the corner quickly and pushed me back into our bedroom, slamming the door. I could smell the whisky. I started to cry while he verbally assaulted me and aggressively gestured toward me. I pleaded with him just to let me get my son, but he wouldn't let me out of the room. His voice kept getting louder and louder until I heard the baby start to cry. I begged him again just to let me get the baby. He grabbed me by the wrists, squeezing them so tight. He threatened me. I told him I was sorry and would give us another chance. I would have said anything just to get to my son. A switch flipped inside of him, and he opened the door. I bolted to the nursery and picked up my son. I knew he was hungry, so I went to the kitchen for a bottle. He followed me, refusing to let us out of his sight. I sat down on the couch, preparing to feed my son feeling so relieved to have him in my arms. He told me he would mix himself another drink and went downstairs to the basement bar. I remember looking at the front door, thinking *I should run.*

Safety and self-preservation kicked in like I had no control over my body. With my son in my arms, I charged for the exit and then ran to the neighbors. I banged on their door, ringing their doorbell for what felt like a hundred times while looking over to see if he realized I was gone. Finally, my neighbor opened the door. "Tanya, what is going on?" she said sleepily.

"Lock the door, shut the lights off, and call the police," I responded quickly.

As I watched him get arrested from my neighbor's front window, I remember looking down at my son and thinking, *"I may not love myself at this moment, but with every cell of my being, I feel unconditional love for you, and I will do anything to protect you."* I had stepped onto dry land after walking through the muddy waters for so long, and I would emerge stronger than ever before.

Having taken the first step toward my freedom, I was now tasked with creating a joyful life for myself and my son. Through personal growth, retreats, courses, and sacred circles, I have been able to work through my pain and fear. I have challenged my body and my mind in the bodybuilding community, showcasing my determination and strength. I have been able to heal my feelings of unworthiness enough to allow an amazing man to love me and my son as his own. He is now my husband and soulmate. I have been called to lead meditation ceremonies to help women transform, reconnect with their voices, and feel supported on their healing journeys. I have learned to release control and trust that I am supported by the Universe. I am mastering my ability to speak powerfully to live a life of purpose and watch what happens in others when they feel called to do the same. I have learned to set clear boundaries within my relationships. Having boundaries is out of love for myself and the protection of the energy that I have worked so hard to regain.

As I shared with you that day almost eight years ago, I felt so much joy. So much joy for keeping my promise to my son and myself. I have reclaimed my power. I have found my voice and have such a beautiful and full life. I show up in this world as my most authentic self, open to receiving all the abundance and beauty the Universe has in store for me.

If you are feeling stuck in your life, choose joy. Be willing to find your voice, your strength, and your confidence. Trust yourself and your intuition as you know what is best for you. Don't allow anyone to dim your light or stop you from shining your light. Lean on your people, find your tribe, and be willing to accept the help you need. The more vulnerable we are to our situations, the more we allow people to flow in and support us. Joy shows up as *you* become your most authentic self. Be open to the abundance, joy, and beauty the Universe wants to give you."

IGNITE ACTION STEPS

- **Meditate** - Focus on the present moment and your breath. Connect with your higher self and become more in tune with your intuition. This will allow your mind to be clear and your thoughts to steam from a place of love and compassion rather than ego.

- **Find Your Tribe** - Surround yourself with people who bring value to your life and who support, love, and give you grace. Connect with those who remind you of your purpose and challenge you to become the best version of yourself.

- **Create Boundaries** - If it's not a heck YES, it's a heck NO. Create healthy boundaries with others and yourself. Do not tolerate disrespect, and be sure to honor your beautiful self.

Tanya Dow — Canada
B.ED in Secondary Education, Reiki Practitioner Level 1&2,
Meditations Facilitator
www.harmonichaven.com
Tanya Dow
havenharmonic

Tina Ritchie

TINA RITCHIE

"Tenacity is the compass that guides us through our storms."

I invite you to embrace the virtues of tenacity and courage when navigating the unknown paths of life. I wish to highlight the power of self-belief in overcoming challenges and remaining steadfast in pursuit of personal goals. My narrative underscores the significance of recognizing and following the subtle cues and guidance from the Universe, whether through signs, symbols, or the support of others. May these experiences encourage you to surrender to the greater plan of the divine and witness the awe-inspiring joy that unfolds along the journey.

THE WHITE FEATHER

The most shocking and disturbing moment of my life was when I arrived at my mother's house for dinner, only to be greeted by a police officer announcing my husband's death. He had been killed in an accident at work and wasn't coming home. I was just twenty-five years of age, and my world stopped. Thinking of our son and our life, everything we knew at the time shattered. I became numb. It was my first experience with death so close to me, and I learned how people can take advantage of the situation in the mindset of grief. People do funny things when people die, and I quickly had to embrace the changes of a future without my husband. I managed to cope with living one day at a time, guided by some support amidst the influence of other people's opinions. I proceeded to move forward with a lump in my throat and a void in my heart, continuing to reflect on words and pictures of the past by constantly repeating the final days prior to his death in my mind.

Memories flooded my heart with warmth and longing as I recalled our last Valentine's Day together. We had reminisced about the wonderful time he had called me to join him on a last-minute vacation to Mexico. Mexico had left an indelible mark on my spirit with its radiant sun, swaying palms, turquoise waters, and warm-hearted people. The allure of that enchanting place lingered within me, Igniting a fire of passion and possibility that would shape the course of my life. My husband's final words to me echoed in my mind, cutting through the bittersweet haze of memories. "You're a great mom; Mexico is your place, and get into real estate."

When he passed, the weight of his absence pressed down on me, and the financial struggles seemed insurmountable. In those dark moments, I couldn't fathom how his words could hold any truth. I was a single parent, navigating life on a meager income with no knowledge of real estate. Yet, despite the despair, a flicker of hope remained — a dream of continuing my education, of carving a path in an industry I knew little about but yearned to explore.

The next chapter of my life was not easy, yet there were glimpses of profound coincidences nudging me to tap into another side of life. As signs and symbols showed up, I had an inner knowing that perhaps they came from my deceased husband. I was still young and curious to explore spirituality, but I did not have enough knowledge. I had learned to pray during childhood and witnessed one or two big miracles that arose. I remember starting to read my way through the pain, taking solace in books that made me realize I wasn't alone in my struggles. Pressure mounted for me to find a new serious relationship, in part to keep me from single parenting. I was very vulnerable, and no one mentioned giving myself time to heal or that mourning comes with grieving and can take years before your heart is ready to feel again.

I coped with deeply conflicted feelings of wanting to be a stay-at-home mom and yearning to be a creative entrepreneur. I needed to provide for my children and gain financial control over my life. The following years in western British Columbia brought forth the harsh reality of Canadian winters, the monotony of rain, traffic-laden commutes, and the burden of an overtaxed system. I fell into the trappings of a very toxic relationship as I juggled running a clothing store and raising four children. My health deteriorated as I took care of everyone else, and symptoms of headaches and backaches became noticeable. When the pain became severe enough, I finally went to the doctor. I was diagnosed with stage three cancer in my female organs.

Again, I was numb. The health, family, marriage, and Mexico dreams were long gone. My mind was in a nightmare, and it was getting worse.

The doctors, with their shiny shoes, were adamant about me having surgery and removing all my female organs. This was a hugely pivotal moment. After always listening to others' opinions, this time, I knew I must awaken the weakness in me and fight for my life. A voice inside said *I could heal myself against all professional opinions.*

I started researching alternative therapies and reached out to healers in the community. I was divinely led to an herbalist and a book, *Living in the Light,* by Shakti Gawain. I had been living in the dark, with pain, sorrow, and guilt, which faded slowly as I received new knowledge through reading. I started to see and feel tremendous healing effects much different than the fear-based opinions of those I had chosen to have close to me. I longed for the tranquility of Mexico and the more holistic way of life there. Fueled by my desire to align with my true self, I started to heal from inside out. With new inspiration, I drank herbs, changed my Western diet, and said no to the Western world doctrine of pharmaceuticals. When I held a new vision with a new story, I became cancer-free.

Yet, I still needed to free myself of another toxin: my unhealthy relationship with my second husband and the father of my next three children. My mother was afraid for me but understood, as she had left a toxic marriage to my step-father. With a new will to live and unfazed by my lack of financial resources, I found the courage to ask her to cosign on a minivan. I started to free myself from all my material possessions. With a small amount of money and all four children in tow, I headed south for a long journey. With each passing mile, the allure of Mexico intensified, a paradise offering freedom and a profound natural love of life.

I showed up to Mexico open to the newness that it would provide, free from toxic behaviors and patterns that no longer served my divine origins. I was greeted by a legendary American real estate broker and a loving Canadian missionary's daughter. These women became my greatest mentors and were pivotal in my spiritual journey and my children's lives. Embracing a career in real estate, I began selling properties to fellow Americans and Canadians. My dedication and prowess propelled me to the pinnacle of sales success, opening doors to numerous opportunities. I felt the glimmer of joy on my newfound frontier.

I embarked on an adventure fueled by passion and determination. With basically no money down other than proof of a written check, we sealed a real estate deal with nothing but a handshake and a promise-to-deliver attitude. This symbolized trust and belief in the vision that was held for the future. My transformation wasn't merely professional but a journey of self-discovery and manifestation. A gift of a book, *Think and Grow Rich*, set me on my path of aligning my desires with reality. As I delved into its pages, a sense of possibility and empowerment began to blossom joy within me. Little did I know that this newfound faith in my own abilities would lead to remarkable manifestations.

After releasing my husband's ashes into the waters of Mexico, a symbolic act of letting go and honoring his memory, I was astounded by the spiritual occurrences that followed. It was as if the Universe responded to my surrender with undeniable signs of alignment. A mansion, once only a distant dream, became my reality. Alongside it came the luxury of hired help and the prestigious role of Director of Sales. An opportunity to work at a world-famous resort materialized, and to my astonishment, it was located in the very same place where I had scattered my husband's ashes. The resort's name even mirrored our two names together, a synchronicity that filled me with awe, wonder, and joy.

Those occurrences held profound spiritual meaning for me. It was as though the unseen forces of the Universe were guiding me, orchestrating a series of events that transcended mere coincidence. As I embraced these signs and surrendered to the flow of life, I felt a deep sense of connection to the divine.

I spread my husband's ashes as a symbol of love and remembrance, but their significance went beyond mere sentimentality. They became a conduit for spiritual guidance and a reminder of our enduring bond. My life was transformed in ways I could never have imagined. It was a testament to the power of faith, resilience, and the profound influence of the unseen forces that shape our lives. As I embraced each journey of growth and self-discovery, those around me noticed a remarkable transformation — a blossoming spirit reflecting the extreme changes within me.

Then, a series of professional wins put me on a path back to Canada and my roots. I quickly realized that I was falling into the dark trappings again. I saw many of my friends' families in debt, divorced, eating poorly, being diagnosed with diseases, addictions becoming the norm, and unhappiness at the forefront. I was personally starting to fail, and I broke the momentum of my financial success. I remember feeling the pain of the surroundings become unbearable, taking me back to those disrupted places I once knew.

I was in my early forties when my world changed again. I found myself on my good friend's couch, waiting to eat lunch she had invited me over for. After talking at length about the relationship challenges we both faced, I walked over to the balcony of her twelfth-story apartment facing the British Properties in West Vancouver, where only a select few lived in wealth. I held out my hands and said out loud an intense prayer. *I AM returning to Mexico to finish what I started to create, and I will receive a substantial amount of money to complete my commitment.*

After the prayer, I surrendered to not knowing and waited for signs from the Universe to present themselves. Before I knew it, my two sons called to say, "Mom, you are not and will not be happy here; let go of everything and come with us to California. We are starting a business there." Going with them was not easy as I had a few days to sort my belongings and donate much of what I owned to a women's shelter, knowing someone else could use them. It's always challenging to let go of what will not serve you, relinquishing complete faith and trust in the universal flow. With just a light suitcase in hand, I went to California, knowing it was halfway to returning to Mexico.

A few weeks after I arrived in California, I received a call from a colleague in Mexico asking me to come back. I took a short flight and arrived amidst the flow of events, forgetting about the prayer. Circumstances led me back to the real estate office, where I searched for desirable properties for sale. One particular beachfront penthouse stood out, offering a massive sales bonus.

Hoping to be the one to receive the bonus, a man walked into the office, visibly disturbed and complaining he couldn't find what he was looking for from other agents. I assured him that I could show him an exquisite penthouse on the beach, and his eyes lit up as we walked into his future purchase. The bonus I received came from a very wealthy, prominent family, and my client and I were invited to close the deal on their yacht.

In a fateful twist, the purchaser had a friend from West Vancouver, where I had recently been. The purchaser's friend was Vice President of a large securities brokerage firm with over 200 sales brokers working with him. In his late sixties, he was proud to see a Canadian girl making more money than his all-male sales team could dream of. Photos of our day on the yacht were taken, and he assured me that if I called him when I returned to West Vancouver, he would give me the pictures.

A few months later, I returned to Canada and visited my friend in that 12th-story apartment. A knowing smile spread across her face as I excitedly shared the news of my big bonus and joyful return to Mexico. Then, she said, "Tina, your prayer came true." The reminder was like a warm embrace, as I was completely wrapped in a sense of faith and connection to a comforting, protective presence I couldn't see. This is when I realized how prayer can work miracles. Moved by this profound 'coincidence,' I felt a sense of joy moving me to action. I decided to call the West Vancouver Vice President and ask where he was located in West Vancouver. It turned out that when I held my hands out in that prayer, he was living in the building across the street, in the penthouse directly adjacent to my friend's on the twelfth floor. Once again, I was in total grace and gratitude for the Divine. My prayer for financial freedom had put the person living across the street in West Vancouver on a yacht with me in Mexico, then brought me back to Canada and his doorstep to collect the photos we took together.

The pictures in my hand were reminders of what I had managed to manifest as I reached out to the Spirit in prayer. I knew then there was another side to life, a spiritual plane of connection that we could tap into and make anything possible. That awareness is what would carry me through a new dark moment of loss into a reaffirmed sense of light and joy. When my mom made a choice to leave this planet Earth, it was then I became aware of patterns and behaviors that were purging; I had to make a decision to let go and surrender and trust the process. As she crossed over, I asked her to give me a huge white feather to let me know she was beside me.

My mom's death led me to a profound realization and a new purpose. Throughout her painful marriage-like relationships, she had not been able to speak her truth or feel equal in a romantic and financial partnership. That bondage that kept her weak showed me how strong I had become and how much work I had done on myself to surpass those types of toxic relationships. During those years, she had not given independence to herself, but she had instilled it in me as her only daughter. In my strength, I managed to go through the seat of justice in the court system after a six-year battle with those who did not honor my Mother's wishes in her final decree. I had to remind myself to have the courage, faith, and trust in the divine light no matter how adversity appeared. With my fork pierced in the ground, I stood for Truth and equality, like every other human who overcomes life's challenges.

The night before the verdict, as I picked up the white binder preparing for court, a huge white feather lay before me! I knew her spirit was there. She was showing me I was on my path and not alone. The next day, on Mexican Independence Day, the Canadian Supreme Court awarded my Mother everything she had wished for. That victory spoke to my heart, as I know how many other women and children have to go through the dark doctrine that still looms in society with the power struggles of toxic codependency.

I returned home to Mexico with a deeper understanding and a joyful purpose. Mastering the art of connecting people with events and properties, my team of like-minded women and I are dedicated to laying the foundation for female empowerment. I have used what I have learned to assist others by providing tools to cleanse emotional, physical, and mental clutter, eat whole foods, and find love for self. I aim to create communities for positive change, with equality between males and females fostering healthy relationships. With gratitude and divine guidance, my vision extends beyond personal success to healing, freedom, and love for the world. I'm embarking on a journey to empower others to manifest their dreams and desires, collectively creating abundance and joy.

Through all my struggles, I have learned that it is important to love yourself, knowing that we are always taken care of even when we don't see the way. Trust in the Universal flow and let go of resistance around old beliefs and fears. Return to love and be in the moment. Be willing to ask for guidance and surrender to what shows up that will lead you freely to your divine bliss and joy.

IGNITE ACTION STEPS

- **Engage** in healing activities like reading inspirational books and seeking guidance.

- **Reflect** on past experiences and lessons to stay resilient and grow.

- **Prioritize** personal healing and growth, focusing on self-care.

- **Embrace** change and adaptability, stepping out of your comfort zone.

- **Cultivate** gratitude and acknowledge blessings.

- **Give back** and empower others by sharing personal experiences and insight.

Tina Ritchie — Mexico, Dubai, Canada, Ireland
Radiant Trailblazer
www.tinaritchie.com
Teamcaboproperties.com
jetsetdiva
tinaritchie8

Vanessa Rivers

Vanessa Rivers

"Life is not something to be survived, but to be cherished and enjoyed."

You have more power over your happiness than you know. I hope that my story will inspire you to wake up every day with childlike excitement about life. Believe in the magic and joy all around and *within* you.

The Doll & The Dinosaur

I sat locked in the back seat of a station wagon with my younger twin brothers, and screamed hysterically as I watched my father repeatedly punch my mother in the face, giving her a black eye, chipping her tooth, and then finally slamming her against the car hood, breaking her wrist. I was five years old.

Even as I write this over thirty years later, my palms are sweating, my heart is racing, and I am right back in that moment feeling like that heartbroken child.

I've learned that our bodies physically attach feelings to traumatic memories. That is why certain memories become triggers for us and induce stress and anxiety. Your body cannot tell the difference between physical and emotional danger.

I have spent my entire life coping with ongoing stress. Like a caged, scared, wild animal, my body is often in a constant fight-or-flight state, waiting for the next disaster to strike. But, by the grace of God, following that traumatic fight, I was put in a situation where I would learn I could control my attitude toward what happened to me.

My parents had been in a violent, ongoing divorce for as long as I could remember, but that momentlocked in the car was just the beginning of what I would endure.

During the divorce, which lasted over ten years, my father's greatest power over my mother was threatening to take us kids away. He used it against her at every turn. Like a fierce mama bear trying to protect her cubs, she'd lash back at him, saying, "If you try to take my kids away, I will f**king kill you!" This, of course, only added fuel to the fire and validity to my father's allegations that our mother was an "unfit parent" and "crazy." Then, Mom would fire back the same accusations. Witnessing their constant screaming felt unbearable.

The court didn't know who to believe so they appointed an attorney for me and my little brothers. The first thing our attorney did was to say that he didn't know who was telling the truth. So he requested psych evaluations of everyone — my mom, my father, me, and my brothers.

The preliminary evaluation determined I "needed further examination." Something about my behavior worried them. Because my father said Mom was an unfit mother and we were in danger with her, a judge decided that "for my safety," I would be sent to the Charter Hospital in Bakersfield, California, where further evaluation could take place in a neutral setting. This behavioral healthcare hospital specializes in acute psychiatric care for children. At five years old, I was taken away from my mother and placed in a mental hospital. I was absolutely terrified.

On the drive to the hospital, I stared out our truck window across miles of barren land dotted with oil wells that looked like giant grasshoppers. Tears ran down my tiny cheeks. Occasionally, Mom looked over and tried to give me a reassuring smile, but I could tell that, like me, she was petrified. There was none of her usual sunny joking, pointing out beautiful scenery, or singing along with Don Henley's soulful voice as it filled our truck. Mom had already tried to explain why I needed to go to the hospital for "a little while," but it didn't make any sense to me.

"Mommy, why do I have to go?" I begged. "I want to stay with you, Mommy. Please don't make me go." I began sobbing uncontrollably.

"Please, I'll be nice to my brothers. I'll do anything. Please don't send me away." Mom kept her eyes on the road, but she reached over, grabbed my hand, and squeezed it in hers. I watched as silent tears streamed down her face.

Reflecting on that memory now that I am a mother, I realize how awful it must have been for her to drive me to the hospital that day — trying to reassure me when she was so scared herself. Out of everything Mom endured, I'm sure that was the hardest thing she went through. I know she would have put up with being beaten by my father every day for the rest of her life if it meant keeping me from being institutionalized. All these years later, I can't even think about that drive to the hospital without crying. But sometimes something "bad" happens so that something *good* can happen.

I only remember bits and pieces from being admitted to the hospital, where children were dealing with severe psychiatric disorders all around me. It was supposed to be a safe space, but it wasn't. I became more depressed than ever. I blamed myself for everything that happened, and I saw the possibility of killing myself as a way to make everything better.

After years of my father raging at all of us and being violent toward our mother, my parents constantly arguing over custody of us, and Dad hounding us relentlessly, I had somehow gotten it in my head that the craziness was *all my fault*. In my child's mind, my birth had ruined everything. I reasoned that *if I hadn't come along, then my parents wouldn't have had anything to fight over. Maybe if I were dead, Dad would leave Mom alone. Then, she and the boys would finally have a chance to be happy and free.*

My first week in the hospital felt unbearable. I drew several disturbing pictures during the evaluation. In one, I drew a giant cactus tree and depicted throwing myself on the huge thorns. In another, I drew a picture of myself jumping off a cliff to my death. I daydreamed endlessly about Mom walking through the door, scooping me up in her arms, and telling me she was there to bring me home for good. I cried myself to sleep every night. All I could think about was how much I missed my mother and my brothers and how badly I wanted to go home.

Children are resilient — even sad, damaged children. Soon, I accepted my situation and tried to make the best of it. There was a special school at the hospital where we did basic work like reading, writing, and math. But what I remember most were the science projects, which I loved.

We built a rocket ship one week, and the whole class went out into the desert to launch it. Watching that mesmerizing orange flash against the barren desert and bright blue sky, I finally felt like I was part of something important. I couldn't wait until my mother arrived so that I could tell her all about it.

Mom visited me in the hospital whenever the rules allowed, sneaking in various animals to cheer me up. My visitors included baby kittens (hidden under her jacket), my rabbit (that she smuggled in a paper bag that jumped up and down in her hands), and even baby goats (that she lifted over the hospital wall into my small, outstretched arms). If I couldn't be at our farm, Mom was determined to bring the farm to me

Gradually, my stay at the facility went from terrifying to bearable. While I still desperately wanted to get out and go home, I managed to find little moments of joy. The brightest part of that place was Bonnie, my psychologist. That woman changed my life forever. She was smart, loving, and compassionate, and I looked forward to our time together. She had a round face kind eyes, and was soft-spoken and encouraging.

I also loved that her office was basically one giant playroom. Looking back, I had no idea I was being evaluated. I just thought I was in Bonnie's warm, wonderful room because she was a loving woman who cared about me and wanted to share all her toys to cheer me up. I remember her asking me questions as I played, but I didn't realize till I was much older than my times playing in her room were actually my 'sessions.' She was trying to meet me on a level where a 5-year-old felt most comfortable — at play.

Months later, the man who would become my stepfather accompanied Mom to one of my sessions. They sat on the other side of the glass and watched as Bonnie asked me to pick out toys that represented my parents. Years later, he would describe this scene to me, saying:

"For your mom, you picked out a pretty doll. For your dad, you picked out Tyrannosaurus Rex. Bonnie later explained to us that she could learn so much about how you felt from that simple exercise. It seemed you saw your dad as a predator who was out to get you."

Until my sessions with Bonnie, I felt powerless to control the chaos that was all around me and growing within me. While my time in the hospital was tough, every day, I grew stronger. Though I was only a little kid, I began understanding how my mind and heart worked together. Bonnie helped me realize that I was an innocent child and none of the family turmoil was my fault. She also helped me believe that I was special and smart and that *my life mattered*.

I only remember bits and pieces of my time with Bonnie, but I do clearly remember one pivotal conversation with her, one moment where everything clicked that changed my entire life. During one of my sessions, Bonnie explained to me that while I could not control what happened to me, I *could* control my attitude towards what happened to me. Her words trailed around my heart like a powerful echo… I knew I had heard this before.

Then, I remembered many times my mother had said, "What makes you beautiful is your attitude toward the world." Like a bright ball of beautiful light, a feeling began to grow in my chest. A deep knowing was washing over me. All of a sudden, I got it. I was only a little kid, but I realized that my power was that I could *choose* to focus on the positives despite the chaos. My power was that I could *choose* to be happy and grateful regardless of what I had been through. I could create whatever life I wanted. I could *choose* to live a life filled with *joy*. The realization that the power was inside me — that it always had been and always would be — changed my life forever.

A few months later, I got out of the hospital, but things did not improve. The chaos got much, *much* worse. My father continued to hound us relentlessly; my mother became completely dependent on alcohol. There were drunken fights. Guns were fired in the house. Fingers were chopped off before my eyes. Mom disappeared for days on end and was eventually diagnosed with the cancer that took her life.

Yet, through it all, I managed to hold on to my power. I could choose happiness. I could choose to focus on the life I would build when I was on my own. I could look past the moments of insanity and cling to the beautiful parts of life and the joy that was growing within me like a rose somehow miraculously sprouting through the cracks in a concrete parking lot. As a child, a seed was planted in my soul that grew until it blossomed into what would become my entire outlook on life. *Life is not something to be survived but to be cherished and enjoyed.*

My childhood wasn't easy, and I was scared a lot, but I also had several people who helped me along the way, especially my Godmother and my Stepfather and his beautiful family. They essentially adopted me and continued Bonnie's work of making me feel special and loved, making me feel like my life mattered despite the insanity I had grown up in.

These important people in my life all shared the same attitude: help people, make the world a better place in whatever way you can, and don't sit around feeling sorry for yourself. No matter how hard things got, you needed to pick yourself up, brush yourself off, and get back to work. This mentality has been ingrained in me since I was young.

I took that advice and ran with it. I stumbled *a lot*, but I never gave up. Eventually, I began to fly. In the thirty years since I left that hospital, I became a globe-trotting travel writer and co-founder of *We Are Travel Girls*. My company's motto is: "Inspire. Connect. Educate. Empower." On our website, we publish stories from female travel writers all over the world, and we feature them on our popular Instagram™ account, using our platform to amplify their voices.

I now fly to the most incredible destinations, soaking up wondrous sights, sounds, tastes, and cultures from every corner of the world. I stay at the best hotels and dine at the best restaurants in the most beautiful cities. I also visit some of the most impoverished places to raise awareness and funding to help empower the local communities.

Perhaps the most empowering thing in my life is being a mother to a beautiful daughter who fills my heart with joy. As I write this, she is only six years old, but she is already one of the most compassionate, loving, smart, and creative people I have ever met. She also has the best father and will never have to endure what I went through. The peace and joy this brings me is immeasurable. This is the life *I* chose.

From looking at my picture-perfect moments on Instagram no one knows what I have gone through to get here. No one knows that every day I wake up, look in the mirror, and thank God that I found a way to focus on the beautiful parts of life — because that sense of gratitude is what saved me. I know happiness is a choice, and my power lies in *choosing* it. My daughter needs a mother who is happy enough to love her the way she she deserves to be loved. I know that every day I get to be alive is a gift. I'm *so* lucky and grateful to be here.

Life doesn't always turn out the way we expect it to. But I wake up every day with a childlike excitement about life. I now live in Malibu — where Sunset Blvd meets Pacific Coast Highway. I run on the beach daily. I take photos of everything like a giddy tourist. I have the best time with my daughter when we're together. She's a constant reminder of just how precious every moment is, especially time spent with loved ones. I am truly happy despite everything I have gone through. My heart is genuinely filled with *joy*.

The Dalai Lama said, "The purpose of our lives is to be happy." My mother said, "What makes you beautiful is your attitude toward the world." Both of these could not be more true. Your inner beauty comes from your gratitude.

I'm continually inspired when I see others refusing to use what they have been through as an excuse not to be happy. I'm also inspired when I witness others achieving their dreams and creating the life they want in spite of every-thing. We all have this power, even though I know sometimes it feels impossible. I'm still my own worst enemy most of the time. But if I have achieved one thing that I am truly proud of, it is the ability to *choose joy*. If I can give you anything from my story, it's that you have the ability to choose it, too. It has always been there within you. Hard things, traumatic things, and seemingly 'bad' things will happen to you over and over again in this life. You can't control what happens to you, but you can control your attitude toward what happens to you. That's where you will find your true power — that's where you will find your *joy*.

Ignite Action Steps

5 Action Steps For Igniting Joy

- **Be a tourist in your own town**. Visit beautiful spots. Take photos. Behave exactly as you would if you were on vacation.

- **Take yourself on a solo date**. Dress up. Book a nice restaurant. Order expensive wine. At dinner, sit and think about how lucky you are to be alive.

- **Watch the sunrise or sunset**. Taking time to reflect at the beginning and end of the day cultivates gratitude.

- **Make time to exercise**, in some form, at least five times per week. The endorphin release you will experience is priceless.

- **Do at least one kind thing** for someone else every single day. Helping others is the key to joy.

Vanessa Rivers — United States of America
Travel Writer, Co-Founder & CEO of We Are Travel Girls
VanessaRivers.com / WeAreTravelGirls.com
VanessaRivers
WeAreTravelGirls

Dr. Willo Boniface

DR. WILLO BONIFACE

"It takes a single moment to transform a mindset and a life."

My intention is for you to feel *unfreakin*-stoppable. My wish is that this story empowers you to say *"Hell Yes!"* to the things that help you GLOW and feel alive. I want you to be the leader of your life and go after your most happy, healthy, joyful existence and wildest dreams with a positive mindset that serves you. Life is too damn short not to.

UNFREAKIN-STOPPABLE

"We have your test results back, and we need to see you in person."

I was standing in a private treatment room with a male doctor I didn't know. It was cold and foreign. Clinical and barren. The smell of hand sanitizer lingered in the air, and the doctor was fidgeting with his pen. I was nervous before I had even walked in, after receiving the dreaded phone call the previous day. I had booked the next available time slot with *any* doctor that would see me. Now, here I was, feeling uneasy in my gut as I took in the scene unfolding, and I just knew. This news wasn't going to be good. The ache in my legs from hours of standing in the waiting room, swaying and shushing to keep my baby calm, was taking its toll. I shifted my weight again with no reprieve. My only source of warmth was my 6-week-old baby girl cradled safely in my arms. Her delicious button nose and bright blue eyes looked up at me as she let out a happy gurgle. She had just begun to smile, and I was her favorite thing. My heart swelled every time I looked at her sweet little face. I felt vulnerable standing in that icy room with her; both of us were restless. I squeezed her tight as the doctor explained what was happening.

"Your pap smear came back abnormal. You have high-grade lesions on your cervix." *Oh sh*t.*

"If we detect lesions in your biopsy we might have to look at further interventions. Worst case scenario, you may need a hysterectomy."

What!?

"Let's not get ahead of ourselves. I will refer you to a gynecologist. Do you have a specialist you would like me to address this to?"

Ahh… ummm.

What just happened?!? I was the type of woman who was always positive, adventurous, and carefree. I usually felt like I could do anything I put my mind to, but this news was *big,* and I didn't know what to think. I felt my vibrant glow drain right out of my body, replaced by a queasy heaviness that felt like it settled in immediately. I knew my life would never be the same again. I already felt different.

The next three years were a blur of biopsies, tests, waiting rooms, hospitals, surgeries, and anxiety. New medical terms, procedures, and body parts I didn't even know existed were raised at every turn… *Bartholin's gland, cone biopsy, high-grade squamous intraepithelial lesions… Ughhhh*! Luckily, I was preoccupied with parenting my two little munchkins and juggling all the balls that come with trying to parent and work while not sucking at absolutely everything. Despite high levels of exhaustion, once everyone went to bed, I meticulously took detailed notes in their baby books. It felt critically important that I capture it all. I was subconsciously driven by the heartbreaking idea that I might not be around to see them grow up.

In the quieter moments, I found myself worrying about what was happening inside of my body, fretting that the lesions had turned cancerous and gone berserk, spreading disease throughout my body. I was hyper-aware of every strange pain as I endlessly googled™ symptoms of cervical cancer and was on high alert. I didn't share my worries with anyone, not even my husband.

Three years after that first lousy appointment, my gynecologist called. Somehow, I knew that I was still in danger, even before the results came back. Something wasn't right in my body and I trusted my intuition like that. It's like when I found out that I was pregnant. I just knew. Of course, I took a pregnancy test, but I didn't need to. The news from my gynecologist was unsurprising but still heavy. She highly recommended a radical hysterectomy as soon as possible — a major procedure to remove the majority of my reproductive organs. I was thirty-four years old at the time and I was terrified that my days were numbered.

While I waited for surgery, other forces were at play in my ultimate unraveling. Due to company reorganization, I was at risk of being laid off in the middle of the pandemic. The financial security of my family was at risk, and that made me feel sick to my stomach. Plus, my extended family exploded after years of unhealthy relationships, which made my heart simply ache for all the people that I love so much.

I remember sitting at my home office on a scorching hot day with zero breeze and no air conditioning to take the edge off the relentless heat. It was weird. Usually, a welcome breeze floated through the window to cool me down, but that day, it was torturously still. A rusty old pedestal fan stood in the corner of the room, meekly pushing hot air around, failing miserably at its one job. This sort of stuff never usually got to me, but that day, I noticed *everything*. I wasn't myself, and I hadn't been for days, but I couldn't quite put my finger on *why*.

I was laboring over an email that was a simple sentence to a friendly colleague, and three hours into the mission I realized that I just couldn't do it. My mind was out of my body, completely unable to focus. I was sweating from the heat, and it felt like butterflies were rising up inside of my body, creeping dangerously up my windpipe and threatening to explode out of me. My throat felt tight as I tried helplessly to swallow it down, but I was out of breath, and the spacious room felt like it was caving in around me. I had to get out of there. Fast!

I ran out of my house and drove to the biggest outdoor staircase I could think of, and I ran up and down those stairs, determined to get that toxic energy out of my body. I forced air into my lungs in desperate, greedy gulps as my legs begged me to stop. The piercing sun scorched my skin, and sweat dripped off my body. My heart pounded in my chest, but I still felt awful, so I kept going as tears rolled down my face.

I finally collapsed at the top of the stairs when I couldn't take one more step. I lay there, panting, crying. A broken woman. I vowed I would never let myself feel like this ever again.

After a while, my breathing regulated itself, and I was able to breathe deeply and slowly, filling my lungs with life. My heart rate eased at its own pace. The pulse I had heard loudly throbbing in my ears and pounding in my chest was now the gentle bounce of a restful heart. I could nearly feel the blood happily swishing through its chambers. The sea breeze cooled my body, and salt crystalized on my skin as the sweat evaporated. The sun felt less harsh as it beamed down on my skin and permeated through me to warm my bones. Everything just felt calmer.

I lay on the grass, salty and sweaty, so much lighter, knowing that I couldn't do anything about the things happening to me at the time. Everyone, including my husband and children… everything, even the cells in my own body… were going to do whatever they wanted. Most of life's circumstances were wildly and beautifully out of my control. It felt like, for the first time, I could be at peace with the idea of trusting and letting go. I felt that old familiar glow come back to me, but it felt different this time, bigger and somehow calmer, like a powerful surge of light building from within.

I rested my hands on my belly as I took deep, easy breaths with my eyes closed, a smile breaking out that felt glorious. At that moment, I became more determined than ever to live whatever life I had left *bigger, MUCH BIGGER*. Full of joy and meaningful moments, adventure and fun, laughter and light. I wanted more of all the good stuff and my brain felt like it exploded with the possibilities. I embraced what was happening and let go of anything I couldn't control. I felt a fierce fire burn inside of me that made me feel *unfreakin-stoppable*.

After that moment, everything changed. I started saying *"Hell yes"* to things that helped me glow brighter and feel alive. I said, *"Hell yes"* to myself, walking to see the sun rise over the horizon every day. I basked in that glorious moment when the day's first rays warmed my face, feeling like the luckiest woman in the world. I would plunge into the ocean and feel the profound sense of freedom and calm that comes with diving under a friendly spilling wave, hearing the muffled sounds of clattering shells tumbling across the sand while I blissfully listened under the surface. On the way home from the beach, I would walk through the park and under the big old fig trees. There was something about those trees, their age beyond the comprehension of a mere mortal. Home to fruit bats and birds, the canopy was fully alive at that time, like a whole world and social structure beyond the worries and busyness of modern human life. I felt blessed to witness it and savored the moment before re-entering the usual hustle and bustle of a midweek morning with a busy family.

I said *"Hell yes"* when my kids invited me into their world. I had to stop myself from the habit of telling them, "I'll be there in a minute," but that minute never came. I started saying a deliberate "Yes" for five minutes, which turned into ten and twenty minutes, then dinner was late, and no one cared. We were lost in time as our imaginations ran wild, and I cherished the joyful squeals of delight as I tickled them. "Again, mum! Again!"

I said *"Hell yes"* to new work opportunities, pushing outside of my comfort zone, stretching and expanding myself to find my limits that never existed. I ambitiously pursued what I wanted in my career, and I got it, despite the uncertainties of the pandemic. It made me realize that all of my ambitious dreams were available to me this whole time.

I said, *"Hell yes,"* when my husband ran his hands across my lower back while we moved around the kitchen. His touch always sent electricity through my body, and I stopped to feel the fire inside of me. We kissed and danced and gave eyes that clearly made plans for later when the kids were in bed, making us both blush in the kitchen. Life went on, joyful and happy. My glow was more vibrant than ever.

The day finally came. I was fully prepared for surgery and gave myself permission to be at peace as they wheeled me into the operating room, calm and ready, not a butterfly to speak of.

By the time I could resume my morning walks to the beach, I might as well have been floating from my sheer gratitude for being able to move my body again. I felt more present than ever with my husband and kids and, something even more profound, I discovered a sense of spaciousness that I didn't think was possible for a working mum in the modern world. I felt like I had time for myself and for others, time to work, rest, and be with my friends, and time to swim and play and go on holidays. A stark contrast to how I felt when I was standing petrified in that cold treatment room all those years ago.

So what changed? Other than having fewer organs in my body, I was working the same number of hours and had the same demands on my time and energy, but my life felt more spacious and joyful. My radical change in mindset and priorities allowed me to get crystal clear on what I wanted, and do more of the things that I loved with the people that mattered the most. I crafted a magnificent vision of my dream life and intentionally set out to make all my dreams my reality. *And guess what?* It's working! You are reading my story right now because I dreamt about being an author, writing my story, and sharing the message that's on my heart. I want other women to radically change their mindset, craft their magnificent vision, and rediscover what matters most to them.

I wholeheartedly believe that when we glow, we can bring our wildest dreams into existence. Glowing is a highly contagious superpower, and now that I have uncovered the secret for myself, I am on a mission to light up the world with glowing women who are embracing joy in their lives. We all want more of the juicy good stuff, and we're going after it. The sheer ambition of my vision for all women to glow makes my heart sing… 100% HELL YES!

I want us all to live big, free, and unbound, fully embracing our joyful life. When we do this, we raise the bar for ourselves, claim our infinite glow, and lead others to theirs. As empowered women, we are obligated to light up others, Igniting humanity to change the narrative and write a bigger, better story than anyone has ever dreamed possible. When younger women and our children watch us, they will see a generation of glowing women. They will see powerful women absolutely thriving, and they will feel unstoppable because we will show them what unstoppable looks like. Women will take their seats at leadership tables around the world, bring heart and light to the conversations that affect us all, and together, we *will* change the world.

You are a leader. This is an invitation to lead yourself to glow brighter. Do it for them, but do it more for you. You are a vibrant force to be reckoned with, go get it!

Ignite Action Steps

The framework I use to dial up a woman's glow is outlined below in three key areas: *Energy, Confidence*, and *Joy*. When a woman has all of these things, she is glowing. I want you to feel your glow and live a vibrant, happy, healthy, and joyful life.

1. **Energy:** The main tool I used to shift my energy was moving my body. Sometimes it required vigorous movement, but mostly it required soul-nourishing gentle steps. Once I made this connection, I committed to walking every day to see the sunrise, rain, hail, or shine — no excuses! I invite you to do something completely life-enriching for yourself every single day. You deserve it.

2. **Confidence:** My confidence has taken many hits over the years. This story is one example of how I had to adjust my expectations and rebuild my confidence. Confidence is a habit; we cultivate it by speaking positivity into ourselves. Our internal language matters. I journal *three affirmations* for myself every day to magnify my courageous confidence. I invite you to take up this high-impact habit to render yourself unfreakin-stoppable.

3. **Joy:** Our joyful life is in the moments, and when I tuned in to the present moment, I truly unlocked a superpower. I keep a daily journal of three things I am grateful for, and I invite you to do the same. Bring your awareness to things that inspire immense joy, and write down how thankful you are for them. I offer an online private journal portal with my clients to keep them accountable for these habits, and the transformations are remarkable. Practicing gratitude will change your life.

Dr. Willo Boniface — Australia
Founder and Director of She's Got Glow,
Lead Glower, Speaker, Author, Proud Mum & Wife
www.shesgotglow.com
shes_got_glow
shes-got-glow
shesgotglow

IGNITE
Joy

WRITE FOR IGNITE™

Moment' and how that pivotal moment has indeed impacted your life. Our goal is that you see the benefits and positivity that have come from that time and realize that in sharing your story, you can ignite the life of another person. Our hope is that the Ignite stories you read have impacted you and that you see how your story could inspire another. If sharing your story feels important, or the idea of writing your Ignite Moment for others to enjoy is percolating in you, please reach out to us **https://igniteyou.life/write/apply/**. We believe every person has a story that deserves to be read. We also know that people learn and feel motivated from reading the triumphs and successes of others, allowing them to feel they can do the same. If your words are longing to come forth, and you want your story to inspire someone else, we want to be there for you to make it happen. Our easy, comprehensive, and enjoyable programs show you exactly how to write your story in a powerful way, and we give you the tools you need to begin your own writing career.

We want to *Ignite a billion lives through a billion words and sharing your story can help make that goal become a reality.*

GET TO KNOW IGNITE

Over seven hundred authors have come to us, and we have made them international best-sellers in both our compilation books and their own solo projects. Individuals who longed to be published but didn't know how to begin have reached best-seller status in a matter of months — in multiple countries, in dozens of categories.
Should you desire to write your Ignite Moment or have an idea for a full book of your own, let us be the ones to support you in reaching your goal.

As the leaders of Empowerment Publishing, we know how to help you craft your book and bring it to the world. Our programs are easy and fun and produce outstanding results. Unlike other publishers, you maintain your copyright, own your content, and receive all your royalties. Your story is yours. Our job is to help you share it with as many people as possible and make it impactful and successful, making people want to read more from you.

Learn more about how you can become a published author with Ignite at:
www.igniteyou.life

GET IGNITE'S 100 WRITING PROMPTS

Ignite your writing with these inspiring writing prompts designed to unleash the writer in you. This FREE e-book contains powerful writing prompts that will help you gain confidence and expertise in yourself and your writing. Use the QR code to access this amazing resource.

THANK YOU

Thank you for being a part of the profound impact we aim to achieve at Ignite!

To the Reader… YOU!

To you, the reader, we thank you for reading and cherishing our stories and for opening your heart and mind to the idea of igniting your own life. We know that you could choose any book off the shelf and spend your valuable time doing many other things, so immersing yourself in the world of Ignite and transporting your imagination into the stories we write is a deeply appreciated gesture. All of our authors, our team, and writers around the world thank you for being an avid reader and making books and stories valuable.

To the Authors

A deep appreciation also goes to each and every author who made *Ignite Joy* possible. It is their powerful and inspiring stories, along with their passion and desire to help others, that will Ignite more JOY within every one of us. Joy can be felt in others when shared in a heartfelt manner, and we thank each author for their desire to want you to find more JOY in your life.

In the spirit of fostering joy, please know that every word written in this book and every letter on the pages has been meticulously crafted not just to inspire you but to transform your thinking. Every individual in this book stepped up to share their stories in the hopes that it fosters more joy in the world. They courageously revealed the many layers of themselves and exposed their fears, challenges, and hardships as few individuals do. Additionally, they spoke authentically from the heart and wrote what was true for them. We could have taken their stories and made them grammatically perfect, following every editing rule, but instead, we chose to leave their unique and honest voices intact so that you felt their essence and individual personality. We overlooked the exactness of perfection to allow individual expression. These are their words, their sentiments, and their vernacular. We let their voice shine in their writing so you would get a true sense of who each one of them is. That's what makes IGNITE so unique. They are authors sharing authentically, with no filters, in a loving way that serves others—stories igniting lives that will, in turn, Ignite Humanity™.

To the Team

A tremendous thank you goes to the IGNITE Publishing™ team, who has been working tirelessly in the background, teaching, editing, supporting, and encouraging the authors to reach the finish line. These individuals are some of the most genuine and heart-centered people on the planet. Their dedication to the vision of IGNITE, along with their integrity and the professionalism they convey, is of the highest caliber possible. They each want you to find inspiration from these stories and use the many IGNITE Moments in this book to rise and flourish in your life. They all believe in you; their dream is for your dreams to come true.

Thanks to the entire team for their support behind the scenes and for going 'above and beyond' to make this a wonderful experience. Their dedication ensured that everything ran smoothly and with elegance.

Production Team: JB Owen, Kristine Joy Magno, Peter Giesin, Mimi Safiyah, Carolina Gold, Brent Casteling, Steph Elliott, and Liana Khabibullina.

Editing Team: JB Owen, Michiko Couchman, Mimi Safiyah, Sarah Cross, and Zoe Wong.

Project Leaders: Nicole S. Freeman and Cheryl A. Rafter.

RESOURCES OUR *IGNITE YOUR JOY* AUTHORS RECOMMEND

Our authors have put together wonderful resources that they themselves have used to help discover more in their lives. We hope that you, too, will utilize the links, offerings, and books listed below and Ignite more joy in your life.

Cheryl A. Rafter
Website:
- www.courageouscomebackcoach.com

Elaine Valerie Thompson
Books:
- *You Can Heal Your Life* by Louise Hay

Website:
- Redox Science - https://elainethompson.redoxlifescience.com
- FlowCode - https://hub.theflowcode.com/members/23393736

Hollis Baley
Offering:
- 7-Day Divine Breath Devotional Practice - https://www.highersanctuary.com

JB Owen
Meditation:
- Affirmations of a Billionaire - https://affirmations.thepinkbillionaire.com

Kari Berridge
Books:
- *Cut the Anchor* by Kari Berridge
- *Done with the Crying* by Sheri McGregor, M.A.

Katarina Amadora
Blog:
- What is Somatica®? https://www.somaticainstitute.com/blog/somatica-sex-relationship-coach/

Meditation:
- Self Love Meditation: https://audio.com/katarina-amadora-1/audio/self-love-meditation

Offering:
- Free Consultation: https://keap.app/contact-us/5720060482027520

Website:
- www.youtube.com/channel/UChTuf7oxJe6hEYNFykU548w
- Heal.me: heal.me/practitioner/katarina-amadora-holistic-health-and-intimacy-coach
- Yelp: /www.yelp.com/biz/amadora-transformations-pleasanton#reviews

Video:
- What is RTT : https://youtu.be/3KCx6nM-x7o?si=wNSMkunXJrq43jtx
- RTT for Attachment: https://youtu.be/fG0EPTWc_Wk?si=yyI-t szcbxlBIwcm
- Heal.me: https://heal.me/practitioner/katarina-amadora-holistic-health-and-intimacy-coach
- Yelp: https://www.yelp.com/biz/amadora-transformations-pleasanton #reviews

Liliana Avila Roque
Audio:
- https://www.menus.kryon.com/freeaudio

Books:
- *Many Lives, Many Masters* by Brian L. Weiss, M.D.

Social:
- https://www.instagram.com/lightcodesandhealing

Website:
- https://adironndaspiritualhealer.org
- https://desarrolloluzdorada.mx
- https://www.leeharrisenergy.com

<u>Lydia Burchell</u>
Books:
The Language of Letting Go by Melody Beattie

<u>Nicole S. Freeman</u>
Website:
- https://www.biblegateway.com

<u>Shirley Jones</u>
Books:
- *The Book of Certitude* by Bahá'u'lláh

<u>Stacie Callan</u>
Books:
- *The Universe Has Your Back* by Gabrielle Bernstein

<u>Tanya Dow</u>
Books:
- *The Power is Within You* by Louise Hay

<u>Tina Ritchie</u>
Books:
- *Living in the Light* by Shakti Gawain
- *Think and Grow Rich* by Napoleon Hill
- *The Light Shall Set You Free* by Norma J. Milanovich and Shirley McCune

Social:
- Facebook Group: Lifestyle via Tina Ritchie: https://m.facebook.com/groups/451458497268220

<u>Dr. Willo Boniface</u>
Audio:
- The Great Reset: The reset button you've been looking for (Free 7-day audio series) www.shesgotglow.com/page/the-great-reset

Offering:
- Glow Mail: An inspirational & thought-provoking newsletter for modern women to glow: www.glowmail.org

PHOTO CREDITS

Ashley Fry: *Janelle with White Creek Ranch Photography*
Cheryl A. Rafter: *Sandra Steier Photography*
Ciara Caston Finley: *Gilmore Photography & Design*
Corinne Erickson: *Stacey Tompkins Photography*
Elaine Valerie Thompson: *Photography by Chanthavee Samountry,*
    Makeup: *Mindy Hair by Laura.*
Hollis Balley: *ANKR Love*
Samountry Makeup: *Mindy Hair by Laura*
Jennifer M. Moore: *Jonathan W. M. Barbee*
Joanne Gauthier: *Vancouver Island Portraits*
Karen Whelan: *Katerina Siviene*
Kari Berridge: *Stacey Tompkins Photography*
Katarina Amadora: *Kersti Niglas*
Katie Allen & Allison Prince: *Crisanto Santa Ana*
Lady JB Owen: *Kersti Niglas*
Leona Wallace: *Wendy K Yalom*
Liliana Avila Roque: *Edgar Blancas Gutiérrez, Estudio 2957*
Lydia Burchell: *John Jennings*
Melissa A. Corrion: *Carissa Anthony Photography*
Melody J. Carberry: *Stacey Tompkins Photography*
Nicole S. Freeman: *Mike The Cameraman*
Nicole Shewaga: *Alonso Reyes Photography*
Shirley Jones: *Randy Woodroffe*
Stacey Tompkins: *Stacey Tompkins Photography with the help of Corinne Erickson*
Tanya Dow: *Jessie McEachern-Jessie Mann Photography*
Tina Ritchie: *Natt Roaro Photography*
Vanessa Rivers: *Kimberly Millard*
Dr. Willo Boniface: *Marty O'Donnell, Shot Studio*

Experience the joy of creativity! We've included some delightful coloring pages for you to unleash your artistic expression. Take a moment to color and create, then display your masterpiece in a prominent place where you can see it every day. Let the colors and creativity Ignite more joy in your heart and remind you of the power of personal expression to brighten your day. Enjoy these pages, add your unique touch, and let the joy flow in you!

JOY

IGNITE
Joy

JOY

IGNITE
Joy

Joy

IGNITE
Joy

Joy

IGNITE
Joy

JOY

IGNITE *Joy*

JOY